THE TRANSFORMATION
OF MEANING
IN PSYCHOLOGICAL THERAPIES

THE TRANSFORMATION OF MEANING IN PSYCHOLOGICAL THERAPIES

Integrating Theory and Practice

Edited by

Mick Power
University of Edinburgh and Royal Edinburgh Hospital

Chris R. Brewin
Royal Holloway, University of London

JOHN WILEY & SONS

Chichester · New York · Weinheim · Brisbane · Singapore · Toronto

Copyright © 1997 by John Wiley & Sons Ltd,
Baffins Lane, Chichester,
West Sussex PO19 1UD, England

National   01243 779777
International   (+44) 1243 779777
e-mail (for orders and customer service enquiries): cs-
books@wiley.co.uk
Visit our Home Page on http://www.wiley.co.uk
or http://www.wiley.com

Other Wiley Editorial Offices

John Wiley & Sons, Inc., 605 Third Avenue,
New York, NY 10158-0012, USA

VCH Verlagsgesellschaft mbH, Pappelallee 3
0-69469 Weinheim, Germany

Jacaranda Wiley Ltd, 33 Park Road Milton,
Queensland 4064, Australia

John Wiley & Sons (Canada) Ltd, 22 Worcester Road,
Rexdale, Ontario M9W 1LI, Canada

John Wiley & Sons (Asia) Pte Ltd, 2 Clementi Loop #02-01,
Jin Xing Distripark, Singapore 129809

Library of Congress Cataloging-in-Publication Data

The transformation of meaning in psychological therapies : integrating
theory and practice / edited by Mick Power, Chris R. Brewin.
p.   cm.
Includes bibliographical references and index.
ISBN 0-471-95826-3 (alk. paper). — ISBN 0-471-97005-0 (pbk. :
alk. paper)
1. Psychotherapy. 2. Meaning (Psychology) 3. Meaning
(Philosophy) I. Power, Michael J. II. Brewin, Chris R.
RC480.5.T736   1997
616.89'14—dc21   96-48034
CIP

British Library Cataloguing in Publication Data

A catalogue record for this book is available from the British Library

ISBN 0-471-95826-3 (cased)
ISBN 0-471-97005-0 (paper)

Typeset in 10/12pt Palatino by Dorwyn Ltd, Rowlands Castle, Hants
Printed and bound in Great Britain by Bookcraft (Bath) Ltd
This book is printed on acid-free paper responsibly manufactured from sustainable forestation, for which at least two trees are planted for each one used for paper production.

CONTENTS

ABOUT THE EDITORS

Mick Power is currently Professor of Clinical Psychology at the University of Edinburgh and a practising clinical psychologist in the Royal Edinburgh Hospital. In the past he has been a Senior Lecturer at the University of London and has worked as a clinical psychologist at Guy's Hospital, and the Bethlem and Maudsley Hospitals. He has also worked for the Medical Research Council and currently acts as a Research Advisor to the World Health Organization. He is one of the founding editors of the journal *Clinical Psychology and Psychotherapy*.

Chris Brewin is Professor of Psychology at Royal Holloway, University of London, where he is co-director of the Cognition, Emotion and Trauma Group, and works in a specialist post-traumatic stress disorder clinic at the West Middlesex University Hospital. He has had a longstanding interest in the social and cognitive processes underlying depression, and more recently has started to investigate similarities between the memory processes involved in depression and post-traumatic stress disorder. He is the author of *Cognitive Foundations of Clinical Psychology*.

CONTRIBUTORS

Editors

Mick Power

Department of Psychiatry,
Royal Edinburgh Hospital,
University of Edinburgh,
Edinburgh EH10 5HF, UK

Chris R. Brewin

Department of Psychology,
Royal Holloway,
University of London,
Egham TW20 OEX, UK

Contributors

Bernice Andrews

Department of Psychology,
Royal Holloway,
University of London,
Egham TW20 OEX, UK

Derek Bolton

Department of Psychology,
Institute of Psychiatry,
De Crespigny Park,
London SE5 8AF, UK

Cynthia Frantz

Department of Psychology,
Tobin Hall,
University of Massachusetts at Amherst,
Amherst,
MA 01003, USA

Paul Gilbert

Department of Clinical Psychology,
Kingsway Hospital,
Derby DE22 3LZ, UK

Leslie Greenberg

Department of Psychology,
York University,
4700 Keele Street,
North York,
Ontario,
Canada M3J 1P3

Ann Hackmann

Department of Clinical Psychology,
Warneford Hospital,
Warneford Lane,
Headington,
Oxford, UK

Jonathan Hill

Child and Adolescent Psychiatry and Psychology,
Royal Liverpool Children's Hospital,
Alder Hey,
Eaton Road,
Liverpool L12 2AP, UK

Ronnie Janoff-Bulman

Department of Psychology,
Tobin Hall,
University of Massachusetts at Amherst,
Amherst,
MA 01003
USA

Phil Mollon

Department of Clinical Psychology,
Lister Hospital,
Coreys Mill Lane,
Stevenage,
Herts SG1 4AB, UK

Juan Pascual-Leone

Department of Psychology,
York University,
4700 Keele Street,
North York,
Ontario,
Canada M3J 1P3

John Teasdale

MRC Applied Psychology Unit,
15 Chaucer Road,
Cambridge CB2 2EF, UK

PREFACE

One of the puzzles about the psychotherapies is why so many different types of therapy work for so many different people so much of the time. For the nearly five hundred or so different psychotherapies, there are proponents who advocate their particular therapy as the biggest and the best, there are satisfied clients who will testify that their lives have been changed dramatically, and, of course, there are vocal groups of detractors who argue that that particular type of therapy doesn't work, shouldn't work, or can't work. There are many alternative ways of coping with the subsequent chaos. Some therapists simply bury their heads in the sand and continue with their favourite techniques. Others, like ourselves, are puzzled and are asking if there are common mechanisms that apply across different therapies that might explain both their effectiveness and their (sometimes) lack of effectiveness?

One of the key factors that has been established as necessary for therapies to be effective is that there should be a good therapeutic relationship between the therapist and the client. We ourselves are strong advocates of this common factor as an essential one before therapy can be effective. However, we believe that the therapeutic relationship, while being a *necessary* factor in effective therapy, is not a *sufficient* one. We argue that a good therapeutic relationship provides the context in which effective therapy occurs, but does not provide the mechanisms through which change or transformation happens. In this book we have asked each of the contributors to consider the possibility that one such key mechanism involves *meaning*. That is, we consider the possibility that therapeutic change, in any form of therapy, requires a transformation of meaning to occur. This change can and should occur at a number of levels for improvement to be maintained, whether in behaviour therapy, cognitive therapy, or psychoanalytic therapy. Our hope is that even though the contributors approach therapy from very different perspectives something of a common framework for approaching the question of therapeutic change emerges from their chapters.

In addition to the contributors themselves, who have in the process of drafting their chapters helped us to articulate our own views, there are a number of other individuals that we would like to thank. These colleagues and friends include Lorna Champion, Jenny Firth-Cozens, Glenys Parry, and Charlie Sharp. They have helped us to clarify our own thinking on the issues of therapy and, although they would disagree with much of what we say, their disagreements have been as valuable as their agreements.

Chapter 1

MEANING AND PSYCHOLOGICAL THERAPY: OVERVIEW AND INTRODUCTION

Chris R. Brewin* and M.J. Power†

The central thesis of this book is that all psychological therapies share a commitment to transforming the meanings that clients have attached to their symptoms, relationships and life problems. This common purpose has, we believe, been obscured by the use of different terminologies, by different conceptualizations of meaning, and by a tendency to focus on what divides therapies rather than on what unifies them. With a few notable exceptions (e.g. Wachtel, 1977), authors have generally preferred to explore the merits of their own brand of psychotherapy rather than to seek common cause with others.

Our thesis should not be taken as advocating eclecticism, the pragmatic willingness to blend different psychotherapeutic theories and techniques as appropriate to each individual case. Nor are we arguing that psychotherapies are effective by virtue of their 'common factors', such as the provision of an accepting, supportive and non-critical relationship. Instead, we adopt the more radical view that it is possible to integrate different psychotherapies at a theoretical level in terms of processes of meaning transformation.

There is little question that issues of meaning form the heart of most forms of psychopathology. In some cases it is the presence of an unwanted or painful meaning that is the problem, in others it is the absence or loss of meaning. Anxious clients are concerned about such things as whether their symptoms mean they are seriously ill or about to die,

*Royal Holloway, University of London, and †Royal Edinburgh Hospital and University of Edinburgh, UK

The Transformation of Meaning in Psychological Therapies.
Edited by Mick Power and Chris R. Brewin. © 1997 John Wiley & Sons Ltd.

whether they will make fools of themselves in public, whether they will be rejected and humiliated, whether they can survive on their own, whether the world is a safe place; depressed clients typically interpret their situation in ways that lead them to conclude that they are bad, guilty or worthless, others are about to or have already abandoned them, and the future is hopeless; paranoid clients are convinced that others have hostile intentions towards them, or that their real value or identity is being systematically overlooked; clients with adjustment disorder or post-traumatic stress disorder (PTSD) typically struggle with questions about why such destructive events have happened to them and how they are to continue now that they can no longer rely on the world that they previously took for granted.

That such a therapeutic integration has rarely hitherto been thought possible attests to the fact that the exercise will not be an easy one. If it is to be valuable, though, it must also be practical. There must be demonstrable gains in terms of general principles that can inform everyday practice and influence outcomes. We have therefore not sought detailed analyses of individual case material relying heavily on interpretation by one individual. Such interpretation, when it emphasizes the joint contribution of the client and the therapist, and their specific historical and cultural context, is known as the hermeneutic approach to meaning (e.g. Ricoeur, 1981). Rather, we have adopted a deliberately limited approach to the study of meaning and have asked our contributors to focus on a small number of regularly occurring themes or processes that will be relevant to the majority of therapists. In this chapter we start by outlining the role of meaning in different schools of psychotherapy and review some evidence that meaning is an important factor in therapeutic outcome.

OVERVIEW OF PSYCHOTHERAPIES

Psychoanalysis

According to Freud and many of his followers, psychological disorders such as anxiety reflect feelings and impulses that are excluded from consciousness because they would be experienced as unacceptable and would conflict with the person's view of his/herself. A variety of defence mechanisms such as denial, repression or projection are employed to exclude such feelings and impulses, which are thought to be often of a sexual or aggressive nature. For example, a person might become depressed and angry with himself rather than acknowledge his anger towards a loved person who had been lost through death or desertion.

Freud proposed, however, that although these defence mechanisms were often effective in hiding the conflict from patients, they could not prevent the emergence of indirect clues in the person's thoughts and behaviour. The nature of the conflict could therefore be detected by a psychoanalyst trained to understand the meanings that are disguised or hidden in everyday events such as dreams and slips of the tongue, and in the patient's behaviour towards the therapist (the transference).

Classical psychoanalysis therefore sought to create situations (talking to a quiet, neutral and unresponsive therapist, or seeing figures in an ambiguous inkblot) in which such unconscious impulses would be as evident as possible. The patients' responses in these situations would contain meanings that were hidden to them, but could be interpreted by an alert analyst attuned to generally important themes and looking for regularities across situations. Later, through a process of interpretation, the analyst would help the patient to become conscious of these hidden meanings, to recognize the unacceptable impulses, and to find alternative ways of gratifying them.

Subsequent psychoanalytic writers diverged from Freud in their views about the centrality of sexuality and aggression. To give only two examples, Jung's theory of archetypes proposed that meaning was in part innately organized and that human beings are predisposed to perceive the world and respond in a variety of complex ways (see Chapter 3 for a more detailed discussion). The nature of the archetypes could be inferred from the study of individual products such as dreams and delusions, and of cultural products such as myths and legends. Bowlby's (1980) influential attachment theory suggested that infants are innately programmed to give high priority to signals of their mother's proximity and responsiveness, and to respond in one of a number of predetermined ways to separation. These early experiences are thought to be stored in memory and to affect the interpretation of subsequent interpersonal events and the course of intimate relationships.

Behaviour Therapy

In contrast to psychoanalysis, behaviour therapy was relatively unconcerned with meaning. Individuals exposed to frightening circumstances might automatically, through unconscious associative learning, acquire the tendency to react in a fearful way to certain stimuli. In contrast, in the face of a reduction in levels of reinforcement, behaviour would automatically decline in intensity and frequency. Psychopathology was regarded as the result of external events, and the individual's subjective interpretation of them was specifically excluded as a cause of emotions and behaviour (see

Power & Dalgleish, 1996, for a detailed account). Thus there was little point in talking to patients about the meaning of their symptoms—improvement was only likely to result from their acting in a different way, or from a change in the contingencies controlling their behaviour.

The behavioural theory of fear acquisition was challenged by several observations, for example by individuals' willingness to seek out frightening experiences deliberately for pleasure and the lack of consequent phobic disorders. Also, it was not found to be the case that fear could be attached to any stimulus with equal facility. Rather, some stimuli appeared to be more 'meaningful' as sources of fear, in the sense that people would more readily become afraid of them given the appropriate circumstances. In response, theorists started to incorporate meaning into their theories, in the form of inbuilt appraisal systems. Seligman (1971) proposed that organisms were innately 'prepared' to respond to certain stimuli as more likely to be the source of fear. Lang's (1979) theory of fear has been among the most influential in the field. He suggested that frightening experiences lead to the storage of a 'fear memory' that incorporates stimulus elements (details of the frightening situation), response elements (details of the person's physiological response at the time), and meaning elements related to their interpretation of the situation (for example, it was perceived as threatening). Fear memories, Lang argued, can be reactivated by encountering real-world cues that have features in common with the stored memory, leading to a re-experiencing of the original fear. Thus behaviour therapy eventually recognized, to a limited extent, the importance of meaning, particularly of perceived threat.

Humanistic Therapy

In client-centred therapy (Rogers, 1959, 1974), psychopathology is seen as arising from discrepancies between the self-concept and the person's experiences. These discrepancies are reduced by the denial or distortion of experiences, but at the cost of rigidity in perceptions and behaviours and vulnerability to anxiety in the face of potentially disconfirmatory evidence. The person is cut off by these defensive manoeuvres from an understanding of the inner world of feelings and the subjective meanings attached to them. Therapy aims to reduce these discrepancies and have clients recognize, own and express feelings and personal meanings that have been hitherto disregarded. This is achieved largely by the creation of a facilitative psychological climate in which barriers to the client's innate drive towards health and self-actualization are removed.

Like client-centred therapy, Gestalt therapy (Perls, 1969) emphasizes that the potential for self-development and positive mental health lies in a greater awareness and acceptance of inner feelings and impulses that have been disregarded as a result of social conditioning. Both place importance on what is happening in the present rather than on analysing and explaining the past. Gestalt therapy has developed a number of techniques for helping clients become more aware of personal meanings, for example by focusing on bodily gestures, posture and sensations, amplifying feelings and motor impulses, and role playing. A major theme is that unwanted meanings are associated with specific emotions, for example anger, and that people escape having to recognize these meanings by avoiding or blocking emotional reactions. Perls believed that a high level of self-awareness was necessary for people to accept themselves fully and take responsibility for their feelings and behaviour.

Cognitive Therapy

In the period from 1950 to the mid-1970s, behaviour therapists developed clearly defined procedures such as desensitization and response prevention that could readily be described and taught. These techniques required little investigation of the individual, only a careful description of the behaviour, its antecedents, and its consequents. However, their usefulness tended to be restricted to the treatment of fairly circumscribed disorders such as specific phobias and compulsions. When behaviour therapists came to address depression and more generalized anxiety disorders, the significance of personal meanings assumed great importance. The investigation of individual thought processes, as recommended by Albert Ellis and Aaron Beck, became the cornerstone of the new cognitive-behavioural approaches.

These new techniques were not embraced, however, without a prolonged period of soul-searching by behaviour therapists. There was great anxiety that investigating individual cognitions was not as 'scientific' or methodologically rigorous as purely behavioural approaches. The new approaches were eventually adopted because they worked, but many expressed unease. The fear was frequently expressed that, in taking this step, behaviour therapy could no longer be so clearly differentiated from psychoanalysis. It was perceived that the project of creating a truly 'scientific' type of therapy was being abandoned for ever in favour of an explicit reliance on subjective interpretation and individual meaning.

Cognitive therapy as promulgated by Beck and Ellis did indeed reinstate the subjective in the assessment and treatment of psychopathology. Their emphasis was largely on the role of faulty reasoning in the creation of maladaptive emotions. Thus errors in thinking, such as faulty assumptions or incorrect interpretation of evidence, could lead to inappropriate levels of anxiety or depression. In early cognitive therapy, therefore, clients were typically viewed as deriving incorrect meanings from their environment that could be corrected by the systematic application of logic. Relatively less attention was paid to the meanings themselves. Beck, however, described the nature of depressive meanings as typically involving guilt, worthlessness, emptiness and hopelessness.

The importance of misinterpretation was also noted in connection with physical symptoms. Storms & McCaul (1976) proposed a common mechanism to account for the exacerbation of a wide variety of anxiety-related behaviours such as stammering, blushing, insomnia and impotence. They suggested that individuals who perceive such symptoms as indicating their own inadequacies or as betraying some personal fault, are likely to experience increased anxiety and a consequent worsening of the unwanted behaviour.

Subsequent development in the theory underlying cognitive therapy for depression has moved in the direction of specifying particular constellations of meaning that are thought to be pathogenic. Beck (1983) distinguished sociotropic individuals, who are highly dependent on others and prone to interpret negative interpersonal events as signalling rejection and disparagement, from autonomous individuals, who are highly dependent on success and prone to interpret negative achievement-related events as signalling incompetence and worthlessness. Very similar ideas have been put forward by psychoanalytically trained theorists (e.g. Blatt & Zuroff, 1992).

The cognitive theory of panic also suggests that specific kinds of misinterpretation underlie many instances of this form of anxiety (Clark, 1988). Individuals who panic are prone to perceive bodily sensations as signalling a catastrophic outcome, such as severe illness, death, loss of control or social humiliation. Patients with post-traumatic stress disorder may similarly misinterpret their symptoms, for example as signs of weakness or madness, thereby prolonging or exacerbating their problems (Ehlers & Steil, 1995). Similarly, with the extension of cognitive therapy to the treatment of personality disorders, further constellations of meaning have been identified that centre on loss of autonomy, mistrust, alienation, restrictions on self-expression, and absence of appropriate limits in interpersonal relationships (e.g. Young, 1990).

Existential Psychotherapy

This type of therapy rests on two philosophical foundations, phenomenology and existentialism (Cohn, 1994). Phenomenology involves giving high priority to the subjective experience of the client, rather than to the therapist's theoretical assumptions. Existentialism is concerned with the individual's capacity for self-reflection, for understanding what it means to be human, and for making important life choices. Part of human existence is seen as the negotiation of a series of life stages, and understanding and coming to terms with death, freedom, isolation and meaninglessness (Yalom's (1980) 'four ultimate concerns'). For the existentialist, all individuals have the freedom to choose how they will respond to circumstances and hence to determine the course of their own lives. As in the case of the humanistic therapy, with which existential therapy is often classed, human beings are believed to have an innate drive to find meaning and purpose in their lives and to realize their potential.

Frankl criticized the tendency to see clients' ideas as nothing more than the product of psychological disorder and noted (1973, p. 33), 'That we make a psychopathological statement about a person does not, therefore, exonerate us from the need to come to grips philosophically with his world view and to examine it for its rightness or wrongness'. Following his experiences in German concentration camps during World War II, he developed what he called 'logotherapy'. This drew on his observations that some individuals, particularly those who retained a faith in their life have a purpose beyond their immediate situation, were better able than others to withstand extreme hardships and deprivation.

For Frankl, the resolution of unconscious conflict or the correction of faulty thinking was not the whole story. He saw logotherapy as an adjunct to psychotherapy, one that recognized central human concerns and restored to individuals their ability to make choices and to take responsibility for their own actions. Issues such as how to accept misfortune, cruelty and death, and how to create purpose and value in everyday activities, were of central importance to everyone, particularly to clients with psychological disorders who had often had more than their share of hardship and suffering. In his view, 'There is no such thing as psychotherapy unconcerned with values, only one that is blind to values' (1973, p. 10).

Constructivist Psychotherapy

This term refers to a meta-theoretical approach rather than to one specific type of therapy. Constructivism holds that people are active construers of their own personal reality, and emphasizes the relativistic nature of these theories of reality in contrast to the view that there is an 'actual' reality that may be accurately or inaccurately perceived. A unitary view of the self is eschewed in favour of a complex self-construct, e.g. a 'dialogical self' (Hermans, Kempen & van Loon, 1992), that is constantly being revised in the service of the individual's purposes.

In practice, constructivist therapy contains many other elements and tends to emphasize the importance of unconscious or tacit learning, the social roots of knowledge in family life (particularly attachment experiences), the development of self-representations that reflect differing and sometimes contradictory life experiences, and the phenomenological exploration of emotional and bodily states (Guidano, 1987, 1991; Mahoney, 1991; Meichenbaum & Fitzpatrick, 1993; Neimeyer, 1993; White & Epston, 1990). In this, the influence of theorists such as Bowlby (1980) and Kelly (1955) is particularly evident. Compared with classical cognitive therapy, constructivist interventions tend to be less structured and didactic, less concerned with reality testing and more exploratory. They attempt to help the client construct a new interpretation of events or a new personal narrative, not necessarily one that is a better fit to 'the facts', but one that is internally consistent and results in less distress.

Some of this work revolves around identifying the metaphors used by clients to describe themselves and their situations, exploring the more complex meanings that may lie behind them, questioning their consequences, and employing alternative metaphors that carry more benign meanings. Problems may be objectified by viewing them as a script or as a metaphoric opponent who has to be outwitted. Perhaps one of the most striking examples of this approach is imagery rescripting, in which distressing images of abuse or humiliation are manipulated mentally, and different, more satisfactory outcomes imagined. Initial reports indicate that this can be highly effective for clients disturbed by memories of early childhood abuse (Smucker & Niederee, 1995).

OVERVIEW OF RESEARCH AND THEORY

This selective review can only cover a few of the many ways in which the role of meaning has been systematically investigated. The aim is once again to illustrate the centrality of meaning within all branches of clinical psychology and psychotherapy, and to set the stage for the more detailed discussions provided by our contributors. We divide this section into work on content and on processes.

Content

Most psychological disorders arise in the context of past or present adversity in the form of stressful life events. Studies of responses to stressors of various kinds have yielded a small number of major themes that direct our attention to those aspects of meaning that are of particular relevance. Bowlby's (1980) work on attachment has been especially fruitful in this regard, and has received much empirical support. Attachment experiences with primary caregivers are seen as the foundation of cognitive representations such as schemas or mental models that provide information about the person's connectedness and value to others who will provide love and support. Unsatisfactory experiences lead to the availability of representations of the self as worthless and deficient, and to representations of others as unreliable, critical or rejecting. These representations may then be activated by thematically similar experiences in later life, leading to self-criticism and self-blame (Andrews & Brewin, 1990; Brewin et al., 1992), and to patterns of relating involving either social anxiety, inappropriate submissiveness, confiding and seeking of reassurance, or compulsive self-reliance with impoverishment of intimate relationships (e.g. Blatt & Zuroff, 1992; Hazan & Shaver, 1987; Zuroff et al., 1995).

Another major theme in depression is helplessness and hopelessness. Experiences of uncontrollable negative outcomes can lead to the formation of cognitive representations of failure that include internal, stable and global causes such as personal deficiencies. In addition to the expectation of personal helplessness in the face of future adversity (Abramson, Seligman & Teasdale, 1978; Seligman, 1975), there may also be an expectation of hopelessness, i.e. not only the self but others are also powerless or unwilling to help (Abramson, Metalsky & Alloy, 1989).

Whether or not these or other pathogenic meanings are deployed in the face of adversity depends on numerous influences, including (a) the fit between the nature of the present adversity and that of the past experiences contributing to the formation of the pre-existing cognitive representations; (b) the fit between the nature of the person's current emotional and physiological responses and that of past responses represented in memory; (c) the existence of alternative meanings and of evidence that can support benign meanings over pathogenic ones; and (d) the availability of mental strategies and resources such as social support that can help to dismiss pathogenic meanings as invalid.

Other research has investigated individual differences in positive meanings such as meaning in life, defined as 'the cognizance of order, coherence and purpose in one's existence, the pursuit and attainment of worthwhile goals, and an accompanying sense of fulfillment' (Reker & Wong, 1988, p. 221). Meaning in life is related (inversely) to negative affect, and somewhat more strongly to positive affect (Zika & Chamberlain, 1992). Individuals with substance-abuse problems have been identified as a group who are particularly likely to view life as meaningless and aimless. Among adolescents, Newcomb & Harlow (1986) showed that perceived loss of control and meaninglessness mediated the impact of negative life events on substance use. Alcoholics have been found to report reduced meaning in life, recovering their sense of purpose as they complete treatment (Waisberg & Porter, 1994). A study of a mixed group of non-psychotic patients receiving psychotherapy indicates that the construct of meaning in life has a more general applicability to psychiatric samples, and that pre-treatment measures of meaninglessness and lack of fulfilment predict the outcome of therapy even when levels of pre-treatment symptoms are statistically controlled (Debats, 1996).

Process

Kelly (1955) proposed that each individual develops a unique set of personal constructs in order to understand the present and predict the future. According to Kelly, personal construct systems differ in how one-dimensional or elaborated they are, and in their ability to account for the data of experience. Anxiety arises, he suggested, when individuals become aware that their construct system is inadequate to comprehend and explain the events with which they are confronted. Psychotherapy acts to free individuals from the limitations of their own construct systems, in part by changing and elaborating the way they construe problematic experiences. In order to achieve this he developed one of the first constructivist therapies.

Bowlby's (1980) attachment theory included detailed discussion of the cognitive consequences of having multiple but contradictory experiences at the hands of caregivers. He suggested that under these circumstances people would develop alternative representations or 'working models' involving themselves and their caregivers. Some would be positive and be associated with high self-esteem and feelings of interpersonal security whereas others would be associated with low self-esteem and negative feelings such as anxiety over abandonment or despair. Both sets of representations would be available to be activated in the appropriate circumstances, and could influence the interpretation of ongoing experience.

The notion of a cognitive structure that, when activated, can influence the interpretation of new stimuli and events, has received powerful support from experimental studies. Evidence reviewed by Eysenck (1992) suggests that anxious patients demonstrate both attentional biases that select threat-related stimuli for preferential processing, and interpretive biases that select threat-related meanings rather than neutral meanings from ambiguous stimuli. These biases do not appear to be present in the absence of an anxious mood.

Bowlby also proposed that the reaction to loss of an attachment figure is a phase of protest and anger which, if it does not succeed in restoring the loss, is followed by a phase of despair. During this period there is an oscillation between conscious preoccupation with the loss and defensive exclusion of related thoughts and reminders. This theory was elaborated by Parkes (1971, 1986) who formulated loss in terms of 'psychosocial transitions'. Psychosocial transitions are major life changes that involve disruption to basic assumptions about one's nature, needs, goals and sources of support. Bereavement, Parkes suggested, consists of the difficult and painful process of abandoning long-held assumptions and adopting new and more appropriate ones.

More recently, other authors have described changes in personal meaning structures following loss or trauma in similar terms. Horowitz (1990) formulated bereavement in terms of changes to 'person schemas', cognitive structures summarizing information about oneself, close others and relationships. He too described the formation of new structures as emerging from a period characterized by alternation between intrusion and avoidance of painful thoughts and memories. Janoff-Bulman (1992) focused principally on the nature of the pre-existing models of the world which the individual carries into the traumatic situation. She argued that PTSD results from the shattering of certain basic assumptions about the world. These are: the assumption of personal invulnerability; the perception of the world as meaningful or comprehensible; and the view of the self in a positive light.

Empirical studies of individuals faced with traumatic experiences such as accidents or assaults confirm that existential questions about the meaning of and reason for the trauma occurring, and about how to rebuild a life in the aftermath, are common (Janoff-Bulman, 1992). The construction of meaningful accounts that attempt to provide explanations for what has occurred appears to be an important part of the recovery process (Harvey, Orbuch & Weber, 1990; Orbuch et al., 1994), and opportunities to develop such accounts by producing a series of narratives promote successful adaptation (Pennebaker, Kiecolt-Glaser & Glaser, 1988). A study of bereaved parents found that the ability to restore meaning after their child's death was linked to the prior existence of a meaning structure that could place the death in context, for example a conviction that the death had a purpose known only by God (Braun & Berg, 1994).

Resistance to acknowledging painful thoughts and memories connected to traumatic events has been repeatedly noted, an observation that has close parallels in the discussion of behavioural and cognitive avoidance by cognitive-behaviour therapists (e.g. Borkovec, Shadick & Hopkins, 1990; Rachman, 1980). The incorporation of denied or warded off elements into a more inclusive script or narrative is an important part both of Horowitz's (1986) theory of trauma response and of the assimilation model, a generic model of psychotherapeutic change based on the acceptance, understanding and transformation of problematic experiences (Stiles *et al.*, 1990).

PLAN OF THE BOOK

This brief review of therapeutic practice, research and theory has identified a number of core questions. Among these are the following: Why do so many authors agree that meaning is important, and how can something so abstract have a causal impact on dysfunctional feelings and behaviours? What are the most important pathogenic meanings and where do they come from? How are such meanings represented cognitively? Can people protect themselves from such meanings? Finally, and most importantly, how do different therapies go about changing pathogenic meanings and what does such change consist of?

The structure of the book is as follows. This chapter and the next one review the empirical and conceptual grounds for the belief that meaning transformation is a pervasive aspect of psychotherapy and is causally related to outcome. Chapters 3, 4, 5 and 6 analyse the biological, cognitive and social factors that determine the way in which meanings are organized and the themes commonly encountered in clients with psychological disorders. Chapter 7 describes the ways in which individuals may protect themselves from having to acknowledge unwanted meanings by using defensive manoeuvres. The next four chapters examine the processes employed to assess and transform meaning in cognitive, humanistic and psychoanalytic psychotherapy with a variety of client groups. Finally, we review the common themes emerging from these widely differing perspectives and discuss the foundations that have been laid for a systematic study of meaning in psychotherapy.

REFERENCES

Abramson, L.Y., Seligman, M.E.P. & Teasdale, J.D. (1978). Learned helplessness in humans: Critique and reformulation. *Journal of Abnormal Psychology*, **87**, 49–74.

Abramson, L.Y., Metalsky, G.I. & Alloy, L.B. (1989). Hopelessness depression: A theory-based subtype of depression. *Psychological Review*, **96**, 358–372.

Andrews, B. & Brewin, C.R. (1990). Attributions of blame for marital violence: A study of antecedents and consequences. *Journal of Marriage and the Family*, **52**, 757–767.

Beck, A.T. (1983). Cognitive therapy of depression: New perspectives. In P.J. Clayton & J.E. Barrett (eds), *Treatment of Depression: Old Controversies and New Approaches* (pp. 265–290). New York: Raven.

Blatt, S.J. & Zuroff, D.C. (1992). Interpersonal relatedness and self-definition: Two prototypes for depression. *Clinical Psychology Review*, **12**, 527–562.

Borkovec, T.D., Shadick, R. & Hopkins, M. (1990). The nature of moral and pathological worry. In R. Rapee & D.H. Barlow (eds), *Chronic Anxiety and Generalized
Anxiety Disorder.* New York: Plenum.

Bowlby, J. (1980). *Attachment and Loss. 3. Loss: Sadness and Depression.* London:
Hogarth Press.

Braun, M.J. & Berg, D.H. (1994). Meaning reconstruction in the experience of
parental bereavement. *Death Studies,* **18**, 105–129.

Brewin, C.R., Firth-Cozens, J., Furnham, A. & McManus, I.C. (1992). Self-criticism
in adulthood and recalled childhood experience. *Journal of Abnormal Psychology,*
101, 561–566.

Clark, D.M. (1988). A cognitive model of panic attacks. In S. Rachman & J.D.
Maser (eds), *Panic: Psychological perspectives* (pp. 71–89). Hillsdale, NJ: Erlbaum.

Cohn, H.W. (1994). What is existential psychotherapy? *British Journal of Psychiatry,*
165, 699–701.

Debats, D.L. (1996). Meaning in life: Clinical relevance and predictive power.
British Journal of Clinical Psychology, **35**, 503–516.

Ehlers, A. & Steil, R. (1995). Maintenance of intrusive memories in posttraumatic
stress disorder: A cognitive approach. *Behavioural and Cognitive Psychotherapy,*
23, 217–249.

Eysenck, M.W. (1992). *Anxiety: The Cognitive Perspective.* Hove, UK: Erlbaum.

Frankl, V.E. (1973). *The Doctor and the Soul.* Harmondsworth: Penguin.

Guidano, V.F. (1987). *Complexity of the Self.* New York: Guilford Press.

Guidano, V.F. (1991). *The Self in Process: Toward a Post-rationalist Cognitive Therapy.*
New York: Guilford Press.

Harvey, J.H., Orbuch, T.L. & Weber, A. (1990). A social psychological model of
account-making in response to severe stress. *Journal of Language and Social Psychology,* **9**, 191–207.

Hazan, C. & Shaver, P. (1987). Romantic love conceptualised as an attachment
process. *Journal of Personality and Social Psychology,* **52**, 511–524.

Hermans, H.J.M., Kempen, H.J.G. & van Loon, R.J.P. (1992). The dialogical self:
Beyond individualism and rationalism. *American Psychologist,* **47**, 23–33.

Horowitz, M.J. (1986). *Stress Response Syndromes* (2nd edn). New York: Jason
Aronson.

Horowitz, M.J. (1990). A model of mourning: Changes in schemas of self and
others. *Journal of the American Psychoanalytic Association,* **38**, 297–324.

Janoff-Bulman, R. (1992). *Shattered Assumptions: Towards a New Psychology of
Trauma.* New York: The Free Press.

Kelly, G.A. (1955). *The Psychology of Personal Constructs* (Vols 1 and 2). New York:
Norton.

Lang, P.J. (1979). A bio-informational theory of emotional imagery. *Psychophysiology,* **16**, 495–512.

Mahoney, M.J. (1991). *Human Change Processes: The Scientific Foundations of Psychotherapy.* New York: Basic Books.

Meichenbaum, D. & Fitzpatrick, D. (1993). A constructivist narrative perspective
of stress and coping: Stress inoculation applications. In L. Goldberger & S.
Breznitz (eds), *Handbook of Stress* (2nd edn). New York: Free Press.

Neimeyer, R.A. (1993). An appraisal of constructivist psychotherapies. *Journal of
Consulting and Clinical Psychology,* **61**, 221–234.

Newcomb, M.D. & Harlow, L.L. (1986). Life events and substance use among
adolescents: Mediating effects of perceived loss of control and meaninglessness
in life. *Journal of Personality and Social Psychology,* **51**, 564–577.

Orbuch, T.L., Harvey, J.H., Davis, S.H. & Merbach, N.J. (1994). Account-making
and confiding as acts of meaning in response to sexual assault. *Journal of Family
Violence,* **9**, 249–264.

Parkes, C.M. (1971). Psychosocial transitions: A field for study. *Social Science and Medicine*, **5**, 101–115.

Parkes, C.M. (1986). *Bereavement: Studies in Grief in Adult Life*, (2nd edn). London: Tavistock.

Pennebaker, J.W., Kiecolt-Glaser, J.K. & Glaser, R. (1988). Disclosure of traumas and immune function: Health implications for psychotherapy. *Journal of Consulting and Clinical Psychology*, **56**, 239–245.

Perls, F.S. (1969). *Gestalt Therapy Verbatim*. Lafayette, CA: Real People Press.

Power, M.J. & Dalgleish, T. (1996). *Cognition and Emotion: From Order to Disorder*. Hove: Erlbaum.

Rachman, S. (1980). Emotional processing. *Behaviour Research and Therapy*, **18**, 51–60.

Reker, G.T. & Wong, P.T. (1988). Aging as an individual process: Toward a theory of personal meaning. In J.E. Birren & V.L. Bengston (eds), *Emergent Theories of Aging* (pp. 214–246). New York: Springer.

Ricoeur, P. (1981). *Hermeneutics and the Human Sciences* (trans. J.B. Thompson). Cambridge: Cambridge University Press.

Rogers, C.R. (1959). A theory of therapy, personality and interpersonal relationships. In S. Koch (ed), *Psychology: A Study of a Science* (Vol. 3). New York: McGraw-Hill.

Rogers, C.R. (1974). Client-centred psychotherapy. In A.M. Freedman, H.I. Kaplan & B.J. Sadock (eds), *Comprehensive Textbook of Psychiatry*. Baltimore: Williams & Wilkins.

Seligman, M.E.P. (1971). Phobias and preparedness. *Behavior Therapy*, **2**, 307–320

Seligman, M.E.P. (1975). *Helplessness: On Depression, Development and Death*. San Francisco: Freeman.

Smucker, M.R. & Niederee, J. (1995). Treating incest-related PTSD and pathogenic schemas through imaginal exposure and rescripting. *Cognitive and Behavioral Practice*, **2**, 63–92.

Stiles, W.B., Elliott, R., Llewelyn, S.P., Firth-Cozens, J.A., Margison, F.R., Shapiro, D.A. & Hardy, G. (1990). Assimilation of problematic experiences by clients in psychotherapy. *Psychotherapy*, **27**, 411–420.

Storms, M.D. & McCaul, K.D. (1976). Attribution processes and the emotional exacerbation of dysfunctional behavior. In J.H. Harvey, W.J. Ickes & R.F. Kidd (eds), *New Directions in Attribution Research* (Vol. 1). Hillsdale, NJ: Erlbaum.

Wachtel, P. (1977). *Psychoanalysis and Behavior Therapy: Toward an Integration*. New York: Basic Books.

Waisberg, J.L. & Porter, J.E. (1994). Purpose in life and outcome of treatment for alcohol dependence. *British Journal of Clinical Psychology*, **33**, 49–63.

White, M. & Epston, D. (1990). *Narrative Means to Therapeutic Ends*. New York: Norton.

Yalom, I.D. (1980). *Existential Psychotherapy*. New York: Basic Books.

Young, J. (1990). *Cognitive Therapy for Personality Disorders: A Schema-focused Approach*. Sarasota, FI: Professional Resource Exchange.

Zika, S. & Chamberlain, K. (1992). On the relation between meaning in life and psychological wellbeing. *British Journal of Psychology*, **83**, 133–145.

Zuroff, D.C., Stotland, S., Sweetman, E., Craig, J.–A. & Koestner, R. (1995). Dependency, self-criticism and social interactions. *British Journal of Clinical Psychology*, **34**, 543–553.

Chapter 2

ON THE CAUSAL ROLE OF MEANING

Derek Bolton* and Jonathan Hill†

THE HISTORICAL PROBLEM

In the 1960s psychoanalysis was severely criticized for being unscientific. The problems identified included apparent lack of objectivity of data, the non-empirical character of its hypotheses (alleged unfalsifiability), and the questionable assumption that meanings are causes (Popper, 1962; also, for example, Clare, 1967). This pressure contributed to the development of the hermeneutic readings of psychoanalytic theory popular in the 1970s, which accepted, more or less reluctantly, the demarcation between understanding and causal, or more generally, scientific, explanation (Habermas, 1971; Klein, 1976; Schafer, 1976; Ricoeur, 1981; and for critical commentary Grünbaum, 1984, 1986).

Psychoanalytic theory, as the main and uncompromising proponent of meaningful explanation of disorder, has carried the burden of the problematic status of meaning in relation to scientific method, but there is a general problem here, not limited to psychoanalysis. It was apparent right from the start in the cognitive science paradigm. Three of its formative influences—transformational linguistics, Artificial Intelligence (AI) theory, and the mathematical theory of communication (MCT)—all in fact explicitly eschewed reference to meaning. Chomsky's theory of language was about syntax, not semantics (Chomsky, 1957; Katz & Fodor, 1963). AI models were also typically concerned with syntax, not semantics (e.g. Pylyshyn, 1980; Graubard, 1988); and MCT dealt in amounts of information, not with its content (Shannon & Weaver, 1949; Dretske, 1983). The

*Institute of Psychiatry and Maudsley Hospital, London, and †University of Liverpool and Royal Liverpool Children's Hospital, UK

The Transformation of Meaning in Psychological Therapies.
Edited by Mick Power and Chris R. Brewin. © 1997 John Wiley & Sons Ltd.

cognitive science paradigm started off surrounded by controversy about the status, definition and role of meaning, and the controversy continues, as will be discussed later.

The problem of meaning in relation to scientific method, and in relation to the scientific world-picture generally, in fact has deep roots in the history of ideas. The last decades of the 19th century saw the emergence of new sciences, particularly history and social science, which had as their subject matter the expression of mind in society. To the extent that these new *Geisteswissenschaften* had their roots in German idealism, rather than in the 17th century dichotomy between mind and matter, knowledge of mind was not a problem for them: the activity of mind in culture and society was a given. But there arose then a fundamentally new problem which remains ours, namely, that knowledge of mind and its expression in activity do not conform readily to the methodological assumptions and rules of the natural sciences. The tension found expression in the celebrated distinctions between *meaning* and *causality*, and between *understanding* and *explaining* (see von Wright, 1971, for a historical, critical review). Human activity is permeated by meaning, understanding of which is a fundamental aim of the cultural sciences. Meaningful phenomena, however, and the way they are known, seem to be different in fundamental ways from the subject matter and methods of the natural sciences. One contrast is that meaningful phenomena (such as a historical event, or a cultural practice) are singular or even unique, whereas natural science deals (mostly) with repeated and/or repeatable phenomena. Another, connected contrast is that physics seeks and uses general causal laws in its explanations, while the cultural sciences produce diverse meaningful accounts of diverse events. A third contrast is more explicitly epistemological. Understanding seems to be subjective, to draw on empathic abilities which vary from person to person, while the methods of observation in the natural sciences are objective, and the results are meant to be the same for all.

The problems of mind and meaning have to do with a tension between meaningful phenomena and scientific method, the method used by the hugely successful paradigm of knowledge, modern natural science. They are distinct from the problems of mind and body, these being primarily the apparent impossibility of causal interaction between the two, and the epistemological privacy of mind. On the other hand it was inevitable that the two problematics became muddled up. This is especially true in psychology, where both the mind/body issues and the problems of meaning and scientific method are of central relevance. The Cartesian framework remained enormously influential, in philosophy and in the sciences, including the new psychology. The older Cartesian problems of mind and body then overlapped and combined with the new problems of mind, meaning and scientific method, both contributing to the idea that meaningful mental (immaterial) states, and the meaningful activity which they allegedly produce, had no clear place in the scientific world-picture. The conflict here was genuine and profound, and has been resolved by splitting: causality as opposed to meaning, explanation as opposed to understanding, behavioural science as opposed to hermeneutic non-science.

THE PROBLEM DECONSTRUCTED BY THE COGNITIVE PARADIGM

The terms of all these problems are, however, ultimately undermined by the cognitive paradigm in psychology. This is the main point to be explicated in the present chapter. The new paradigm, particularly in its role as successor to conditioning theory and behaviourism, posits mental or cognitive states as implicated in the regulation of behaviour (Gardner, 1985; Baars, 1986). In this context meaning makes its appearance under the heading of the 'information' carried by the mental or cognitive states, and what matters in this context, namely, the regulation of behaviour, is *semantic information*, information with *content*, which is about the environment and specifically about organism–environment interactions, and which is correct or incorrect, etc. Mental (or cognitive) states have to be semantic, to carry this kind of information, if they are to be any use in the regulation of action. So theory has to posit these semantic properties, as encoded in the acting being.

So are these explanations causal? A polemical argument will do here. You can do hermeneutic analysis on a text, dream or discourse, and this can be described as non-causal non-science, but this construction does not suit cognitive-behavioural psychology. The best science of behaviour we have, the legitimate heir to behaviourism and conditioning theory, posits semantic states regulating behaviour. How can it be said that experimental cognitive-behavioural psychology is doing hermeneutics?!

This polemic, however, just indicates that the framework of the science/hermeneutics distinction has fallen apart. Behind the polemic is a rational argument. The aim of cognitive-behavioural science is not (just) to make sense of, to feel that one understands, nor is it just to retrodict events. A primary aim is to predict, to find necessary and/or sufficient conditions of the living being behaving in this way or that, interacting with the environment in such and such a way so as to achieve certain results. There is no viable alternative to construing the explanations in cognitive-behavioural science as being causal.

On the other hand, surely causes have to be material? Yes, certainly if the only other choice is 'immaterial'; in other words, if we are still confined within the thought space of 17th century dualism. In that case, we can say that the causes of behaviour must be in the material brain, and this is obviously consistent with the fact that brain damage puts paid, more or less, to action.

Thus we have the position that *both* cognitive, semantic states *and* brain states cause behaviour. Now while these dual forms of explanation might look problematic sitting together, the behavioural and brain sciences have no trouble with them in practice (as opposed to philosophical reflection), because it is fundamental to theory that:

- brain states are semantic (they encode/process/regulate behaviour according to information).

This may be called for convenience the 'encoding thesis'. It is fundamental to the cognitive-behavioural paradigm, and is critically important. It marks the end of both the meaning/causality distinction, and of the mind/matter distinction, because it says, first, that semantic states are causal, and it implies, second, that the brain as *res extensa* is also *res cogitans*.

OBJECTIONS TO THE ENCODING THESIS

In fact the otherwise innocent-looking encoding thesis comes under *massive* pressure, the main thrust of which is as follows:

- Surely the brain cannot (really, literally) be semantic—because it really is just material/physical . . .

And then:

- . . . it must be the brain which is (really, literally, after all is said and done) doing the causing, and when we speak about semantic states doing this, we are speaking 'as if', as a mere aid to prediction (*sic*), or we are conceptually confused, or just plain wrong . . .

On the one hand there is indignation from *physicalism* at the idea of causality which is not ultimately a matter of physical events covered by physical laws (in which semantics definitely have no place). On the other hand there is protest from *hermeneutics* at the idea of meaning being taken out of its context of social activity and tied somehow to (mere) physical events in the brain.

Physicalist perspectives on cognition are dominant in North American philosophy, while the hermeneutic tradition in psychology is strongest in Europe. Considering the physicalist approaches, key players in the debate on the role of meaning in mental causation include the following, discussed in more detail in Bolton & Hill (1996). Stich (1983) accepted that cognitive states have a causal role and can be identified with brain states, but argued that there is no need to credit them with semantic properties. In fact, Stich went on, cognitive science should jettison meaning, which is essentially vague and observer-relative. Putnam (1975) argued that 'meaning ain't in the head', because it is defined by reference to external (physically defined) environmental features. Fodor (1982) correctly identified a problem here for cognitive science: causes have to be internal, local and proximate, and if meaning 'ain't in the head' it cannot be causal. Fodor's Language of Thought hypothesis (Fodor, 1975, 1987) has semantic mental states as causal, but only because they have syntactic properties which map onto neural states which also have a syntax; these do the causing of behaviour according to physical laws.

Dennett (1987) emphasizes and explicates the logic of the Intentional Stance as opposed to the Physical Stance in explanations of systemic functioning: the Intentional Stance, with its use of information-processing concepts, helps to predict, but it may or may not pick our causes, and if it does they are physical causes. Davidson (1963, 1970) has influentially argued that reasons are causes, because they are identical with neural states, but the causing really goes on at the physical level and the causal laws are physical. According to Davidson the language of reasons has an unlawlike—anomalous—relation to neural states, and is in fact in a business other than defining causes and making predictions, namely, the business of rationalizing action, bringing behaviour under rational norms.

These various positions have in common the assumption that causality, whether of billiard balls or human action, is regarded as fundamentally a matter of physical events covered by physical laws, and the language of meaningful mental states is either not causal, or is so only insofar as it mimics physics.

The conclusion can also be reached from the hermeneutic side of the dichotomy, by stressing the non-scientific autonomy of meaning, as can already be seen in Davidson's sophisticated position. Following Wittgenstein (1953), for example, it can be said that meaning (language, signs) belongs to activity as a whole, perhaps specifically to language-users, embedded in forms of life and culture. It may then appear to be a 'conceptual error' to attribute meaning to the brain, and to suppose that brain states encoding meaning cause behaviour (Hacker, 1987). Or again, in contrasting what he calls the 'second cognitive revolution' to the more familiar first, Harre (1994, p. 39), writes:

> It seemed as if behind what we were doing there was another set of cognitive goings on, the processing of information. There are no other *cognitive*

goings on. There are just the neurophysiological processes running in the brain and nervous system and the discursive processes engaged in by skilled actors in the carrying out of this or that project. Neurophysiological processes are governed by the causality of physics and chemistry, discursive activities are governed by the rules and conventions of symbol use.

ATTRIBUTIONS OF MEANING ENABLE PREDICTION OF ACTION

There is, therefore, a formidable array of otherwise disparate views converging on the idea that meanings are not causes, and specifically that they are not causes because they are not encoded in neural states. As against all these considerations—which are primarily philosophical—there is, as already mentioned, the practice of cognitive psychology and cognitive neuroscience, which proceeds with remarkable naïvety on the assumptions that animal and human behaviour is best modelled by positing regulation by (or causation by) semantic, information-carrying states, that of course it is also true that the brain regulates behaviour, including on the basis of information coming in from the environment, and that these two points are quite compatible because what the brain does is process encoded information.

So what is the resolution of the apparent conflict here? It is true that you do not see meaning (or information) in the brain with the naked eye, microscopes, EEGs, PET or MRI. But no one thinks that you have to be able to 'see' posits in scientific theory. The posits are valid because they play an essential role in theory-driven predictions. Semantic properties get attributed to the brain *that* way.

But further then, the 'causal laws' invoked by cognitive-behavioural science, concerning stimuli, the interaction between information-carrying states, and the regulation of behaviour, are (pretty obviously) not physical laws, however broadly construed, i.e. not mechanical, not thermodynamic, not chemical, not physiological (unless the physiological processes are being described as information-processing).

This is what runs up against physicalist preconceptions, the idea that there can be causal laws which do not map onto, reduce to, which are not true in virtue of, physical laws covering physically defined events. But why should this idea be so unpalatable? Perhaps because a too literal, too 17th century, view of reality is adopted, as composed of 'objects', which must be physical objects (as opposed to mental objects), following laws explicated by physics. The 20th century view, by contrast, is that reality is better conceived in terms of patterns of energy or activity, in which case the thought that physics picks out some of these but not all is at least thinkable. It is crucial to biology, for example, that living beings are sensitive to patterns which do not map onto physical kinds, e.g. food as opposed to toxins. Social animals are sensitive to the meaning of behaviours, to patterns of intentionality in Dennett's sense, even though, as is well known, these do not correspond to physically defined motor movements. Causal laws covering the behaviour of living beings typically invoke sensitivity to these patterns, and the whole story is grounded in, has to remain compatible with, but soon exceeds, what is of interest to physics.

COGNITIVE-BEHAVIOURAL CAUSAL LAWS HAVE INCREASING SPECIFICITY

We can now note a further characteristic of cognitive-behavioural laws which distinguishes them from physics: they become *more local* and *less general*. In phylogenesis, living beings are increasingly differentiated, and, what amounts to the same, they become sensitive to increasingly diverse aspects of the environment. Indeed, the notion of environment itself becomes accordingly more differentiated and diverse. The physical environment, which is essentially the same for all, accounts for less and less of the variance in behaviour. Thus the biological, zoological and ethological textbooks deal not with living beings in general but with the behaviour and information-processing systems of this or that species, or species/ environment nexus. In human beings differentiation and specificity are elaborated further in ontogenesis, associated with high capacities of learning. Individuals as well as species learn, and this individualism is reflected in increasing specificity of the rules governing behaviour. There are by all means generalities, for example that the experience of uncontrollable aversive events leads to helplessness, but what these generalities amount to in particular cases may be highly specific, applicable, in the limiting case, to just one case. What counts as '(insufficiently) controllable' will depend on many inner and outer circumstances, and also what counts as '(too) aversive', and so on.

Consider, for example, the following case. A 25-year-old woman was involved in a relatively minor road traffic accident, and in the immediate aftermath was left feeling terrified and abandoned by the roadside. Over the following weeks she developed symptoms of misery, loss of interest, sleep disturbance, concentration difficulties, and feelings of worthlessness. She was preoccupied with distressing, intrusive thoughts about the accident, but specifically with fears of damage (which she did not suffer), and terror and abandonment (which she did).

What is the explanation of this major depressive episode? There was no reported psychiatric history, so it was not a simple matter of relapse. There were certainly signs characteristic of post-traumatic stress, but the predominant signs were of depression, not stress. This was so far unpredictable.

About four weeks after the accident the woman was lying in bed, feeling dreadful, and was suddenly hit by an image 'like being hit on the back of the head by a hammer'. It was an image of being sexually assaulted as a child by a friend of the family. She had recollections of being seriously assaulted only twice, but remembered having to go back to the house many times, so she had many experiences of helpless fear. The woman had not remembered these incidents since childhood, prior to the road traffic accident. The emotional state that she got into after the accident, fear and abandonment, presumably cued the recall of the child sexual abuse, according to principles of state-dependent learning and recall. This has nothing to do with being in therapy (the recall was before any therapy), nothing to do with action against the perpetrator (who was by this time dead), and nothing to do with compensation (if anything, the recall might possibly count against a compensation claim in connection with the road traffic accident).

There are general explanatory principles invoked here, for example that childhood sexual abuse involves terror of damage and isolation, that defence against these experiences may involve splitting and forgetting, that recall of the events is more likely in a similar cognitive-emotional state. But their application in particular cases can be highly specific, or individual. It is not necessary to suppose that any other human being has gone through just this sequence of events. Bearing in mind all the contexts, it is indeed unlikely that anyone else has. Thus, for example, this particular young woman's experience was conditioned by the care she had from parents, which she recalls as extremely good, and which protected her from intrusions from the childhood trauma, until she was 25 and happened to be involved in a particular kind of accident.

We may summarize the main point as follows:

- Causal explanations in biopsychological science become increasingly specific, up to and including, in the case of human beings, explanations in terms of the 'personal meanings' of events and actions.

COGNITIVE STATES NOT NECESSARILY CONSCIOUS

It is clear in all this that the cognitive-affective states regulating behaviour are not necessarily conscious, e.g. amenable to self-report. The idea that they should be is just a hangover from the Cartesian concept of mind, and has nothing to do with the cognitive-behavioural explanatory paradigm. What matters in this paradigm is that cognitive-affective states regulate behaviour. Articulation in language is altogether a different issue (Nisbett & Wilson, 1977; Dennett, 1991; see Chapter 4, this volume).

DISORDER AND THE CAUSAL ROLE OF MEANING

This point is critical to the understanding of disordered psychological states, which typically intrude into consciousness or into behaviour, without the person having a clear idea how or why. The result indeed is apparently as incomprehensible as an epileptic fit, a meaningless intrusion into normal mental life. Indeed it always is a *possible* explanation of disordered mental states that they are caused by a lower-level disruption of normal information-processing. 'Lower-level' means: by a physical or chemical lesion interfering with the information-processing function of biological systems. Cerebral atrophy, electrical discharges and psychotropic drugs are examples of this 'bottom-up' type of causal explanation, and they have nothing to do with meaning.

This is the paradigm explanation for the so-called Medical Model in Psychiatry (Szasz, 1961). It is supported by the occasional discovery of physico-chemical causes, but also by an *a priori* line of thought, as follows:

- Well, anyway, meanings can't be causes in the abnormal case because they have run out. So we have to look at lower level causes, brain–behaviour relationships after all.

But the question of where the limits of meaning lie presses hard. Generally there are meanings in abundance over and above what is available to any one individual or culture at any one time, and they regulate activity. They include what readily feels familiar, but also meanings which are not, or which are hardly, comprehensible to us. The limits are vague and negotiable. This of course feels like hermeneutics and sociology and makes the scientific mind uncomfortable. But the implication of the line of thought we are tracking here is that if we want the best scientific explanation of human behaviour—not just to understand the behaviour, but to give causal, predictive explanations—then we have to take on board, find out about, the systems of beliefs, and world-pictures, which guide and regulate the behaviour. This applies equally whether the behaviour and beliefs are ours or not, whether they are scientific experimentation, or the practices of tribal magicians. Some would reject such a prospect for behavioural science, but the grounds are specious. Specifically, the fact that meaning has run out for any particular person or group so far says as much about these observers as about the cognitive processes regulating activity.

Alternatives to the Medical Model in Psychiatry suppose that meaning is disrupted not by lower-level causes but by *more meaning*. They typically invoke intrusion by cognitive-affective states, typically resulting from earlier traumatic, forgotten or at least unaccommodated experiences. This was the psychological model of explanation of mental disorder envisaged at the start by Freud, and in a much simpler way by Watson. Freud saw further that intolerable mental states would be deflected from consciousness, and, one might add, from access to control over action. Deflection may involve a variety of mental strategies generally known as 'defences', such as denial, splitting and projection (e.g. Sandler, 1988; see Chapter 7, this volume).

The point of the line of argument followed through this chapter is that the form of explanation which appeals to semantic states (to intrusion of intolerable states, and defences against them) is *also causal*, is as causal as explanation in terms of, for example, cerebral atrophy. It is, however, a different form of explanation to that appropriate in the physical sciences, and invoked in the medical model of mental disorder, because it essentially turns on the *intentionality* (or the semantics) of the processes involved.

Intentional-causal processes may also have a role in disorder primarily caused by non-intentional processes. The system as a whole attempts to act despite the deficit, making meaningful compensations or adjustments to it. For example, if people with schizophrenia have suffered early neuro-developmental disturbance (Murray, 1994) which disrupts the ordering and hence prediction of experience by learnt regularities (Hemsley, 1994), then the question arises—for the living being—of how to carry on for the best notwithstanding this disadvantage. Strategies might include restriction of experience, by behavioural means, or cognitive, perhaps by 'delusions' (Garety & Hemsley, 1995). We are then back in the business of trying to understand behaviour in terms of meaningful processes.

This point applies whenever there is a physical, non-intentional disruption to activity, whether it be a broken leg, a physical illness, a maladaptive gene, brain insult, or mental impairment. What needs understanding/explaining is what the disruption means to the person as a whole, how he or she adapts to it, and makes sense of it. What appear as 'symptoms' will probably be for the most part the result of meaningful adaptations to the underlying problem, and the causal models which form the basis for invention will largely invoke intentional, meaningful causation (Bolton & Hill, 1996).

COGNITIVE-BEHAVIOURAL SEMANTICS AS A RESEARCH PROGRAMME

The prediction of the line of thought outlined so far is that meaning will assume increasing importance in cognitive-behavioural science, whether applied to the mind in order or in disorder. The context will be research programmes already in the cognitive science paradigm:

- abstract (mathematical, computational) problems about how information can be encoded and processed
- neurophysiology and neurochemistry.

The first, AI, is largely (not only) an abstract investigation of syntax, and the second determines its realization in the brain. A further aspect of this neuroscience programme is:

- the study of which brain structures process particular kinds of information.

This study, revolutionized by functional PET and MRI, can be concerned with content, in defining which areas of the brain are implicated in, for example, fear response to a particular stimulus (e.g. Hoehn-Saric & Benkelfat, 1994). But the methodology is generally limited to gross functions, such as attention, language or fear, served by correspondingly large areas of the brain, and the content it can study is generally limited to what is controlled by stimuli which can be presented in the scanning machine.

In the context of these scientific research programmes, the implication of the line of thought sketched in this paper is that there will also be:

- a *cognitive-behavioural science of semantics*, elucidating the 'meanings' which regulate behaviour.

This programme will have to run independently of AI and neuroscience. In particular, the study of the brain will be no substitute for it. Rather, they are different enterprises with a creative tension between them. The cognitive-behavioural theory of meaning is paramount in the sense that it defines *what* the brain is doing (and ultimately for what purpose). AI and neuroscience between them define *how* it does it.

All this is uncontroversial while we stick to meanings in the scientific paradigms, when we think of conditioning, the acquisition of S–S or S–R linkages, and perhaps even the acquisition of expectations, or language processing and visual imagery. But these are elements only in the organization of complex animal behaviour, and specifically of human behaviour. The cognitive-behavioural science of meaning has to be *much* wider than this, and has to be concerned with content.

THE EPISTEMOLOGY OF MEANING IS BROAD-BASED

So what is the epistemology of meaning? How do we know what meanings regulate behaviour? Or to put the point another way: what matters to human beings, what are their goals, what is the kind of thing they need to know relevant to achieving them, and so on. Here it has to be remembered that what the person is inclined to say is at best a partial, not necessarily valid, guide. Broadly speaking the epistemology of meaning includes the following building blocks.

Biological/evolutionary theory. (See Chapter 3, this volume.) An axiom of this theory is that the function of biological systems is in general terms to aid survival. This applies equally to the information-processing systems which are of special interest in the cognitive science paradigm. We may infer that information-processing is fundamentally in the service of adaptive action. Some goals are necessary for all living beings, such as energy consumption. We know on the basis of evolutionary theory, for example, that need for food and mating are powerful drives that will regulate at least some information-processing and behaviour, even if the person or the culture may choose to ignore this. We also know from biological theory that other factors assume high importance for social animals, such as status in the group. It should be emphasized that there is here no suggestion that human meanings in some sense all 'reduce to' basic biological drives. Rather, human meanings have many layers, of which one fundamental one is the biological. There are others.

Developmental psychology. (See Chapter 5, this volume.) Evolutionary theoretical, biological considerations merge seamlessly into developmental psychology. What we see there includes the fundamental importance of early patterns of communication, care and attachment (Bowlby, 1969; Sroufe & Waters, 1977; Stern, 1985; Crittenden, 1992).

Social sciences. To the biopsychological theory of meaning are added the social sciences. The progression of the sciences reflects human development, and it is this development which cognitive-behavioural semantics seeks to track: living beings grounded in evolutionary nature and elaborated in culture. It is impossible to know what meanings are regulating behaviour without understanding culture. Superficially the same event may have very different meanings between societies. A certain kind of practice may be innocent according to one set of values, but sin to be avoided or concealed in another, and so on. Of course all this is obvious. All that has ever been controversial is whether or not these socially constructed meanings have anything to do with the 'hard science' of causally explaining and predicting behaviour. The argument of this chapter is that meanings as encoded in the brain are implicated in the causation (regulation) of behaviour, and this point is the same whether the meanings are cultural or biologically determined drives and preoccupations.

The broad nature of meaning reflects diversity in ways of change. Some meanings are innate, as specified by evolutionary theory, some are innately maturing, specified by developmental psychology, and some are learnt from experience. Meanings of all those kinds of origin interact with the theory that we learn from our family, teachers and cultural media. Meanings change in all these ways, and the processes are generally open to view. Or what passes for change is the acquisition of alternative repertoires; so old meanings never die, they just get superseded, remaining still accessible for re-enactment given the right cues.

RETROGRESSIVE AND PROGRESSIVE META-THEORIES

This new cognitive-behavioural semantics certainly looks less than attractive to the scientific eye. It encompasses so much, extends vaguely off into cultural studies including semiotics, and has a vague empirical basis, with principles of change looking as much like politics as science. There is undoubted pressure to keep alive something like the old science/hermeneutics distinction. This conservativism leads to retrogressive claims, basically repetitions of what is familiar in the old dualist, positivist paradigms. These include statements to the effect that the most important (basic, fundamental) science consists of studying the brain and brain–behaviour relationships *as opposed to* meaningful mental states. According to this view the future lies in the new and ever more sophisticated neurotechnologies which will tell us about the fundamental causal processes, or in behavioural and ultimately molecular genetics. One can ignore mental meaningful states, and the quite distinct methodologies they require, such as textual analysis, or conditions of acceptance of interpretations, or theoretical work on meaning, personal and cultural. Why should a *scientific* research council fund that sort of thing? And so on. The problem with this old way of looking at things is that it just cannot account for the fact that meaning (causally) regulates behaviour, and that any causal model of the behaviour which omits this fact will be for that reason drastically inadequate.

On the other side of the same coin, there are the claims that personal, family and social meanings are a matter for hermeneutics *as opposed to* causal science, and are out of reach of scientific theory and investigation. According to this line of thought, understanding a semiotic agent, one for whom meaning matters, has nothing to do with science, which can only misrepresent and distract from what really matters, which is fundamentally a matter of relating, and so on. One sign of the problem in all this is that the study of meaning is left stranded. There is no clear way that we might set out from here to study, for example, adult sequelae of childhood adversity, or how one kind of risk factor for the development of psychopathology interacts with others, or with protective factors, and so on.

Of course, the views sketched above have nothing to do with a particular set of empirical data, or even with this or that theory. They are more a matter of ideologies, or what can be called 'meta-methodological principles'. These are assumptions that say what kind of methodologies are worth pursuing, what kind of data are worth collecting. Hence typically they can never be confirmed or disconfirmed by any experience or experiment: they claim all of a certain kind of data, and dismiss as entirely irrelevant, typically with more or less concealed contempt, all the rest.

The hermeneutic exercise in its 20th century form is fundamentally a reaction, and a necessary dialectical response, to the hegemony of the methodology of physical science, particularly in the empiricist and positivist forms it took from the 17th to the 19th century. But that science too had to be constructed, and can and has been deconstructed. It took a great deal of intellectual work, over a century or so, to conceive of nature as infinite, absolute, geometrical space, and to work out the concept of experiment (Burtt, 1932; Koyré, 1968). So far as our time is concerned, it was only a few decades ago that meaning was seen as nothing to do with causation of behaviour, notwithstanding that human life is pervaded by meaning and is unimaginable without it, and it was only a few decades before that that mental states were considered irrelevant.

The present task is therefore to accommodate meaning within a transformed scientific paradigm. Scientific enquiry has to adapt to increase its sensitivity to mental states and meanings, and hermeneutics (or semiotics) will have to get used to becoming more scientific, to thinking how it might answer questions about measurement and causality, concerning, for example, risk factors, outcomes, evaluating interventions, and so on. These will be the progressive theory-shifts.

To avoid giving any impression that this will be straightforward, let us by way of conclusion return to one aspect of the meaning/science distinction that was mentioned at the beginning of the chapter, namely, that understanding, as opposed to scientific explanation, typically involves empathy.

The cognitive science paradigm, coming from the scientific side of the divide, has had to approach meaning cautiously, being indeed in something like an approach–avoidance conflict about it. In sketching some elements of the semantics which belongs in the paradigm, we have emphasized the use of scientific theory, biological, psychological and social. The assumption is that knowledge of mental states and meaning essentially involves theory. The theory is to the effect that such and such kinds of activity are typically regulated by such and such kinds of meaningful, information-carrying states, all this being relativized to species, cultures, etc. Well known work on the day-to-day knowledge of mind and meaning has followed this approach, the idea being that adults, children, and indeed animals, use a 'theory of mind' to find their way in social activities (Premack & Woodruff, 1978; Davies & Stone, 1995a). So far, so quasi-scientific. However, there has been increasing and inevitable interest in reviving a much older epistemology of mind, the one based in 'empathy'. This has been proposed in the philosophy of mind and is currently a live issue in developmental psychology (Davies & Stone, 1995b). There are suggestions, speculative at present, that something like empathy, or 'mental simulation', plays a fundamental role in knowledge of other minds, that it is a fast, cheap (in terms of computing time and resources) and cheerful way of knowing in the flux of interaction between living beings where speed and good enough accuracy can be a matter of life and death.

Empathy has of course long been familiar in psychoanalytic theory under the heading of counter-transference, but it will be a particularly wild card in cognitive-behavioural science. Its future in basic science and clinical work is difficult to foresee. Empathy has generally been seen as an alternative way of knowing to theory, but the dichotomy here between empathy and theory is probably misleading (Bolton, 1995). Empathy without theory tends to be just a simple rule: it is with them as it is now (with me). Empathy in this sense might deal primitively with basic emotional states, such as loss or anger. For empathy to work effectively in anticipating the other, however, it has to take account of differences, and this is where theory becomes involved. Theory helps to define relevant differences between self and the other, differences in perspectives, in experiences and in cognitive-effective states generally. By contrast non-empathic use of theory just fails to see what is going on in the present particular case (oneself or the other).

In this sense empathy has a role in understanding mental states analogous to the role of sense-perception in knowing physical nature. Ironically sense-perception *was* problematic for modern physics, in theory though not in practice. The 17th century problem was that sense-experience was *relative* (just like empathy in fact), not up to knowing the absolute objects in space, which were known rather by mathematical theory (Burtt, 1932). However, theory never did tell you what was in front of your eyes. Kant famously broke down the previous dichotomy between conceptual understanding and sensible intuition, in a way summed up in the dictum: 'Thoughts without content are empty, intuitions without concepts are blind' (Kant, 1781; discussed in, e.g., Strawson, 1966). The analogue in the case of knowledge of mind would be this: 'Theory without content is empty; empathy without theory is blind'.

REFERENCES

Baars, B. (1986). *The Cognitive Revolution in Psychology*. New York: Guilford.
Bolton, D. (1995). Self-knowledge, error and disorder. In M. Davies & A. Stone (eds), *Mental Simulation: Evaluations and Applications*. Oxford: Blackwell, pp. 209–234.
Bolton, D. & Hill, J. (1996). *Mind, Meaning, and Mental Disorder: The nature of Causal Explanation in Psychology and Psychiatry*. Oxford: Oxford University Press.
Bowlby, J. (1969). *Attachment and Loss: I. Attachment*. London: Hogarth Press.
Burtt, E.A. (1932). *The Metaphysical Foundations of Modern Physical Science*. London: Routledge & Kegan Paul.
Chomsky, N. (1957). *Syntactic Structures*. The Hague: Mouton.
Clare, A. (1967). *Psychiatry in Dissent*. London: Tavistock.
Crittenden, P.M. (1992). Treatment of anxious attachment in infancy and early childhood. *Development and Psychopathology*, 4, 575–602.
Davidson, D. (1963). Actions, reasons, and causes. Reprinted in D. Davidson, *Essays on Actions and Events*. Oxford: Clarendon Press, 1980, pp. 3–19.
Davidson, D. (1970). Mental events. In L. Foster & J. Swanson (eds), *Experience and Theory*. MIT Press. Reprinted in D. Davidson, *Essays on Actions and Events*. Oxford: Clarendon Press, 1980, pp. 207–227.
Davies, M. & Stone, A. (1995a). *Folk Psychology*. Oxford: Blackwell.
Davies, M. & Stone, A. (1995b). *Mental Simulation: Evaluations and Applications*. Oxford: Blackwell.
Dennett, D. (1987). *The Intentional Stance*. Cambridge, MA: MIT Press.
Dennett, D. (1991). *Consciousness Explained*. Harmondsworth: Penguin.
Dretske, F. (1983). Precis of *Knowledge and the Flow of Information*, with peer commentary. *Behavioral and Brain Sciences*, 6, 55–63.
Fodor, J. (1975). *The Language of Thought*. New York: Crowell.
Fodor, J. (1982). Cognitive science and the twin earth problem. *Notre Dame Journal of Formal Logic*, 23, 116–117.
Fodor, J. (1987). *Psychosemantics*. Cambridge, MA: MIT Press.
Gardner, H. (1985). *The Mind's New Science: A History of the Cognitive Revolution*. New York: Basic Books. (Reprinted in 1987 with new Epilogue.)
Garety, P. & Hemsley, D. (1995). *Delusions*. Oxford: Oxford University Press.
Graubard, S.R. (ed.) (1988). *The Artificial Intelligence Debate: False Starts, Real Foundations*. Cambridge, MA: MIT Press.
Grünbaum, A. (1984). *The Foundations of Psychoanalysis: A Philosophical Critique*. California: University of California Press.
Grünbaum, A. (1986). Precis of *The Foundations of Psychoanalysis: A Philosophical Critique*, with peer commentary. *The Behavioral and Brain Sciences*, 9, 217–284.
Habermas, J. (1971). *Knowledge and Human Interests*. (Trans J.J. Shapiro). Boston: Beacon Press.
Hacker, P. (1987). Languages, minds and brain. In C. Blakemore & S. Greenfield (eds), *Mindwaves. Thoughts on Intelligence, Identity and Consciousness*. Oxford: Blackwell, pp. 485–505.
Harré, R. (1994). The second cognitive revolution. In A. Phillips-Griffiths (ed.), *Philosophy, Psychology and Psychiatry*. Oxford: Blackwell.
Hemsley, D. (1994). Perceptual and cognitive abnormalities as the bases for schizophrenic symptoms. In A. David & J. Cutting (eds), *The Neuropsychology of Schizophrenia*. Hove: Lawrence Erlbaum, pp. 97–116.
Hoehn-Saric, R. & Benkelfat, C. (1994). Structural and functional brain imaging in obsessive-compulsive disorder. In E. Hollander, J. Zohar, D. Marazziti & B.

Olivier (eds), *Current Insights in Obsessive Compulsive Disorder.* Chichester: Wiley, pp. 183–211.

Kant, I. (1781) *Kritik der reinen Vernunft.* English translation: Meiklejohn, J.M.D. (1934). *Critique of Pure Reason,* London: Dent.

Katz, J. & Fodor, J. (1963). The structure of a semantic theory. *Language,* **39,** 170–210.

Klein, G.S. (1976). *Psychoanalytic Theory.* New York: International Universities Press.

Koyré, A. (1968). *Metaphysics and Measurement: Essays in the Scientific Revolution.* London: Chapman & Hall.

Murray, R. (1994). Neurodevelopmental schizophrenia: the rediscovery of dementia praecox. *British Journal of Psychiatry,* **165,** 6–12.

Nisbett, R. & Wilson, T. (1977). Telling more than we can know: verbal reports on mental processes. *Psychological Review,* **84,** 31–59.

Popper, K.R. (1962). *Conjectures and Refutations.* New York: Basic Books.

Premack, D. & Woodruff, G. (1978). Does the chimpanzee have a theory of mind? *The Behavioural and Brain Sciences,* **4,** 515–526.

Putnam, H. (1975). The meaning of 'meaning'. In *Mind, Language and Reality.* Cambridge: Cambridge University Press, pp. 215–271.

Pylyshyn, Z.W. (1980). Computation and cognition: issues in the foundations of cognitive science, with peer commentary, *Behavioral and Brain Sciences,* **3,** 111–169.

Ricoeur, P. (1981). *Hermeneutics and the Human Sciences,* (trans. J.B. Thompson). Cambridge: Cambridge University Press.

Sandler, J. (ed.) (1988). *Projection, Identification, Projective Identification.* London: Karnac Books.

Schafer, R. (1976). *A New language for Psychoanalysis.* New Haven, CT: Yale University Press.

Shannon, C. & Weaver, W. (1949). *The Mathematical Theory of Communication.* Illinois: University of Illinois Press.

Sroufe, L.A. & Waters, E. (1977). Attachment as an organizational construct. *Child Development,* **48,** 1184–1199.

Stern, D. (1985). *The Interpersonal World of the Infant.* New York: Basic Books.

Stich, S. (1983). *From Folk Psychology to Cognitive Science.* Cambridge, MA: MIT Press.

Szasz, T.S. (1961). *The Myth of Mental Illness: Foundations of a Theory of Personal Conduct.* New York: Harper & Row.

Strawson, P.F. (1966). *The Bounds of Sense.* London: Methuen.

Von Wright, G.H. (1971). *Explanation and Understanding.* London: Routledge & Kegan Paul.

Wittgenstein, L. (1953). G.E.M. Anscombe & R. Rhees (eds), *Philosophical Investigations.* (Trans. G.E.M. Anscombe). Oxford: Blackwell.

Chapter 3

THE BIOPSYCHOSOCIOLOGY OF MEANING

*Paul Gilbert**

Psychological meaning, in contrast to philosophical or textual meaning, probably depends on two essential things: consciousness and feelings. In the absence of either, it is difficult to conceptualise an entity creating 'meaning'. Tomkins (1981) suggested that emotions make things matter to us. Without them, he argued, nothing may matter—with them anything can. In his theory it is emotions and our capacity 'to feel' that give rise to meanings. However, emotions evolved to nudge, entice and compel the seeking of certain goals. Most human goals, beyond those to sustain life, are social (Nesse, 1990). Meaning and emotion are locked together in a multitude of social relationships, e.g. those of love, friendship, jealousy, social status, shame, revenge, grief, etc. The emotional experiences we consider to be the most personally meaningful are usually social. This chapter explores *why* the social domain is the arena for our most powerful emotions and meanings.

We could, of course, start an exploration of meaning in a different place and consider *what is meaningful*; that is, ask questions about what it is that makes human life meaningful (Baumeister, 1991). In this approach meaning arises from goals, ambitions and plans. These may include goals to have self-worth, to make money, to exert control over one's destiny, to find loving relationships, etc. These goals are either considered to be rewarding in themselves or are associated with anticipated rewards. Meanings and goals are linked together via emotions (Oatley, 1992). What is sometimes missing in this approach is reflection on why certain goals come to matter more than others. Why are some social goals so universally pursued?

---

*Southern Derbyshire Mental Health Trust and Derby University, Derby, UK

The Transformation of Meaning in Psychological Therapies.
Edited by Mick Power and Chris R. Brewin. © 1997 John Wiley & Sons Ltd.

Another approach to meaning is to explore the 'hows' of meaning and focus on our cognitions: our attributions and attitudes and ways of evaluating things. Many authors in this volume speak to this important theme. While beliefs and attributions are important for therapeutic understanding and intervention, they do not touch the bedrock of our humanness. The purely cognitive approach to meaning can be criticised for the same reasons that the purely social theories of meaning can be criticised. Both leave out of the analysis concern with the biological and archetypal themes of human nature. Such a critique was put forward by Halton (1992) when he argued that:

> Contemporary culture theory is, for the most part, a form of sensory deprivation. Those who proclaim culture to be a 'system of symbols and meanings' make an uncritical assumption that culture, symbols, and meanings neither touch nor are deeply touched by organic life. Indeed the ideologues of culture theory tend to regard any concern with the relations between culture and organic nature or evolution as a threat to the hegemony of the cultural system over meaning. (p. 36)

Some cognitive theorists, however, do suggest that cognitions can only exert the powerful impacts they do because they touch the biological in us. Anxiety floods us when our interpretations relate to danger and trigger innate fight/flight systems (Beck, Emery & Greenberg, 1985). Beck et al. (1985) also hypothesise the existence of 'danger schema' which act like evolved threat-detection systems. (e.g. of heights, snakes, social exclusion, etc; see also Marks, 1987). From an evolutionary perspective it was adaptive to respond to danger quickly. For example, it may be better for an animal to assume that the sound in the bushes is a predator and run away than to stay put to gather more evidence. One can make the first type of mistake many times and survive (i.e. to overestimate the danger) but to miss the presence of a predator (underestimate the danger) is a mistake one only makes once. Indeed, in many contexts overestimating a danger is more adaptive than underestimating it. This is a kind of 'better safe than sorry reasoning' (Gilbert, 1993). Thus the brain evolved to minimise the cost of mistakes but not mistakes themselves. There is, in fact, increasing evidence that some cognitions seem to work via very rapid information-processing systems that are designed for speed rather than accuracy (Epstein, 1994; Epstein et al., 1992). These fast-track processing systems use heuristics, take short cuts to reach conclusions quickly, use crudely integrated information, are reliant on affect and how something feels, are preconscious and possibly rely on earlier experience and conditioned emotional responses. *Fast track* modes of functioning may be reliant on more primitive, earlier evolved appraisal–response systems, encoded in limbic and sub-limbic areas (Bailey, 1987; Buck, 1988; MacLean, 1985).

This chapter explores another road to meaning, one that is concerned with the evolution of mind and the evolved social basis of our personal meanings. The evolved motives (e.g. for love, attachment, power and sex) are major ingredients to the sense of self. The central argument is that both personal meaning and a sense of self are creations shaped in part by experience and in part by evolved biological processes. The brain is not a plasticine entity, free to create any type of meaning. Various potentials for a social life (e.g. to form loving attachments, sexual relationships, etc.), and thus create both a sense of self and meaning, exist by virtue of humans having evolved into a certain type of animal.

THE ARCHETYPES OF MEANING

Few now accept the *tabula rasa* view of human psychology. Rather it is recognised that the human infant comes into the world prepared to become a viable representative of the species (Schore, 1994). If all goes well the child will form attachments to his/her care-givers, acquire language, develop cognitive competencies, form peer and sexual relationships, and so forth. In other words there are innate components to our meaning-making. This is not a new idea, for its origins can be traced back to Plato and Kant, but the person most associated with attempts to illuminate the innate nature of the human capacity to create meaning was Jung (1875–1961).

Jung rejected Freudian libido theory because of his growing belief that the psyche was not made up of competing drives, as Freud insisted, but rather of various internal meaning-making and action-directed systems. These systems he called 'archetypes'. Archetypes influence the unfolding of development (e.g. to seek care, to become a member of a group, to find a sexual partner and become a parent, and to come to terms with death; Stevens, 1982). Jung believed that the source of many of our passions and aspirations is archetypal. He also suggested that many archetypal themes of human life are enacted in the rituals, stories and myths of all societies. The themes of grief, envy, shame, jealousy, guilt, deception, remorse, distrust, abandonment, exploitation, heroism, sacrifice and so forth will be known in all cultures.

Jung postulated that humans, as an evolved species, inherit specific predispositions for thought, feeling and action. These predispositions exist as foci within the collective unconscious and serve to guide behaviour, thoughts and emotions. He distinguished the *collective unconscious* from the personal by suggesting that the *personal unconscious* represented those aspects of personal experience that are rooted in real events. They had at one time been conscious but were either forgotten or repressed. The collective unconscious, however, is the realm of the inherited universal predispositions—the internal motivating systems that form the bedrock of species-typical behaviours. He suggested that:

> . . . The archetype in itself is empty and purely formal, nothing but a *facultas praeformandi*, a possibility of representation which is given a priori. The representations themselves are not inherited, only the forms, and in that respect they correspond in every way to the instincts, which are also determined in form only. The existence of instincts can no more be proved than the existence of the archetypes, so long as they do not manifest themselves concretely. With regard to the definiteness of the form, our comparison with the crystal is illuminating inasmuch as the axial system determines only the stereometric structure but not the concrete form of the individual crystal. This may be either large or small, and it may vary endlessly by reason of the different size of its planes or by the growing together of two crystals. The only thing that remains constant is the axial system, or rather, the invariable geometric proportions underlying it. The same is true of the archetype. In principle, it can be named and has an invariable nucleus of meaning but always only in principle, never as regards its concrete manifestation . . (Jung, 1972, pp. 13–14)

So Jung was first and foremost concerned with those various universals common to humanity. He attempted to articulate the internal psychic mechanisms that (across various cultures and time) brought into existence (into relationship) various universal life themes, myths, rituals and stories. These life themes (for attachments, seeking sexual partners, joining groups, forming social ranks, worshipping gods, etc.) arise, he argued, from some kind of pre-wiring, or preparation, of our psychology. Thus, as will be noted shortly, Jung saw the mind as a mixed structure, made up of various motives and modules.

Interestingly, Jung's friend and Nobel prize-winning author, Hermann Hesse, never really understood all the controversy about archetypes. He said that as far as humans are concerned, writers had known about them for centuries and if they could not feel them within themselves and connect with them, they could not write stories. In fact, story-telling is an interesting human activity, for despite thousands of years and many differences in cultural styles and language, from the ancient Egyptian, Greek, Indian and Chinese cultures, we are able to understand the themes of all the stories humans have ever written. Whatever the textures of culture, they are surface textures that do not cover the deeper meanings of human life.

RECENT APPROACHES TO ARCHETYPES

For reasons to do with Jung's mystical interests, writing style and the dominance of Freudian and behavioural psychology, the concept of archetype has remained a vague and somewhat peripheral idea in psychology. Yet in the past 20 years concepts and ideas pertaining to innate potentials for the construction of meaning have become increasingly prevalent. For example, Coon (1992) opens his introductory text on psychology with this graphic depiction:

> You are a universe, a collection of worlds within worlds. Your brain is possibly the most complicated and amazing device in existence. Through its action you are capable of music, art, science, and war. Your potential for love and compassion coexists with your potential for aggression, hatred . . . Murder? (p. 1)

What Coon and other researchers suggest is that we are not unified selves, despite our experience of being so. Rather we are made up of many different possibilities for the creation of meaning. Our brain is a modular system (Gazzaniga, 1989) with old and new evolved components (MacLean, 1985). So as Ornstein (1986) points out:

> The long progression in our self-understanding has been from a simple and usually 'intellectual' view to the view that the mind is a mixed structure, for it contains a complex set of 'talents,' 'modules' and 'policies' within . . . All these general components of the mind can act independently of each other, they may well have different priorities.
>
> The discovery of increased complexity and differentiation has occurred in many different areas of research . . . in the study of brain functions and localisation; in the conceptions of the nature of intelligence; in personality testing; and in theories of the general characteristics of the mind. (p. 9)

In some ways both Coon and Ornstein are offering a modern exposition of the archetypal nature of the human mind. And they echo another Jungian idea—that although we often think of ourselves as somehow whole and integrated individuals, this may be an illusion. In fact, Jung suggested that integration and wholeness are psychological feats—maturational accomplishments. We are made up of many different talents, abilities, social motives, emotions, and so on. Not only are we worlds within worlds, but it is these internal modules that give us our sense of, and varieties of, meaning.

This mixed bag of motives and meaning-creating modules (archetypes) can give rise to the experience of not one self but a variety of possible selves (e.g. Rowan, 1990). These possible selves or sub-personalities can feel different things and play different parts when we are in different states of mind. In therapy we can even learn to name these different selves and speak with them. We can recognise the bullying self, the perfectionist self, the vengeful sadistic self, the sexual self, the forgiving self, and so on. The sub-personalities are created by the way different

Table 3.1   A cognitive view of meaning and psychological problems

Problem	Thoughts
Panic	I am going to die from these symptoms.
Social anxiety	I will do something so that I will make a fool of myself and be rejected.
Depression	I am a bad, weak or inadequate person and the future is hopeless.
Paranoia	People are out to get me.

modules come together in the mind. Another way to think of this is as the potential to enact different social roles (Gilbert, 1989, 1992).

It is also recognised that we reason and create meaning differently in different states of mind. Indeed, the cognitive approaches to psychological problems focus on the way a person thinks and creates meaning. These approaches note that certain styles of thinking are associated with certain types of problem (Table 3.1).

All these developments, be they in conceptualising the mind as a modular system, or as a mixed array of possible selves, or as having a variety of possible roles, or variations in cognitive construing, speak to the archetypal—to the evolved nature of mind. Increasingly, cognitive theory pays due regard to the evolutionary dimension in the creation of personal meaning and styles of thinking (Beck et al., 1985; Beck, Freeman & Associates, 1990).

Given these various approaches to meaning and the fact that there is growing interest in the innate and evolved dimension of the mind, we are now in a position to explore in more detail what an evolutionary approach might add to our understanding of personal meaning.

EVOLUTION AND MEANING

Jung did not really understand Darwinian theory—although the concept of archetype is quite compatible with it—nor did he have much insight into the workings of the brain. There was not the evidence then, as there is today, of the enormous changes that take place in the brain with and during maturation (Schore, 1994). However, modern evolutionary theory agrees with Jung to the extent that, while there is a great potential for individual variations associated with varied developmental and cultural environments, the human brain is attuned to be a highly social organ.

Many of our most exciting and troublesome passions and meanings revolve around social situations and outcomes: in our sexual jealousies, our fear of shame, our seeking of close relationships, our desire to belong

Table 3.2   Some dimensions of happy and unhappy social situations

Happy situations	Unhappy situations
Loved and wanted	Unloved and unwanted
Close to others	Abandoned
Accepted and belonging	Not accepted, and rejected
Have friends	Do not have friends
Accepted member of a group	An outsider or ostracised
Have something of value to offer others	Have little of value to offer others
Appreciated and valued by others	Being taken advantage of; criticised, put down
Feel attractive to others	Feel unattractive to others
Have status and respect	Do not have status and respect
Winning	Losing

to a group, to have friends and avoid being excluded. If we think about happiness many of the things associated with happiness revolve around social goals, as depicted in Table 3.2.

A key question is: how did these various archetypal possibilities come into existence? One answer to this is related to gene frequencies in populations. For example, consider animals who are subject to predation. Those animals who inherit the capacity to detect predators quickly and take evasive action are likely to survive better than those who are poor at detecting predators and/or are slow to react. Over time the more proficient predator avoiders will survive and leave more genes behind than those who are poor predator avoiders. To take another example, if caring for offspring means that more offspring survive and reproduce (in certain ecological niches) then the genes for caring will gradually spread through the population. The key idea is that any trait (e.g. predator avoidance, caring) which increases the chances of its genes being passed on to succeeding generations will be selected for (Trivers, 1985). Thus evolutionary theory suggests that universal forms of behaviour will evolve if they increase the chances of the genes of their carriers being passed on to succeeding generations. This is called 'inclusive fitness'. However, it is important to recognise that this does not mean that animals and humans are motivated to increase the number of offspring they leave behind or even that they have any conscious concern with inclusive fitness. As Fox (1986) points out:

> . . . sociobiology speaks of organisms maximising their reproductive success or inclusive fitness or whatever. It is not at all clear that this describes the outcome of various of their activities. After all, it is commonplace that animals do not know they are reproducing, much less maximising, anything. What they are doing is accumulating resources or power, for which they are proximately motivated. If they get all these right, then maximum

reproductive success should follow. But it is these intermediaries they are motivated to achieve, not the success itself. This is no less true of humans. They will strive to accrue resources of all kinds—wealth, power, access to sex—and normally reproductive success (inclusive fitness) will follow. But it is equally possible that a consideration such as the enormous expense involved in raising offspring to a point where they too can accrue these things might well lead them to limit families . . . Again, there is no real discrepancy here since they are not in this argument motivated to maximise reproductive success per se, but those things that will, in the normal course of events, lead to it. (p. 193)

The basis of sociobiology is that social behaviour, and the propensity to have feelings and passions about our social relationships, arises by virtue of the kind of species we have evolved into. Certain kinds of social relationships (e.g. attachment, sexual) are both biologically and psychologically meaningful. Thus many of our goals are biosocial (Gilbert, 1989). The reason that some forms of social relating matter more than others is because the enactment of certain social behaviours have had important inclusive fitness pay-offs. To put this another way, the evolutionary approach to meaning begins by asking what are the most common social (adaptive) problems that humans have evolved ways of recognising and solving (Buss, 1991). Solutions to certain adaptive problems (e.g. how to survive when one is born as a helpless infant) throw light on the most common and typical types of biosocial goals and motives. A rough classification, of such universal biosocial goals which, while not comprehensive, captures some of the more important, can be suggested as follows:

1. *Care eliciting and seeking.* These involve the motives to elicit and seek care, support and help from others. The 'need for others' to survive is active from the first days of life and motivates desires to be cared, helped and protected. It continues throughout life in increasingly complex ways.

2. *Care giving.* The propensity to invest time, energy and resources in others, such that the other survives and prospers, is essential if care eliciting and seeking are to be effective. If humans had no interest in helping others then our social relationships would look very different from how they look today.

3. *Cooperation and the formation of alliances.* The propensity to form groups and work cooperatively (which involves aggression inhibition, sharing, affiliation, friendships and reciprocal behaviour) is another hallmark of the behaviour of humans and indeed of many mammals.

4. *Mate selection and sexual behaviour.* Why sex evolved at all is a complex question (Ridley, 1994), but sexual behaviour has played a salient role in

primate evolution and social behaviour. Not only is the timing of sexual maturity part of our biological endowment, but so too are a set of motives that lead to it. These involve attracting, being attracted to, courting, conception and mate retention.

5. *Ranking behaviour (status).* Since humans are group-living animals, once in a group some will do better than others. This gives rise to competitive behaviour and the formation of social ranks. In humans, these ranks can form around various attributes such as strength, attractiveness, talent and so forth. The motive to gain rank and avoid losing rank shows up in the salient predisposition for humans to compare themselves socially with others (Gilbert, Price & Allan, 1995) and avoid being seen as inferior. Status is one of the most salient social variables that influence the quality of alliances and mates that one can attract.

These various biosocial goals give rise to personal meaning because they form a template for the construction of self–other roles. These involve the way that the self and other are construed. Table 3.3 offers a simple depiction. You will note that the sexual domain is not included here. This is not because its importance is devalued but because sexual behaviour can involve various social behaviours. For example, it can be used to express affection, to dominate or simply to have 'one-off' encounters (see below). Thus, self and other constructions in sexual encounters vary as to the nature of the encounter.

MENTALITIES

These kinds of social cognition and behaviour enable social communication, which involves sending signals to and receiving signals from

Table 3.3 Core social roles

	See self as:	See other as:
Care receiving	Obtaining inputs from other(s): care, protection, safety, reassurance	Source of: care, nurturance, protection, safety, reassurance
Care giving	Provider of: care, protection, safety, nurturance	Recipient of: care, protection, safety, nurturance
Cooperation	Of value to other, sharing, appreciating, contributing, affiliative	Valuing, contribution sharing, appreciating, affiliative
Competition/rank	Contestant, status/rank, inferior–superior, hostile–attractive	Contestant, status/rank, inferior–superior, hostile–attractive

conspecifics in order to form certain types of relationship. Such communications enable conspecifics to organise themselves into relationships according to role (e.g. parent–child, dominant–subordinate, supportive ally, sexual partner). Hence, the signals exchanged between conspecifics are not random but involve signals indicating particular interactional patterns of behaviour (e.g. to form friendship and alliances, sexual receptivity and interest, and preparedness to challenge or back down to a challenge).

Gardner (1988) pointed out that evolutionary stable social roles (e.g. for attachment, sexuality or to gain dominance) represent *states of communication* which are understandable and readable in other conspecifics. However, crucially they are internally generated states that automatically coordinate patterns of affect, behaviour and appraisal in the individual expressing them. As such, communicative states are responsible for signalling intent and need (Gardner, 1988). They guide and coordinate the behaviour of an animal in a manner recognisable to (and hence allowing, facilitating or calling forth a response from) conspecifics.

Patterns of relating (attachments, sexual love, fighting with opponents) are mediated by innate mechanisms which Gilbert (1989) referred to as mentalities. The activation of a mentality orientates the individual to adopt certain social roles and behaviours and generates certain states of mind. This is a similar position to Gardner (1988), who argued that various communication states are mediated by 'deeply homologous neural structures'. When these neural structures are stimulated and activated they cause an animal to demonstrate a special readiness to assume distinctive social behaviours. For example, falling in love involves combinations of emotions, increases the desire to be close to the loved other and orientates lovers to behave in certain ways to each other. Losing a loved other stimulates patterns of emotions (sadness, pining) and behaviours (searching). Caring for others involves feelings of empathy and care, and seeking opportunities to help or look after the other. Competing with others involves very different patterns of affect, cognition and behaviour—such as aggression or fear. Social behaviour is expressed to gain advantage over the other or avoid losing out to the other. Thus, Gilbert (1989) suggested that some states of mind are reflections of the activation of different mentalities; e.g. care seeking, care giving, sexual, cooperating and competing.

Care Eliciting and Care Seeking

It is now accepted that mammals are biologically set up to care for their offspring, and their offspring to need caring for. Without such biological predispositions there is no reason why offspring and parent would have much interest in each other. Most fish species do not have such concerns, and following birth offspring simply disperse.

The care seeking–care giving interaction gives rise to social bonds that are often regarded as forms of attachment (Schore, 1994). The evolution of attachment relations was underpinned by a complex biology and development of limbic brain areas (MacLean, 1985). It is now known that disruptions to attachment relationships, especially child–parent relationships, can have profound biological affects. The infant does not *learn* that disruption of attachments (loss of access to a caring other) is aversive, he/she is biologically prepared for it to be so. Research on the psychobiology of attachment shows that many stress hormones and monoamine systems are affected by discontinuities in attachment relationships and some of these can have long-term effects (Hofer, 1984; Reite & Field, 1985; Schore, 1994). In later life most find the loss of a valued attachment relationship intensely painful and it often activates states of grief, pining and searching.

Bowlby (1969, 1973, 1980, 1988) was one of the first to suggest that humans are born with an innate need for attachments and innate potentials to develop complex working models of attachment relationships. These working models function to answer questions like: are there others who care for me? are they available? can I trust them? can I function without them? In this sense the focus is on care-eliciting and care-seeking behaviour. According to the experiences a child has with his/her parents these internal working models or schema (Safran & Segal, 1990) can come to function in various ways; that is, the construction of meaning in and about close relationships varies according to the experience of them. When parents are available and loving towards a child, the child tends to develop internal models of attachments that are based on trust and self-confidence. Attachment objects thus function to control arousal (calming and exciting) and can be looked to for support, help and emotional pleasures. In neglectful or abusive relationships, however, the arousal mediation of attachments does not function in the same way. The abuser becomes a focus of fear rather than calming or affection. Consequently, an attachment object who has not functioned to calm or excite may leave the child with a disturbed attachment system. This disturbance may show itself as a fearful distrust of close attachments (the experience of being uncared for) and serious problems in how care is elicited or sought out. However, although an abused person may believe that supportive, loving relationships are unavailable, and thus avoids closeness and seeking affection from others, this does not necessarily mean that their yearning for closeness ceases. Indeed, they may never feel comfortable with their defensive avoidance or aloofness and may seek to find a substitute in God or a pet. For such people therapy may awaken deep and painful (archetypal) needs and yearnings to feel loved and protected.

The desire to be loved and close to others permeates much of our social behaviour and relationships and gives meaning to them (Birtchnell, 1993; Gilbert, 1989). This is reflected not only between parent and child but between sexual lovers, friends, leader–follower and in our relationships with a deity (God). Some argue that it is the basis of a need for belonging (Baumeister & Leary, 1995).

Caring Giving

Humans are not only capable of the most destructive and cruel behaviours (as in war and torture) but also the most caring and compassionate. The innate potential to care has given rise to various psychological competencies such as empathy and sympathy. Fogel, Melson & Mistry (1986) define care-giving as:

> The provision of guidance, protection and care for the purpose of fostering developmental change congruent with the expected potential for change of the object of nurturance. (p. 55)

The orientation of caring may be expressed to other humans, animals, inanimate objects (e.g. the family car) or the self. It takes in the concept of 'looking after'. Fogel et al. (1986) note four dimensions of caring which include: (1) choice of object (as noted above); (2) expression of caring and nurturant feelings; (3) motivation to care and nurture; (4) awareness of the role and need for caring. However, care is an expensive resource to dispense and it is not given equally to any who seek it. We are highly motivated to care for those with whom we are genetically related. For example, a mother who has just given birth wants to take home her own child, not just any child from the delivery room. Great distress is caused if there are mistakes in identification.

There are, however, other considerations that come into play when it comes to caring. Evolution theory predicts that care-giving will be greatest when it gains status, is likely to be repaid and/or where it is directed to kin. However, much depends on the cost and nature of the threat that requires help. As both the threats and costs of caring increase, Burnstein, Crandall & Kitayama (1994) note that:

> a) Natural selection favors those who are prone to help others as a function of the latter's relatedness, potential fecundity, or other features indicating a recipient's capacity to enhance the donor's inclusive fitness, and b) this effect is especially strong when help is biologically significant (e.g. the

recipient will not survive otherwise). Such a heuristic is demonstrated in several studies involving hypothetical decisions to help: In life-or-death situations, people chose to aid close kin over distant kin, the young over the old, the healthy over the sick, the wealthy over the poor and the pre-menopausal women over the postmenopausal women; whereas when it is a matter of an everyday favor, they gave less weight to kinship and opted to help either the very young or the very old over those of intermediate age, the sick over the healthy, and the poor over the wealthy. (p. 773)

There may also be gender differences in caring behaviour, with women being more focused on emotional forms of caring and males on instrumental and practical solutions (Gilligan, 1982). The degree to which these differences are innate or the result of socialisation remains a matter of debate and research, but the vast majority of people would like to see themselves as caring rather than uncaring, selfish and egotistical. Thus caring does seem to be one activity that gives meaning to our social roles.

Cooperation and the Formation of Alliances

Care-seeking and care-giving often play a role in the formation of alliances and cooperativeness. Argyle (1991) suggests that cooperation is the basis of sociability. Cooperative behaviour evolved in the context of group living, and can involve aggression inhibition, conformity, sharing, affiliation, friendships and reciprocal exchanges. However, not all cooperative behaviour is affiliative and there are times when cooperation occurs to avoid punishments. Armies and work organisations may cooperate to achieve common goals but there may not be much affiliation between the ranks. Cooperation normally relates to an awareness that there are mutual gains in working together and resisting serious infighting. Thus, we should distinguish between cooperativeness that is held together by shared goals and that which is held together by more intimate emotional attachments.

Our ability for *intimate* cooperation probably begins very early, in the shared joys and attuned interactions between the child and the care-giver. Later it matures into experiences of friendship and companionable relating based on mutual pleasure, desire to be with, respect and valuing (Heard & Lake, 1986). Recently, Baumeister & Leary (1995) have argued that the need to belong is an innate human need. Hence the desire to belong may well relate to some archetype(s) to be with like or similar others on whom one can depend and be valued by.

Cooperation and conformity probably evolved from the need to form, and benefits of forming, alliances. Very few male primates make it to the top without allies, and in females alliances are essential for gaining rank (Kevles, 1986). These alliances are usually kin-based. For humans, people thrive best in mutually supportive networks of familiar and friendly others rather than hostile strangers. Positive social relationships are a key to happiness and mental health (Argyle, 1990; Baumeister & Leary, 1995). Bailey, Wood & Nava (1992) have suggested that the more intimate our cooperation (as in therapy) the more we want to be treated like kin, gaining the same degree of commitment and feelings of being valued and cared for.

In cooperation there is also a pressure (and desire) to *conform*. This conformity may arise from following fashion, working on the same research, sharing religious beliefs and so forth. There can be an archetypal pressure to reduce differences, and to become warier of others the more different from us they appear to be. Evaluations of conformity, reciprocality and sharing are key social concerns and convey to people that they are (and will be) accepted, valued and appreciated. Finding a place within a group and gaining a sense of belonging allow the self to feel reassured by its fellows and benefit from a *mutual sharing of help and support*.

Many patients speak of feeling like *outsiders*, never having had much of an experience of fitting in and belonging. For some this feeling of being an outsider can be associated with paranoid anxieties, depression and envy. Much may depend on whether one feels an inferior or superior outsider.

Cooperation depends on reciprocation. Non-reciprocation can give rise to a variety of different types of adult problems (McGuire & Troisi, in press). It can activate feelings of being exploited or unappreciated. Failures in reciprocation can unleash much anger and resentment. It does not matter if they are the broken promises of help, love or affection, or the broken treaties of nations. Failures in reciprocation, evidence of exploitation and cheating ignite anger. Some patients attempt to form cooperative and caring relations with rejecting and punitive individuals under the false belief that there must come a point when, if they give (invest) enough, they will be reciprocated (the other will increase their investment in the relationship). Those stuck in such relationships may feel they have invested too much to leave, or they will lose too much by leaving (e.g. access to accommodation and other resources) or are fearful of being alone. So they remain entrapped in very unrewarding relationships. Such patients may feel very subordinate in these relationships. When this is the case the anger can be inhibited. As one patient said, 'I know that he is cheating on me, and does not give much affection but if I say anything I am frightened he will get angry or may leave me. I still try though, and hope one day he will come to love me again.'

Mate Selection and Sexual Behaviour

The sexual attachment bond cannot be seen as a re-run of infant-parent attachments but is a different form of attachment (Gilbert, 1989). There are, however, some behaviours (such as looking into each other's eyes and yearning to be close) that are common to both. However, if a lover is unavailable (e.g. is working away) this will not necessarily disrupt the bond. What will disrupt the bond is sexual cheating and feeling that one is being used in a non-reciprocal way by one's lover. This concern is not seen in infant–parent relating. The sexual attachment bond evolved for reproduction, to sire offspring, and in this context the attractiveness of the mate and potential faithfulness play a salient role in how meaningful a sexual liaison will be.

That humans are highly motivated by and for sex is undisputed, as is the fact that puberty is the time when the evolved mechanisms for adequate sexual behaviour are triggered. What makes sex meaningful, however, is more complex. Research suggests that meaningful sexual relationships may vary between the genders. One reason for this is that male reproductive interests may be served by mating with many females and investing in just a few or one. However, in the case of females there is considerably more investment of time and energy in bringing viable offspring into the world and helping them survive. Research suggests that men are more attracted to women younger than themselves, who have characteristics of beauty that suggest good genes (e.g. complexion, body symmetry and wide hips) and find one-night stands more pleasurable than women do. The social status of the woman, especially in one-night stands, seems unimportant to men. Men are also likely to be more aggressive and to guard women with whom they seek to form long-term relationships (Buss, 1994).

According to Wilson & Daly (1992) men can treat women as *property* and recruit the psychology of entitlement, ownership and control. There are three central ideas about why this is so:

1. Men (unlike women) cannot guarantee that their mate's offspring are their own. Thus, they have to be careful not to invest in a female whose offspring may be sired by someone else, and thus be cuckolded. Over evolutionary time those who were not bothered by such concerns would lose out in inclusive fitness terms to those who were more cautious.
2. Human males do invest in their offspring, at least more than many other primates, and females tend to select for (signals of) high rather than low investing males. So being cuckolded could be costly.
3. However, male reproductive interests can be served by cuckolding other males, or at least gaining 'control' over (or inseminating) more than one female.

Wilson and Daly (1992) suggest that 'women as property' is a core mindset of men:

> . . . whose operation can be discerned from numerous phenomena which are culturally diverse in their details but monotonously alike in the abstract. These phenomena include socially recognised marriage, the concept of adultery as a property violation, the valuation of female chastity (and virginity), the equation of the protection of women with protection from sexual contact, and the special potency of infidelity as a provocation for violence. (p. 291, brackets added)

Meaningful sexual relationships for women, however, are more likely to arise in relationships where there are emotional closeness and signs that the man does indeed care for her and her offspring. Moreover, women will be influenced in their attraction to a man by his status, especially in making a long-term commitment (Buss, 1989, 1994; Ridley, 1994). However, recent work suggests that the relationship between traits of status/dominance and altruism/agreeableness in female preference is complex. For example, agreeableness/altruism seems a more attractive trait to women than dominance/status in some contexts. Indeed, when men are non-altruistic (disagreeable), dominance may have little effect on attraction. It is as if women search first for altruistic tendencies and only then are concerned with status—echoing the view that for women a man's personality is important in attraction (Jensen-Campbell, Graziano & West, 1995). It may be, of course, that if men had to choose between traits for beauty or faithfulness in a long-term partner, they also might prefer faithfulness and altruism. Trustworthiness is likely to be a key trait that both genders select for in long-term partners.

An evolutionary approach to sexuality does not in any sense reduce the need for social analysis, for it is clear that social values shape sexuality and behaviour (e.g. see Barkow, 1989; Fisher, 1989). It is in the social domain that many of the various forms of sexual behaviour can be found. It is obvious that Chinese foot binding and female circumcision are not found in the genes. Such behaviour may be socially amplified aberrant effects of male efforts to control female sexual behaviour. And it is social changes, not biological ones, that will (and did in the case of Chinese foot binding) bring about changes.

Competing for Status

Humans are highly motivated to gain self-esteem and become accepted and valued in their social relationships. The biological reasons for this are that high rather than low status carries many advantages. High(er) status individuals make more attractive sexual partners, more attractive allies and exert more control over social activities and resources in general. There are two ways to gain status. The first is by simply overpowering others, threatening others and winning conflicts (of interest) by force and imposing one's will. The second way is by courting favourable judgements from others and being chosen by them, that is, to be attractive to them (Barkow, 1989; Gilbert, 1989; 1992; Gilbert, Price & Allan, 1995). In the second case, the desires are to be wanted, valued and chosen by others. Raleigh et al. (1991) reviewed the evidence for the role of affiliative behaviour in status acquisition and maintenance and the role of serotonergic mechanisms in status enhancement. Drugs that increase a primate's dominance do so by increasing social approach and social affiliation and *reducing aggression*.

The importance of social status, social recognition and creating good (attractive) impressions on others (i.e. impression management) has been known and written about for hundreds of years. Fukuyama (1992) gives this concise overview of the issue. He writes:

> The concept underlying 'recognition' . . . is as old as Western political philosophy itself, and refers to a thoroughly familiar part of the human personality. Over the millennia, there has been no consistent word used to refer to the psychological phenomenon of the 'desires for recognition': Plato spoke of *thymos*, or 'spiritedness', Machiavelli of man's desire for glory, Hobbes, of his pride or vainglory, Rousseau, of his *amourpropre*, Alexander Hamilton of the love of fame, and James Madison of ambition, Hegel of recognition, and Nietzsche, of man as the 'beast with red cheeks.' All of these terms refer to that part of man which feels the need to place *value* on things—himself in the first instance, but on the people, actions, or things around him as well. It is the part of the personality which is the fundamental source of the emotions of pride, anger, and shame, and is not reducible to desire, on the one hand, or reason on the other. The desire for recognition, is the most specially political part of the human personality because it is what drives men to want to assert themselves over other men and therefore into Kant's condition of 'asocial sociability'. It is not surprising that so many political philosophers have seen the central problem of politics as one of taming or harnessing the desire for recognition in a way that would serve the political community as a whole. Indeed, the project of taming the desire for recognition has been so successful in the hands of modern political philosophy that we citizens of modern egalitarian democracies often fail to see the desire for recognition in ourselves for what it is. (pp. 162–163)

All cultures have ways of dispensing social status (Barkow, 1989) and taking it away—as in shame (Kaufman, 1989). Humans are highly motivated to gain status, recognition and to make good impressions, and to avoid losing them. Shame and humiliation (involving loss of status) are among the most feared of social outcomes, even when no physical damage to the self may occur. In so far as human status may depend on affiliation, then shame may be aversive because it reduces opportunities for positive, status-enhancing social affiliations.

These innate tendencies (to avoid shame and loss of status) are harnessed by societies and cultures in different ways so that the exact behaviours that give rise to status vary from culture to culture. For example, Overing (1989) has compared two very different Amazonian groups, shaped by different ecologies and hunter–gathering patterns: The Shavante and the Piaroa. The Shavante value hunting and warrior values. Children are gender-segregated from an early age. Boys are brought up to be aggressive and 'bellicose', to recognise male superiority in terms of the products of their contributions to the group and political decision-making. Women are excluded from political decision-making and many of the rituals of manhood involve demonstrations of fearlessness and an aggressive control over females. These are the behaviours that gain status. Women, on the other hand, are trained to value certain attributes in men and be shaming of fearful men. The Piaroa, in contrast, are quite different. They are not gender-segregated and the kind of male behaviour valued by the Shavante would be considered as evidence of 'lack of control' and as sub-human—something to be pitied. Tranquillity, emotional control and the rights of individual members (male and female) are valued equally and gain status. Warrior values are seen as highly disruptive to the group and are shamed. The ability to be social and tranquilly cooperative is considered to be the most important (and thus valued) characteristic of being human. Hence, even if a person knows they could or can perform a certain role competently, if this role is not valued by others, they may gain little pleasure from it.

What such comparisons suggest is that status and prestige are important to all humans, but the exact behaviours that gain or lose them vary from culture to culture. Whether it be the aggressive male defending and proving his manhood, the anorexic taking pride in his/her loss of weight, the scientists struggling to win a Nobel prize, or the patient who is too fearful and ashamed to reveal a history of abuse, there seems little doubt that how we think we are seen in the eyes of others creates salient personal meanings. And the tendencies to compare ourselves with others and seek favourable social comparisons are biologically powerful and derived from old, evolved social dispositions (Gilbert, Price & Allan, 1995).

Status, like attachment, is also known to have various biological mediators. It is now known that the social variations of rank (e.g. between dominant and subordinate) are associated with different behaviours and biological states (Henry & Stephens, 1977; Henry, 1982; Price et al., 1994; Sapolsky, 1989, 1990a,b). Moreover, there might also be differences between secure and insecure dominant animals (e.g. the latter being more aggressive, with higher levels of stress hormones) and secure and insecure subordinates (Sapolsky, 1990a,b). Gilbert (1992) suggested a distinction between voluntary and involuntary subordinate positions. For example, voluntary subordinate positions might pertain to a teacher–student relationship, or any relationship where a person feels secure with others being in leader positions, and can rely on them (but does not necessarily wish to form a close attachment with them). Involuntary subordination is being in a one-down position against one's will. It is somehow enforced and can be associated with an acute sense of feeling inferior to others, defeated, vulnerable to other people's attacks, put down, marginalised, thwarted in aspiration and trapped.

Therapy Issues

Being cared for, caring for, cooperating, sex, and gaining status and being valued are only some of the more central archetypes of the evolved human mind, but they suggest that many of the themes and conflicts that patients suffer will centre around them. Thus, we should not be surprised that people come to therapy with issues and difficulties in the following areas.

Care seeking

Some patients feel unloved or uncared for and have problems in their close attachment relationships. They seem unable to elicit enough care or closeness to feel comfortable or trusting. They may feel acutely vulnerable to abandonment and being on their own. This style is sometimes called 'anxious attachment'. At the other extreme are people who find it difficult to tolerate close relationships and prefer to avoid them because of lack of trust or fear of obligation. Some feel that asking for help is shaming and a sign of weakness (e.g. Fisher, Nadler & Whitcher-Alagna, 1982).

Caring giving

Some patients find it difficult to create meaningful roles where they can care for others, or at least give something to others that is meaningful. They may feel that nobody needs them and it matters little if they live or die. Some may feel that they are only a burden. At the other extreme are those who feel others depend on them too much. They may feel burdened with obligations to care and may have a strong wish to escape—for which they may also feel guilty. They may have beliefs that the needs of others must always be put before their own. Yet a third type of problem arises when a person appears to have little or no interest in caring for others. They appear to lack empathy or basic compassion and are prone to be exploitative and harmful to others to serve their own ends. It is not only individuals who can behave like this—one group can exploit and be harmful to others, and lack any concern or care for them. Group-induced 'psychopathic' behaviour is far more common than is perhaps recognised.

Cooperation

Some people feel that they are exploited by others. Although they see themselves as highly cooperative, individuals who share and help others, others do not (in their view) reciprocate enough. This often elicits anger and at times demands on others which others find aversive (McGuire & Troisi, in press). Difficulties in cooperation can take many forms, but there is growing recognition that, be it due to lack of social skill or of opportunity, reduced sociable cooperation is associated with unhappiness (Argyle, 1991).

Sex

Some problems revolve around sexual relationships. Some may find their sexuality difficult and/or confusing. Some (usually women) can feel exploited and used. They may lose interest in sex as a result. Problems of sexual jealousy and sexual infidelity are common across cultures and are typical arenas for conflicts and even violence.

Status

Perhaps the most common reason for people to come to therapy is that their social relationships are going poorly. They come because they have lost confidence in themselves and feel shamed or humiliated and inferior. They make negative social comparisons with others and are often highly critical of their own self-presentations and performances. The basic themes centre around inferiority and worthlessness.

However, others would seem to have overvalued ideas of their own status, importance and entitlement, sometimes referred to as narcissistic grandiosity (Wink, 1991). Recently, an inflated sense of self has been linked to violence (Baumeister, Smart & Boden, 1996).

A key problem in therapy is often how to help people see that they may well be making errors, treating themselves or others unreasonably, yet not shame them in the process. Indeed, it is not uncommon to find that one needs to help people develop a more caring approach to either themselves and/or others—i.e. maturation of an internal caring mentality (Gilbert, 1989).

These arenas of therapy allow us to engage in all the dramas of being human—dramas that are timeless and vary little from culture to culture. These include grief, envy, shame, jealousy, guilt, deception, distrust, abandonment, exploitation, and so forth (Gilbert, 1992). All these themes are the sources of our most powerful meanings and misery. As cognitive therapists (e.g. Young, Beck & Weinberger, 1993) begin to plot and list the various schema that come up in therapy it may be useful to consider that these are archetypal experiences to which all of us are potentially vulnerable.

CONCLUSION

Some might argue that it is a big step to move from the evolution of mental mechanisms, descriptions of biosocial goals and mentalities to personal meaning. Personal meaning, it might be said, arises from a personal hierarchy of innumerable possible goals. For example, a person might risk and even seek humiliation, or become celibate for the love of his/her God. Or a person may forego long-term close relationships to seek a career. Evolutionary theory does not predict the precise goals that any one individual will choose in any particular context, but only describes the typical themes that arise in human social life (Gilbert, 1995).

This chapter has focused on the themes of caring, cooperation, sex and status as some of the more common human themes that organise personal meaning. Although by no means exhaustive, and many others can be suggested, the central idea is that many of the things that give us our deepest sense of personal meaning are archetypal. It is our sensitivity to the archetypal in us that allows us to engage in therapy. Although therapists must be sensitive to cultural variations and contexts in meaning making, there is also a sense in which we are all the same. If we are uncared for, abused and humiliated, cheated and exploited, abandoned and rendered outsiders—suffering is likely. An evolutionary approach does suggest what should be or is acceptable. It is not a justification for capitalist economics or autocratic governments, for these are moral issues. Rather, an evolutionary approach suggests what we might expect in certain contexts, e.g. in contexts of harsh male competition, violence is more likely in young males at the margins of society (Archer, 1994). In situations where there is vigorous competition for status with many losers there will be increasing rates of depression, anxiety and violence (Wilkinson, 1996). Political commentators who make calls for community values are in fact recognising that humans have certain needs that are archetypal.

REFERENCES

Archer, J. (1994, ed.). *Male Violence*. London: Routledge.

Argyle, M. (1991). *Cooperation: The Basis of Sociability*. London: Routledge.

Bailey, K.G. (1987). *Human Paleopsychology. Applications to Aggression and Pathological Processes*. Hillsdale. NJ: Lawrence Erlbaum.

Bailey, K.G., Wood, H. & Nava, G.R. (1992). What do clients want? Role of psychological kinship in professional helping. *Journal of Psychotherapy Integration*, **2**, 125–147.

Barkow, J.H. (1989). *Darwin, Sex and Status*. Toronto: Toronto University Press.

Baumeister, R.F. (1991). *Meanings of Life*. New York: Guilford.

Baumeister, R.F. & Leary, M.R. (1995). The need to belong: Desire for interpersonal attachments as a fundamental human motivation. *Psychological Bulletin*, **117**, 497–529.

Baumeister, R.F., Smart, L. & Boden, J.M. (1996). Relation of threatened egotism to violence and aggression: the dark side of high self-esteem. *Psychological Review*, **103**, 5–33.

Beck, A.T., Emery, G. & Greenberg, R.L. (1985). *Anxiety Disorders and Phobias: A Cognitive Approach*. New York: Basic Books.

Beck, A.T., Freeman, A. & Associates (1990). *Cognitive Therapy of Personality Disorders*. New York: Guilford Press.

Birtchnell, J. (1993). *How Humans Relate: A New Interpersonal Theory*. Westport, CT: Praeger.

Bowlby, J. (1969). *Attachment: Attachment and Loss, Vol. 1*. London: Hogarth Press.

Bowlby, J. (1973). *Separation, Anxiety and Anger. Attachment and Loss, Vol. 2*. London: Hogarth Press.

Bowlby, J. (1980). *Loss: Sadness and Depression. Attachment and Loss, Vol. 3*. London: Hogarth Press.

Bowlby, J. (1988). Developmental psychiatry comes of age. *American Journal of Psychiatry*, **145**, 1–10.

Buck, R. (1988). *Human Motivation and Emotion*, 2nd edn. New York: Wiley.

Burnstein, E., Crandall, C. & Kitayama, S. (1994). Some neo-darwinian rules for altruism: Weighing cues for inclusive fitness as a function of biological importance of the decision. *Journal of Personality and Individual Differences*, **67**, 773–807.

Buss, D.M. (1989). Sex differences in human mate preference: Evolutionary hypotheses tested in 37 cultures. *Brain and Behavioral Sciences*, **12**, 1–49.

Buss, D.M. (1991). Evolutionary personality psychology. *Annual Review of Psychology*, **42**, 459–491.

Buss, D.M. (1994). The strategies of human mating. *American Scientist*, **82**, 238–249.

Coon, D. (1992). *Introduction to Psychology. Exploration and Application: Sixth Edition*. New York: West Publishing Company.

Epstein, S. (1994). Integration of the cognitive and the psychodynamic unconscious. *American Psychologist*, **49**, 709–724.

Epstein, S., Lipson, A., Holstein, C. & Huh, E. (1992). Irrational reactions to negative outcomes: Evidence for two conceptual systems. *Journal of Personality and Social Psychology*, **62**, 328–339.

Fisher, J.D., Nadler, A. & Whitcher-Alagna, S. (1982). Recipient reactions to aid. *Psychological Bulletin*, **91**, 27–54.

Fisher, S. (1989). *Sexual Images of the Self: The Psychology of Erotic Sensations and Illusions*. Hillsdale, NJ: Lawrence Erlbaum Associates.

Fogel, A., Melson, G.F. & Mistry, J. (1986). Conceptualising the determinants of nurturance: A reassessment of sex differences. In A. Fogel & G.F. Melson (eds),

Origins of Nurturance: Developmental, Biological and Cultural Perspectives on Caregiving. Hillsdale, NJ: Lawrence Erlbaum Associates.

Fox, R. (1986). Fitness by any other name. *Behavioral and Brain Sciences,* **9,** 192–193.

Fukuyama, F. (1992). *The End of History and the Last Man.* Harmondsworth: Penguin.

Gardner, R. (1988). Psychiatric infrastructures for intraspecific communication. In M.R.A. Chance (ed.), *Social Fabrics of the Mind.* Hove: Lawrence Erlbaum Associates.

Gazzaniga, M.S. (1989). Organization of the human brain. *Science,* **245,** 947–952.

Gilbert, P. (1989). *Human Nature and Suffering.* Hove: Lawrence Erlbaum Associates.

Gilbert, P. (1992). *Depression: The Evolution of Powerlessness:* Hove: Lawrence Erlbaum Associates and Guilford Press.

Gilbert, P. (1993). Defense and safety: Their function in social behaviour and psychopathology. *British Journal of Clinical Psychology,* **32,** 131–154.

Gilbert, P. (1995). Biopsychosocial approaches and evolutionary theory as aids to integration in clinical psychology and psychotherapy. *Clinical Psychology and Psychotherapy,* **2,** 135–156.

Gilbert, P., Price, J.S. & Allan, S. (1995). Social comparison, social attractiveness and evolution: How might they be related? *New Ideas in Psychology,* **13,** 149–165.

Gilligan, C. (1982). *In a Different Voice: Psychological Theory and Women's Development.* Cambridge, MA: Cambridge University Press.

Halton, E. (1992). The cultic roots of culture: In R. Munch & N.J. Smelser (eds), *Theory of Culture.* Berkeley, CA: University of California Press.

Heard, D.H. & Lake, B. (1986). The attachment dynamic in adult life. *British Journal of Psychiatry,* **149,** 430–438.

Henry, J.P. (1982). The relation of social to biological process in disease. *Social Science Medicine,* **16,** 369–380.

Henry, J.P. & Stephens, P.M. (1977). *Stress, Health and the Social Environment: A Sociobiologic Approach to Medicine.* New York: Springer Verlag.

Hofer, M.A. (1984). Relationships as regulators: A psychobiologic perspective on bereavement. *Psychosomatic Medicine,* **46,** 183–197.

Jensen-Campbell, L.A., Graziano, W.G. & West, S.G. (1995). Dominance, prosocial orientation and female preference: Do nice guys really finish last? *Journal of Personality and Social Psychology,* **68,** 427–440.

Jung, C.G. (1972). *Four Archetypes.* London: Routledge.

Kaufman, G. (1989). *The Psychology of Shame.* New York: Springer.

Kevles, B. (1986). *Females of the Species: Sex and Survival in the Animal Kingdom.* Cambridge, MA: Harvard University Press.

MacLean, P.D. (1985). Brain evolution relating to family, play and the separation call. *Archives of General Psychiatry,* **42,** 405–417.

Marks, I.M. (1987). *Fears, Phobias, and Rituals: Panic, Anxiety and their Disorders.* Oxford: Oxford University Press.

McGuire, M.T. & Troisi, A. (In press). *Darwinian Psychiatry.* New York: Oxford University Press.

Nesse, R.M. (1990). Evolutionary explanations of emotions. *Human Nature,* **1,** 261–289.

Oatley, K. (1992). *Best Laid Schemes: The Psychology of Emotions.* Cambridge: Cambridge University Press.

Ornstein, R. (1986). *Multimind: A New Way of Looking at Human Beings.* London: Macmillan.

Overing, J. (1989). Styles of manhood: An amazonian contrast in tranquillity and violence. In S. Howell & R. Wills (eds), *Societies at Peace. Anthropological Perspectives.* London: Routledge.

Price, J.S., Sloman, R., Gardner, R., Gilbert, P. & Rhode, P. (1994). The social competition hypothesis of depression. *British Journal of Psychiatry*, **164**, 309–315.

Raleigh, M.J., McGuire, M.T., Brammer, G.L., Pollack, D.B. & Yuweiler, A. (1991). Serontonergic mechanisms promote dominance acquisition in adult male vervet monkeys. *Brain Research*, 181–190.

Reite, M. & Field, T. (eds) (1985). *The Psychobiology of Attachment and Separation*. New York: Academic Press.

Ridley, M. (1994). *The Red Queen: Sex and the Evolution of Human Nature*. Harmondsworth: Penguin.

Rowan, J. (1990). *Subpersonalities: The People Inside Us*. London: Routledge.

Safran, J.D. & Segal, Z.V. (1990). *Interpersonal Process in Cognitive Therapy*. New York: Basic Books.

Sapolsky, R.M. (1989). Hypercortisolism among socially subordinate wild baboons originates at the CNS level. *Archives of General Psychiatry*, **46**, 1047–1051.

Sapolsky, R.M. (1990a). Adrenocortical function, social rank and personality among wild baboons. *Biological Psychiatry*, **28**, 862–878.

Sapolsky, R.M. (1990b). Stress in the wild. *Scientific American*, **262**, January, 106–113.

Schore, A.N. (1994). *Affect Regulation and the Origin of the Self: The Neurobiology of Emotional Development*. Hillsdale, NJ: Lawrence Erlbaum.

Stevens, A. (1982). *Archetype: A Natural History of the Self*. London: Routledge & Kegan Paul.

Tomkins, S.S. (1981). The quest for primary motives: Biography and autobiography. *Journal of Personality and Social Psychology*, **41**, 306–329.

Trivers, R. (1985). *Social Evolution*. California: Benjamin/Cummings.

Wilkinson, R.G. (1996). *Unhealthy Societies: The Afflictions of Inequality*. London: Routledge.

Wilson, M. & Daly, M. (1992). The man who mistook his wife for a chattel. In J.H. Barkow, L. Cosmides & J. Tooby (eds), *The Adapted Mind: Evolutionary Psychology and the Generation of Culture*. New York: Oxford University Press.

Wink, P. (1991). Two faces of narcissism. *Journal of Personality and Social Psychology*, **61**, 590–597.

Young, J.E., Beck, A.T. & Weinberger, A. (1993). Depression. In H.D. Barlow (ed.), *Clinical Handbook of Psychological Disorders*. New York: Guilford.

Chapter 4

CONSCIOUS AND UNCONSCIOUS REPRESENTATIONS OF MEANING

*M.J. Power**

INTRODUCTION

The idea that there may be two different types of processing in the mind has a long history. Perhaps the most familiar of these has been the distinction made between the conscious and the unconscious (see Ellenberger (1970) for the definitive history), but a range of other related distinctions have also been made, including primary process versus secondary process, automatic versus controlled, rational versus emotional, and impulsive versus realistic (see Hilgard, 1962). The fact that so many similar distinctions have been proposed is of course insufficient evidence to confirm the reality of the distinction, any more than the fact that half-a-million Americans claim to have been abducted by aliens is proof of the existence of Creatures From Mars. The abundance of such distinctions does, however, merit careful examination of the possibility that there could be two qualitatively different types of process that occur in the mind and that these may lead to the generation of two categories of meaning. In order to provide the historical context for current views on the subject, two separate but extremely influential traditions within psychology will be considered, the first originating in the work of the German 19th century polymath, Hermann von Helmholtz (1821–1894), and the second in the work of Sigmund Freud (1856–1939). In addition, however, it will also be argued that the work of Pierre Janet (1859–1947) must be considered for an integrated model of the unconscious to be developed.

*Royal Edinburgh Hospital and University of Edinburgh, Scotland

The Transformation of Meaning in Psychological Therapies.
Edited by Mick Power and Chris R. Brewin. © 1997 John Wiley & Sons Ltd.

SOME HISTORICAL BACKGROUND

Helmholtz

The main tradition in the study of the unconscious that has influenced modern cognitive science stems from the work of Helmholtz. Innovative studies of the visual system led Helmholtz to publish a series of volumes which formed the *Handbook of Physiological Optics* (1856–1866). In the *Handbook* he noted a range of puzzling questions about vision that included the following:

1. Why are there no breaks in the visual field despite the existence of the blind spots in each eye?
2. How do the two views that we have of the world through our binocular vision combine to produce a single unitary perception?
3. Why is the visual system vulnerable to the experience of a range of visual illusions?
4. How do we judge distance through stereoscopic vision and how do a number of constancies (e.g. of size, colour and shape) operate?

In order to explain these and other phenomena, Helmholtz argued that there was a need to postulate the existence of a Perceptual Unconscious whose operation was apparent from the range of Unconscious Inferences or Conclusions that led to the phenomena in question. These inferences were considered to have an empiricist and associationist basis, that is, they were learned during early experience through association and experience, they were irresistible, and they were inductive because they generalised to new experiences. Helmholtz's work demonstrated very dramatically, therefore, how the visual system automatically creates a meaningful visual world in which the observer is placed. This meaningful world is, however, partly created through the imposition or addition of material to the imperfect input. Meaning is created automatically as an interaction between new input being combined with stored experience of the world.

This Helmholtzian tradition of the importance of low-level unconscious or automatic processes is a cornerstone of modern cognitive psychology, which, as I will discuss later, has broadened the need for such processes well beyond vision in order to include almost all basic cognitive skills. An important point to note, however, is that both the Helmholtzian Perceptual Unconscious and more recent cognitive science proposals consider conscious and unconscious processes to operate in cooperation with each other rather than in opposition to each other, in contrast to the way that they are considered to operate in the Freudian model (e.g. Neisser, 1967).

Freud

The second major tradition is provided in the work of Sigmund Freud. In fact, through the course of his writings Freud proposed not one but several models of the unconscious. The key proposal was Freud's shift from earlier 'descriptive' models in which the unconscious was viewed as a storehouse for old memories to a 'dynamic' model in which the unconscious played an active role in our everyday thoughts and actions (see Ellenberger, 1970). Freud was in fact a great admirer of Helmholtz (Wilhelm Fliess' Christmas present to Freud in 1898 was a two-volume set of Helmholtz's lectures); he based his principle of constancy of psychic energy directly on the conservation of physical energy which Helmholtz had drawn together in the Laws of Thermodynamics. If psychic energy fails to be expressed through the proper channels, Freud argued, it will be transformed into other forms and expressed as symptoms, parapraxes and dreams. For example, Freud initially considered anxiety to be transformed libidinal energy (Breuer & Freud, 1895), arguing that the hyperventilation and over-arousal characteristic of anxiety bears more than coincidental resemblance to sexual excitement and orgasm! Later, however, he altered his views on anxiety when he proposed that anxiety was no longer transformed psychic energy but was the ego's reaction to an unacceptable impulse or idea that had to be kept out of consciousness (Freud, 1926). The energy model was nevertheless retained in a more sophisticated form in the later structural theory.

In contrast to Helmholtz, Freud viewed basic cognitive processes as part of the preconscious rather than the unconscious and, in addition, considered them to be veridical rather than distorted; thus, in the later structural theory (*The Ego And The Id*, 1923) cognitive processes are viewed as part of the ego, one of whose main functions is reality testing. Meaning generated by perceptual mechanisms is therefore a true representation of reality, even though we know from Helmholtz's work onwards that perceptual processes are inherently distorted. Freud (e.g. 1915) considered the unconscious to be composed of two parts. The first part is innate and composed of the basic drives and their associated energy. The second part is the repressed and consists of material that was once conscious but which is no longer so. The unconscious is considered to display a number of characteristic or 'primary process' features including an absence of contradiction or negation, timelessness and irrationality (see e.g. Power & Brewin, 1991); at the primary process level, therefore, meaning is qualitatively different and not subject to the same logical limitations that would be applicable to ego-based secondary processes.

Janet

A third tradition in the study of the unconscious stems from the work of Pierre Janet (1889). Brief mention will be made of it because of continued interest in revised versions of Janet's proposals (e.g. Hilgard, 1986) and because of the relevance of the approach for modularity approaches in modern cognitive science (e.g. Fodor, 1983; Gazzaniga, 1988). Janet argued that in certain vulnerable individuals dissociations of the mind can occur; such dissociations are apparent in hysteria, in fugue states, somnambulism, and multiple personality disorder. In these dissociations, a part of the mind comes to act autonomously and independently of the self or the ego. Whereas in the healthy individual the mind acts in an integrated fashion, Janet proposed that in vulnerable individuals there is a failure of such integration and a splitting of the mind occurs. For example, in extreme cases such as the multiple personality disorders (or 'dissociative disorders of identity' in DSM-IV, (American Psychiatric Association, 1994) terminology), although there may be one dominant personality, there are one or more additional personalities of which the dominant personality is sometimes unaware; dominance, however, switches between personalities under appropriate circumstances, as in the nighttime prowling of Dr Jekyll's alter ego, Mr Hyde.

Janet's proposal that dissociation was limited to only 'weak-minded' individuals was challenged early on by Breuer & Freud (1895) in *Studies on Hysteria*. They stated:

> In complete opposition to Janet's views, . . . in a great many cases what underlies dissociation is an excess of efficiency, the habitual co-existence of two heterogeneous trains of ideas. (pp. 312–313).

In addition, Breuer & Freud proposed that:

> There are no doubt a whole number of activities, from mechanical ones such as knitting or playing scales, to some requiring at least a small degree of mental functioning, all of which are performed by many people with only half their mind on them. (p. 313)

Finally, they conclude that:

> The duplication of psychical functioning, whether this is habitual or caused by emotional situations in life, acts as a substantial predisposition to a genuine pathological splitting of the mind. (p. 314)

Through explicitly linking the automatisation of simple cognitive skills with emotional processes and of more major dissociations within the personality, Breuer & Freud pointed to a crucial mechanism by which repeated patterns of meaning generation can come to occur automatically if they are repeated often enough.

This revision of Janet's proposals concurs in fact with a more recent revision proposed by Hilgard (1977/1986) called neo-dissociationism in which dissociation is considered a potential feature for any individual, not only those with an hereditary weakness. Hilgard has for example argued that hypnotic phenomena must be understood as dissociations of consciousness in which control may be relinquished and handed over to another individual.

AN INTEGRATED APPROACH?

We have argued elsewhere that a broad-based cognitive science approach can offer the possibility for integration of the three key historical approaches to the unconscious, as represented in the works of Helmholtz, Freud and Janet (Power & Brewin, 1991). The emphasis on modular processing in current cognitive formulations parallels the possibility of dissociations within Janet's approach, especially when taken in the modified form presented by Breuer & Freud quoted above, in which they liken the splits to those that occur in highly automated cognitive skills. Although it is necessary to jettison certain aspects of the Freudian unconscious, especially the emphasis on drive-based psychic energy, this step has already been taken in many more recent psychodynamic approaches (e.g. Fairbairn, 1952; Holt, 1967). In addition, Freud's proposal that perceptual and mnemonic processes are not distorted but are veridical, would have to be rejected in the light of the tradition stemming from Helmholtz in which a range of cognitive processes have been found to be inherently distorted.

The proposed integration of these three approaches must step beyond the Helmholtzian focus on low-level perceptual and cognitive skills in order to embrace the fact, as emphasised by Freud and Janet, that the unconscious has a dynamic effect on our thoughts and actions and is not simply limited to coffee-table demonstrations of visual illusions. The possibility that the unconscious includes relatively high-level processes related to goals, plans and the generation of emotions in addition to low-level cognitive processes provides a very different model than is characteristically considered in cognitive science. However, rather than discuss this broader cognitive model in the abstract, we will be specific and focus on the generation of emotion as presented in a recent application of these ideas (Power & Dalgleish, 1997).

TWO ROUTES TO EMOTION

The SPAARS Approach

In order to be specific about the application of the proposed integrated model of conscious and unconscious processing, the model will be considered in its recent application to the generation of emotion. Power & Dalgleish (1997) have presented the so-called SPAARS model (or the 'Schematic, Propositional, Associative, and Analogical Representation Systems' Model), illustrated in Figure 4.1. The main features of the SPAARS approach are that a number of different representation systems are involved in the processing of information (cf. Teasdale's ICS approach presented in Chapter 9). Incoming information is processed by a range of analogical systems that include the visual, auditory, olfactory, tactile and kinaesthetic systems: for simplicity these have been grouped together as the Analogical Representation System. The output from the analogical systems may then feed through one or more of the three remaining systems: the Associative, the Propositional, and the Schematic Model. The Associative System is that traditionally associated with the unconscious. It combines a range of influences that, we have argued, include:

1. The innate basic emotions of Sadness, Happiness, Fear, Anger and Disgust;

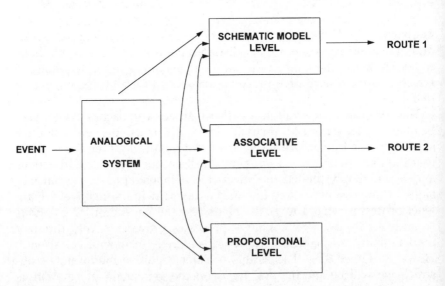

Figure 4.1 An outline of the SPAARS approach illustrating two distinctive routes to the generation of emotion

2. Other biological factors, for example, the effects of drugs, hormones and diet;
3. Learned associations between inputs and responses, in the manner suggested by modern learning theories (e.g. Mackintosh, 1983);
4. Automated sequences from oft-repeated appraisals.

The pathway from the Analogical System to the Associative System is labelled 'Route 2—the Automatic or Direct-Access Route' (see Figure 4.1). The emphasis on direct access reflects the fact that emotion generation via this route may be fast and automatic. Although the individual may become aware of an emotion that is generated via this route, the emotion could be inhibited either consciously or unconsciously. For example, an unwanted or unacceptable emotion such as sadness in Western men might be experienced momentarily but then 'choked back' or inhibited. In extreme cases, however, the individual need never be aware of an emotion such as sadness, but only be aware of its absence; individuals who use an excessive repressive coping style may seldom experience negative emotions such as sadness, anxiety and anger, even though physiologically they are hyper-aroused (e.g. Myers, Brewin & Power, 1992; see also Chapter 7). The SPAARS model would suggest in such cases that the processing of relevant events still occurs automatically, but the outputs from the direct access route are actively inhibited: they fail to reach consciousness, but they do impact on other relevant physiological systems.

The pathway from the Analogical System to the Schematic Model System is labelled 'Route 1—the Appraisal Route' (see Figure 4.1). This pathway involves the controlled processing of appropriate events or situations; controlled processes can be conscious or partly conscious, though their crucial feature is that they make resource demands on a central limited-capacity working memory. The emotions generated via this route can sometimes occur quickly or, by contrast, they can occur extremely slowly if some ambiguity in a situation needs to be resolved before it is clear which emotion is most appropriate. To give an example, you have just landed on a certain Greek island and as you are walking along the road an elderly man cycles past while making an unfamiliar hand gesture towards you and uttering something in Greek. Under the circumstances you do not know whether to laugh, cry, or get annoyed; only later in the taverna does the proprietor explain that it was a welcoming greeting to strangers and you feel a positive warm glow. However, a couple of days later you mention the situation in passing to the travel rep, who explains that the gesture and accompanying utterance questions your mother's sexual habits and that the proprietor of the taverna probably did not want to upset you on your first evening. You now feel furious!

Like this example, most of the complex situations and relationships that we engage in, unfold in complex and often unexpected ways; the actual emotions we experience may therefore vary considerably as new information becomes available to us.

The cornerstone of the appraisal route is the generation of a Schematic Model which, typically, is constructed out of a combination of pre-stored schema-like information which is dynamically combined with current information to form the current dominant mental model; that is, although the construction of a schematic model involves controlled processes, nevertheless, automatic processes in the other systems may contribute to the final model. The term 'Schematic Model' was coined by Teasdale & Barnard (1993) in order to capture this interplay between stored information and the dynamics of the current situation; although the term 'schema' has been used in a variety of often inconsistent ways in both cognitive and clinical psychology, the hope is that this new use will have sufficient specificity to be useful. This form of representation therefore is the highest level holistic synthesis of all relevant information, a synthesis that provides the main contrast with the associative level of semantic representation. Its content cannot simply therefore be expressed in verbal or propositional form (cf. Johnson-Laird, 1983) and there are many situations where one may be advised to avoid words or leave the task of attempting to articulate the schematic model to poets and novelists. Indeed, information that is expressible in a verbal form belongs properly to the Propositional System rather than to the Schematic Model System.

The Propositional System within the SPAARS approach is not considered to give rise to emotion directly but only indirectly through the Schematic Model and Associative Systems (see Figure 4.1). Although we considered in detail whether or not the Propositional System might provide a third route to emotion (Power & Dalgleish, 1997), it was unclear how such a route might be distinguishable from the other two. For example, the emotional impact of swear words and taboo words may often be independent of the propositional truth-value, and appears to be a direct association to the words or phrases themselves (e.g. 'Sh*t!'). The emotional impact of utterances which, however, do depend on their propositional truth-value (e.g. 'You're fired!' or 'I do!') take us well beyond the simple truth-value to Schematic Models with considerable depths of unarticulated implications; it is the process of appraisal and the construction of Schematic Models that seem crucial, not simply an analysis of the truth-value of a proposition which merely provides the starting point from which the appraisal process might begin (see Power & Dalgleish (1997) for a detailed discussion).

The SPAARS approach is of course not the only dual or multi-level approach to emotion. One notable approach is that of Leventhal (e.g.

Leventhal & Scherer, 1987), who has argued for three routes to emotion: first, an innate-based sensory motor level; second, an automatically activated schematic level; and third, a propositionally based conceptual level. SPAARS combines the first and second levels in the form of the Associative route, because we consider the innate basic emotions as developmental starting points which are subsequently modified through experience. A similar dual route distinction is made by Brewin (1989) who has argued for verbally accessible memories (VAMs) and situationally accessible memories (SAMs) in relation to emotion reactions. Although this model has many features in common with SPAARS, especially in its emphasis on automatic and controlled processes, there are also important differences. For example, SPAARS describes in greater detail the schematic models that underlie the production of emotion. Also, in SPAARS the associative route is not only driven by key situations but by activity in one or more of the other representation systems as well. The important point, however, is that the SPAARS approach is now one amongst several that emphasises the fact that emotion may be generated via two or more routes.

SOME IMPLICATIONS OF TWO ROUTES TO EMOTION

Rather than consider further detail of the SPAARS theory, it will be more profitable to outline some of the possible implications of the proposal that there are two routes to emotion both in relation to the emotional disorders and in relation to the possibilities for therapeutic change.

One of the characteristics of emotions is that they are typically short circumscribed reactions that last from a few seconds to a few minutes (e.g. Ekman & Davidson, 1994). The puzzle therefore is to understand how emotional disorders, which are typically chronic and long-standing, can arise from such short, time-limited reactions. One suggestion is that there may be feedback loops within the system that can maintain an emotional reaction; thus, Teasdale & Barnard (1993; see Chapter 9) have suggested that the so-called Propositional and Implicational level systems within their ICS approach could 'interlock' and continually activate each other, as illustrated in Figure 4.2.

Within the ICS model, therefore, thoughts of being a failure could serve to maintain a Schematic Model of SELF-AS-FAILURE which in turn could generate further thoughts, and so on. The outcome of this cycling is that an emotion such as sadness might be maintained for longer than would normally be the case. Although we agree with Teasdale & Barnard that such a process is important, in the SPAARS approach we have pointed to

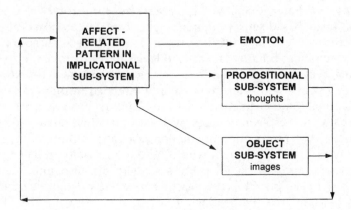

Figure 4.2 An example of 'interlock' between subsystems within Teasdale & Barnard's (1993) ICS approach

a more powerful positive feedback loop in which two emotions become 'coupled' together and thereby maintain each other potentially over considerable lengths of time (see Figure 4.3). In fact, there are at least two possible ways in which emotions can be coupled within SPAARS. First, the generation of one emotion can lead to the generation of a second emotion, for example, anger might invariably lead to the genera-tion of fear in some individuals for whom the experience or expression

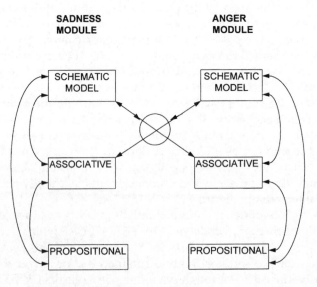

Figure 4.3 An example of emotion 'coupling'

of anger was not allowed. Second, the same event could lead to two different appraisals which in turn lead to two different emotions. For example, in the SPAARS analysis of problematic grief reactions, we have suggested that two key basic emotions involved in grief, the emotions of sadness and anger, may come to be coupled together and thereby maintain the individual locked in grief over long periods of time.

Mr L was constantly troubled by the loss of his son, five-and-a-half years previously. He was angry with his son for abusing drugs which led to him developing AIDS and dying unnecessarily. He was angry with medicine for not having developed a cure for AIDS. He was angry with his son's girlfriend for not allowing his son to be buried where Mr L knew his son wanted to be buried. But most of all, he was angry with himself for the uncontrollable episodes of crying that regularly overwhelmed him.

In addition to the possibility that two emotions can couple together and maintain the individual in a complex emotional disorder, there are of course other possible outcomes of the existence of two routes to emotion which have implications for emotions and the emotional disorders. One such possibility hinted at earlier is that conflicting emotions can be generated via the two different routes. There are numerous minor everyday examples where one might 'force' oneself, for example, to experience and express happiness toward a work colleague's success, or sadness at his or her failure, even though the 'real' emotion experienced might be anger in response to the success and happiness in response to the failure. A possible SPAARS analysis would be that the expected emotion for the situation may be generated via the appraisal route, while being aware of a contrasting emotion being generated via the associative or direct access route. Much more damaging, however, are the families in which a child may be prevented from expressing certain 'negative' emotions, especially when these may be natural responses to extreme circumstances, such as in physical and sexual abuse (see Andrews, Chapter 5). For example, John Bowlby (1973) pointed to this possibility in relation to important attachment figures as follows:

> During therapeutic work it is not uncommon to uncover gross inconsistencies between generalisations a patient makes about his parents and what is implied by some of the episodes he recalls of how they actually behaved and what they said on particular occasions. Sometimes a generalisation refers in broad and glowing terms to a parent's admirable qualities, some or all of which are called sharply in question when episodes of how he or she had actually behaved and/or spoken are recalled and appraised. (p. 62).

As a further illustration of the two routes, consideration will be given to the case of Mr L who, as mentioned above, was bereaved from the loss of his son through AIDS, but who had also more recently lost his wife when she had died of a heart attack.

Mr L had first presented to his GP with globus and had been investigated for cancer of the throat. The tests had proven negative and he was then referred for behaviour therapy, because he was having difficulty swallowing solid food because of the lump in his throat. A cognitive behavioural programme had been designed that included relaxation training and graded exposure to increasingly solid food. The therapist initially made some progress with this approach, but eventually the therapy seemed to grind to a halt and the therapist terminated treatment. Mr L. was eventually re-referred because the globus was getting worse. On initial questioning Mr L still wondered if he might have cancer of the throat.

The meaning attributed to the symptom by Mr L was that he had cancer of the throat; this schematic model led to the generation of anxiety. The first therapist's model was that Mr L's *belief* that he had cancer of the throat caused the increased tension in his throat in certain situations, in the manner of the vicious circle outlined for Clark's (1986) cognitive therapy for panic. Although the therapist and Mr L had different schematic models about the lump in the throat, both agreed that the model led to the generation of anxiety. However, within the SPAARS model we would consider the possibility that there was an alternative direct-access level of meaning or emotion generation route; namely, that the experience of the loss of two significant relationships through death were both associated with extreme grief and that these reactions to loss are basic innate responses. The role for schematic models in this account was to inhibit the expression of sadness, because Mr L believed that sadness and tears were weak and unmanly. So why would the inhibition of sadness lead to a lump in the throat rather than some other somatic symptom? Apart from the everyday sense that emotions such as sadness can be choked back or swallowed, Mr L had also found his wife shortly before she died gasping for air because of an asthma attack. His most terrifying memory was a vision of his wife gasping for breath, unable to breathe. What is suggested therefore is that the patient's (or therapist's) preferred meaning or model may lead to one emotion, but there may be a different level of meaning at which a more complete understanding of the process can be achieved. This suggestion, of course, implies that meaning, like emotion, can be both conscious and unconscious, and that the conscious meaning may be out of tune with the unconscious (see Bolton & Hill, 1996; see also

Chapter 2). Only through understanding both can the therapist make progress in therapy and can lasting therapeutic change be attained.

By no means all emotional disorders necessitate that the two routes are in conflict with each other, but, instead, they may compound each other in their effects. For example, in the case of Post Traumatic Stress Disorder (PTSD) the two routes may be involved in different ways (Brewin, Dalgleish & Joseph, 1996; Power & Dalgleish, 1997). The experience of a traumatic event leads many people to experience recurrent flashbacks, nightmares, and intrusions connected to the trauma. These phenomena are often of a low-level, analogical nature: the smell of burning, the crackle of fire, the taste of smoke, and the brightness of flame may come to be associated with anxiety being generated via the direct-access or associative route. Indeed, where such phenomena are the main feature (particularly when combined with avoidance), behavioural approaches may provide the treatment of choice. In contrast, some individuals who experience traumatic events present primarily with 'shattered assumptions' about the world (e.g. Janoff-Bulman, 1992; see Chapter 6). That is, their experience of trauma invalidates core beliefs or schematic models about, for example, the safe and just nature of the world; the world becomes an unsafe place and people are now seen to be completely untrustworthy. In these cases, anxiety would seem to be generated via the appraisal route and the treatment of choice is more likely to be cognitive therapy involving therapeutic work on the invalidated core schema. Of course, some individuals present with a panoply of shattered beliefs and intrusive phenomena coupled with avoidance; in such cases combined cognitive and behavioural approaches would seem to be the most warranted (see Power & Dalgleish, 1997, for further discussion).

THERAPY AND THERAPEUTIC CHANGE: SOME COMMENTS

The identification of two qualitatively different types of processes, each of which can lead to the generation not only of different emotions but also of different goals and plans, and different levels of meaning, has important implications for therapy and therapeutic change. One of the important features of controlled processes is that they are easily accessible to consciousness and are readily modifiable (e.g. Power & Brewin, 1991; Schneider, Dumais & Shiffrin, 1984). In theory, therefore, problems based on faulty schematic models and the generation of emotion via the appraisal route should be more amenable to fast therapeutic change (e.g. Brewin, 1996), while noting the proviso that many patients want low-level symptom change without wanting to change their higher-level models. Such Fast Change processes are probably evident in David Clark's (1986) adaptation of cognitive therapy for panic. In this approach the individual suffering from panic attacks is considered to catastrophically misinterpret certain bodily stimuli; for example, a beating heart is interpreted to mean an impending heart attack, shortness of breath to signal imminent suffocation, dizziness to indicate a brain tumour, and so on. That is, the individual appraises a bodily sensation to indicate physical threat and thereby experiences panic; a faulty schematic model is constructed in the process which serves to maintain the panic. Clark's cognitive therapy for panic is based therefore on the presentation of an alternative schematic model to the sufferer (Teasdale & Barnard, 1993); through a combination of education about anxiety and the testing out of an alternative model during the experience of panic, a more appropriate schematic model can be developed which is less debilitating for the individual. The construction of this more appropriate schematic model could take place relatively quickly, even within a single session, because it is potentially a Fast Change process.

Unfortunately, most therapeutic change is based on Slow rather than Fast Change processes. Although the patient who responds quickly and successfully to cognitive therapy for panic may experience a dramatic Road to Damascus transformation of meaning, nevertheless, the low-level analogical–associative phenomena should still be present. That is, although individuals no longer believe that they are going to die of a heart attack, they will still experience a pounding heart when they visit the supermarket on a Friday evening (or whatever situation is crucial); these phenomena are likely to continue to be triggered associatively in the critical situations, and should only gradually begin to change despite the fast alteration of schematic models. In fact, it seems likely that much of the change that is aimed for in therapy is of the Slow Change variety; habitual patterns of thinking, acting and relating may become the focus for change in therapy, but the actual processes through which these changes occur are on a slow track, because they are based on the alteration of associatively based representations. Indeed, the initial attempts to change associative reactions may consist of increasing the individual's awareness of when such processes are automatically triggered, and then gradually learning to intervene earlier in the automatic sequences as they are run off.

The distinction between Slow Change and Fast Change, between automatic and controlled processes, and between direct-access and appraisal-generated emotion is also captured in the common distinction made between intellectual change and emotional change. Patients in therapy often report that while intellectually they believe or feel one thing, emotionally they believe or feel another. Beck et al.'s (1979) handling of this phenomenon was to claim that the two are merely aspects of the same process (see also Teasdale, Chapter 9). However, the two-route approach emphasises that these phenomena are qualitatively distinct and that conflicting emotions can be generated via the two routes. Moreover, it is clear that during positive change in therapy, patients are likely still to be aware of the older habitual patterns while attempting to replace them with more recent, healthier ones. 'Intellectual' change may therefore be experienced as preceding 'emotional' change; the point made within the SPAARS approach is that *both* are forms of emotional change, so one is not more valid than the other.

There are of course many other clinical implications of the two routes to emotion approach captured within SPAARS (see Power & Dalgleish, 1997). A final one that will be highlighted is the role of Negative Automatic Thoughts (NATs) within the cognitive therapy model (e.g. Beck et al., 1979). When translated into the SPAARS model, the proposal that NATs lead to emotion would be an example of activity in the Propositional System which would not, in itself, lead to the generation of emotion. The effect of NATs is most likely to be through feeding into the appraisal system and thereby contributing to the construction of a relevant schematic model (cf. Teasdale & Barnard, 1993; Chapter 9). However, it would also be possible for highly automated sequences to feed through from the Propositional System (see Figure 4.1 earlier) via the Automatic Route. Whichever of these two routes occurs, the crucial point is that although some emotions may be indirectly linked to NATs, many emotions do not involve NATs in their generation. Chasing NATs in cognitive therapy may sometimes be a fruitless exercise, because there are no NATs to be caught! Moreover, we believe that our patients have been telling us this fact for a long time when they report that they had no thoughts in a particular situation, that the emotion came over them 'out of the blue'. The practice of cognitive therapy needs therefore to be altered to incorporate the Automatic Route to emotion generation.

CONCLUSIONS

Three key approaches to the unconscious were briefly reviewed. The earliest, that of Helmholtz, focused on low-level automatic processes involved in perception. This tradition is still highly influential in modern cognitive science and has been broadened to include a range of other cognitive skills, not just perception. The second and best known approach is that of Freud. Freud's emphasis on the dynamic nature of the unconscious was his major contribution and one that must be maintained in any modern approach to the unconscious. The third approach, that of Janet, has not been as widely known as Freud's, but has continued to have an influence nevertheless. An amended version of Janet's dissociation theory, perhaps surprisingly first suggested by Breuer & Freud (1895), seems very much in line with a number of modern cognitive theories. We have argued elsewhere (Power & Brewin, 1991) that an integrated approach to the unconscious needs to draw together the strengths of these three traditions while avoiding some of their weaknesses. The net effect of this integration is that two qualitatively different types of processes need to be considered in a vast range of activities. The focus in this chapter has been on the role of these two routes in the generation of emotion (Power & Dalgleish, 1997). The existence of two routes has substantial implications for working with the emotional disorders and for considerations of therapeutic change. The fact that there are two routes suggests that therapeutic change need not be experienced as a unitary process, but rather as different systems potentially changing at different rates. For example, schematic models could in theory change very quickly, whereas associative processes change much more slowly. Although successful therapy should ultimately involve changes in both systems, different methods and different techniques may be more powerful for one type of change than for the other.

REFERENCES

American Psychiatric Association (1994). *Diagnostic and Statistical Manual of Mental Disorders (Fourth Edition) (DSM-IV)*. Washington: American Psychiatric Association.

Beck, A.T., Rush, A., Shaw, B. & Emery, G. (1979). *Cognitive Therapy of Depression*. New York: Guilford Press.

Bolton, D. & Hill, J. (1996). *Mind, Meaning, and Mental Disorder: The Nature of Causal Explanation in Philosophy and Psychiatry*. Oxford: Oxford University Press.

Bowlby, J. (1973). *Attachment and Loss (Vol. 2): Separation*. London: Hogarth Press.

Breuer, J. & Freud, S. (1895). *Studies on Hysteria*. In The Pelican Freud Library, Vol. 3. Harmondsworth: Penguin (1974).

Brewin, C.R. (1989). Cognitive change processes in psychotherapy. *Psychological Review*, **96**, 379–394.

Brewin, C.R. (1996). Theoretical foundations of cognitive-behavior therapy for anxiety and depression. *Annual Review of Psychology*, **47**, 33–57.

Brewin, C.R., Dalgleish, T. & Joseph, S. (1996). A dual representation theory of post-traumatic stress disorder. *Psychological Review*, **103**, 670–686.

Clark, D.M. (1986). A cognitive approach to panic. *Behaviour Research and Therapy*, **24**, 461–470.

Ekman, P. & Davidson, R.J. (1994). *The Nature of Emotion: Fundamental Questions*. New York: Oxford University Press.

Ellenberger, H.F. (1970). *The Discovery of the Unconscious: The History and Evolution of Dynamic Psychiatry*. New York: Basic Books.

Fairbairn, W.R.D. (1952). *Psychoanalytic Studies of the Personality*. London: Tavistock.

Fodor, J.A. (1983). *The Modularity of Mind: An Essay on Faculty Psychology*. Cambridge, MA: MIJ Press.

Freud, S. (1915). *The Unconscious*. In The Pelican Freud Library, Vol. 11. Harmondsworth: Penguin (1984).

Freud, S. (1923). *The Ego and the Id*. In The Pelican Freud Library, Vol. 11. Harmondsworth: Penguin (1984).

Freud, S. (1926). *Inhibition, Symptoms and Anxiety*. In The Pelican Freud Library, Vol. 10. Harmondsworth: Penguin (1973).

Gazzaniga, M.S. (1988). Brain modularity: Towards a philosophy of conscious experience. In A. Marcel & E. Bisiach (eds), *Consciousness in Contemporary Science*. Oxford: Oxford University Press.

Helmholtz, H. von (1856–1866). *Treatise on Physiological Optics* (3 Vols). New York: Optical Society of America (1924).

Hilgard, E.R. (1962). Impulsive versus realistic thinking: An examination of the distinction between primary and secondary processes in thought. *Psychological Bulletin*, 59, 477–488.

Hilgard, E.R. (1977/1986). *Divided Consciousness: Multiple Controls in Human Thought and Action*. New York: Wiley.

Holt, R.R. (1967). Beyond vitalism and mechanism: Freud's concept of psychic energy. In J.H. Masserman (ed.), *The Ego*. New York: Grune & Stratton.

Janet, P. (1889). *L'Automatisme Psychologique: Essai de Psychologie mentale sur les Formes Inferieures de l'Activite Mentale*. Paris: Alcan.

Janoff-Bulman, R. (1992). *Shattered Assumptions: Towards a New Psychology of Trauma*. New York: Free Press.

Johnson-Laird, P.N. (1983). *Mental Models*. Cambridge: Cambridge University Press.

Leventhal, H. & Scherer, K. (1987). The relationship of emotion to cognition: A functional approach to a semantic controversy. *Cognition and Emotion*, 1, 3–28.

Mackintosh, N.J. (1983). *Conditioning and Associative Learning*. Oxford: Oxford University Press.

Myers, L.B., Brewin, C.R. & Power, M.J. (1992). Repression and autobiographical memory. In M.A. Conway, D.C. Rubin, H. Spinnler & W.A. Wagenaar (eds), *Theoretical Perspectives on Autobiographical Memory*. Dordrecht: Kluwer.

Neisser, U. (1967). *Cognitive Psychology*. New York: Appleton-Century-Crofts.

Power, M.J. & Brewin, C.R. (1991). From Freud to cognitive science: A contemporary account of the unconscious. *British Journal of Clinical Psychology*, 30, 289–310.

Power, M.J. & Dalgleish, T. (1997). *Cognition and Emotion: From Order to Disorder*. Hove: Psychology Press (Erlbaum, UK).

Schneider, W., Dumais, S.T. & Shiffrin, R.M. (1984). Automatic and control processing and attention. In R. Parasuraman & D.R. Davies (eds), *Varieties of Attention*. Orlando, FL: Academic Press.

Teasdale, J.D. & Barnard, P.J. (1993). *Affect, Cognition and Change: Re-modelling Depressive Thought*. Hove: Erlbaum.

Chapter 5

EARLY ADVERSITY AND THE CREATION OF PERSONAL MEANING

*Bernice Andrews**

The type of psychological distress and disorder for which people seek treatment is typically preceded by events and situations which are per-- ceived as being particularly upsetting and disturbing. There is in fact evidence that common mental health problems such as depression and anxiety are usually triggered by severe events and major life difficulties judged by researchers to be objectively threatening (Brown & Harris, 1978, 1989). But there is a wide variation in reactions. At one end of the spectrum are individuals who weather most storms with equanimity, at the other are those who become distressed by what appear to others to be the smallest vicissitudes of everyday living. The individual meaning at- tached to events is argued to play an important role in explaining varia- tions in response (e.g. Brown, 1989). Within this psychosocial perspective, meaning is seen as a function of the interplay between the individual's external world (that is, the actual features and context of events that may happen) and his or her internal world (that is, personal attitudes and schemas concerning self and others). I will argue that early experience has a bearing on both, inasmuch as it has the propensity to shape the current context of peoples' lives as well as the way they perceive themselves and others within that context. This model rests on the assumption that stress- ful events evoke different but interrelated layers of meaning.

At the most immediate level particular features of events may possess universal evolutionarily derived meanings which make them especially pernicious. Loss, rejection, humiliation and entrapment have all been

*Royal Holloway, University of London, UK

The Transformation of Meaning in Psychological Therapies.
Edited by Mick Power and Chris R. Brewin. © 1997 John Wiley & Sons Ltd.

implicated (Bowlby, 1973; Brown, Harris & Hepworth, 1995; Gilbert, this volume, Chapter 3). Loss events may involve the death of a loved one, or enforced separation, or the loss of employment or other role. Such events often involve rejection, as in the case of being fired from a job for not measuring up, or being thrown over by a loved one. Humiliation often occurs as a result of being publicly seen as having failed in some way. Another potent form of humiliation involves being physically beaten, or sexually abused. Abuse also often involves an element of entrapment, that is being trapped in a punishing situation. This can occur where the abuse is perpetrated by a partner or close family member and there is little opportunity to escape because of limited resources. Although these features of events are universally aversive, for those with adverse child-hoods they may well provide cues that activate prior autobiographical memories and habitual cognitive and affective coping mechanisms. In this way, the aversive meaning attached to the current situation may be intensified.

The context in which events occur, for example the existence of ongoing life difficulties, and future goals and plans, together with the quality of social support, may also affect meaning (Brown, 1989; Oatley & Bolton, 1985). For example, stressful events arising from existing life difficulties are associated with a higher risk of subsequent depression than experience of other stressful events (Brown, Bifulco & Harris, 1987), and women who receive no support from close friends or family when a crisis occurs have a higher onset rate of depression than others receiving support (Brown et al., 1986). But the current context of people's lives is at least to some degree a function of personal biography; ongoing life difficulties and the quality of personal relationships often have their origins in much earlier experiences, and are likely to be construed within this deeper context.

The emerging picture of the link between early adversity and meaning is one of considerable complexity. In what follows I will elucidate some of the issues, and draw attention to the emerging themes, using detailed illustrations from my own research.

EARLY ADVERSITY AND THE CURRENT CONTEXT OF EVENTS

Meanings Arising from a Match between Current Life Difficulties and Early Adversity

There is considerable evidence that women who receive inadequate parental care in childhood are at increased risk of experiencing poor social conditions in adulthood. The most common route is through their propensity to make unwise choices when selecting long-term partners. This often occurs as a result of unplanned pregnancies, or a general lack of planning.

In one prospective study of young women brought up in institutional care as a result of a breakdown in parenting, it was found that those who committed themselves too hastily and for the wrong reasons were more likely to end up with a deviant, unsupportive spouse (Quinton, Rutter & Liddle, 1984). Other research has shown that women reporting 'lack of care' in childhood, involving parental indifference and neglect, are more likely to become pregnant before marriage, which in turn leads to a greatly increased risk of ending up with an unsupportive and violent spouse (Andrews & Brown, 1988a; Harris, Brown & Bifulco, 1987). From the results of our investigation of biographical factors associated with marital violence (Andrews & Brown, 1988a), we concluded that women who experienced lack of care in childhood have a more immediate need to be loved and cherished than women whose early needs have been met. As part of this they may be susceptible to the attentions of possessive, dependent men whose own needs and backgrounds make them more likely to resort to violence in close relationships.

A major consequence for women of having a deviant or unsupportive partner is that it increases the likelihood of living in poor social conditions either with the spouse or alone, because marital breakdown is more common (Harris et al., 1987; Quinton, Rutter & Liddle, 1984). Poor social conditions for males also appear to be related to early family breakdown and institutional rearing, this effect being mediated, as in females, by lack of planning in early adulthood (Rutter, Quinton & Hill, 1990). Lack of planning for work appears to be a key factor for males. Evidence from studies of both men and women therefore suggests that early adversity involving inadequate parental care can set individuals on a trajectory of chronic life stress from adolescence and the early reproductive years right through into adulthood. Of course, this is by no means inevitable. While the risk of poor social conditions in adulthood is greatly increased by early adversity, many escape through careful planning (Quinton, Rutter & Liddle, 1984) and by finding a supportive partner (Harris, Brown & Bifulco, 1987).

One of the effects of being caught up on a trajectory of chronic life difficulties is an increased risk of experiencing objectively stressful life events (Brown, Bifulco & Harris, 1987). As already mentioned, Brown and colleagues showed in their longitudinal study of 400 women in Islington, London, that stressful life events 'matching' previously measured long-term difficulties were associated with a particularly high onset rate of depression. A firm finding in the life-events research concerning the role of specific meaning has been the importance of loss (Brown & Harris, 1978). Brown and colleagues argued that these matching events carry extra meaning, often underlining the fact that something had already been lost, or had never really been possessed. For individuals with no good experience of early parental care this particular type of meaning must carry a special poignancy.

In summary, people with early adverse parenting are more likely than others to experience the type of pervasive life difficulties that make stressful life events a common occurrence. Life events occurring in such a context have a particularly severe impact because of their meaning, and this might be even more deleterious for those with poor childhoods.

An example of such a process comes from the research I was involved in with George Brown.* It concerns a single mother who experienced a very difficult childhood where she suffered a good deal of neglect and abuse. Her parents threw her out in her teens when they discovered she was pregnant. The father of her child came after her, and they married, but he was dissatisfied and resentful from the start, as he felt obliged to disrupt his studies and work to support the family. She suffered very severe violence at his hands for a number of years, and eventually left when she felt her life was in danger. Two years later her former husband was killed in self-defence by another woman to whom he had been violent, an event for which she felt responsible. The single mother had chronic financial difficulties, with no support from anyone in the family for the three children. Furthermore, her son in particular had emotional and behavioural problems with which she had to contend. He eventually left home after an argument and severed all contact. Very soon after this she heard that he had committed a serious crime and was being sent to prison. At this point she became severely depressed. One of the features of the depression was her deep feeling that she was alone in the world with no one to help her. She feared going out because she said it was as if she had a label attached to her that everyone could see announcing 'R is alone'. She was a naturally gregarious and remarkably resourceful person with good self-esteem despite all the odds, but the severe event involving her son proved to be too much, occurring as it did in the context of major life difficulties related to a string of tragic circumstances stretching right back to her childhood. The current event served to intensify feelings of isolation that had been an objective feature of her earliest experiences. Coupled with this was the notion that not only had she failed with her husband, but she had failed with her son.

---

*Some details of the women described in the examples presented have been changed to protect their anonymity

Meanings Influencing the Use and Impact of Social Support

When severe life events are experienced, their meaning is likely to be affected by the responses of others in the immediate social network. The protective or 'buffering' role of social support has been demonstrated in a number of studies (see Alloway & Bebbington, 1987; Cohen & Wills, 1985). We have already seen that women with adverse childhoods are more likely to end up with deviant and unsupportive partners. They are also less likely to receive adequate social support in times of crisis (Andrews & Brown, 1988b). Bowlby's (1973, 1980) model provides a plausible explanation for this finding. He proposed that early representations of self and others are the result of experiences with primary attachment figures. Negative mental representations are based on childhood experiences such as never attaining a stable and secure relationship with parents, and being told repeatedly that one is unloveable or inadequate. Following this model, the mental self-representation of women who have not received adequate parental care would be one of being unworthy of others' support. By the same token, the representational model of others would be one involving rejection and unresponsiveness.

From a not unrelated perspective, it has also been proposed that the negative effects of adverse childhood experiences, particularly those involving any type of abuse, should be considered in terms of adaptational failure (Wolfe, 1987). Wolfe proposed that adaptation to the immediate predicament may be a functional or reasonable response to an extreme set of circumstances, but is dysfunctional in terms of developmental adaptation to the more general environment. For example, avoidance of an abusive caregiver is also seen as an adaptive response. However, avoidance might generalise to non-family members and become dysfunctional in later life when proximity to and support from others in times of stress can serve as a buffer against psychological distress and disorders such as depression. There is some evidence of such a process from a study of abusive mothers who were themselves abused in childhood (Egeland, Jacobvitz & Paptola, 1984); these mothers were more emotionally isolated than non-abused parents, withdrawing and avoiding intimate, supportive relationships with a partner.

Avoidance may, however, be just one strategy adopted by those with adverse childhoods. Further analysis of the Islington women revealed that those reporting early lack of care and maternal antipathy were very much more likely than others to turn to unsuitable or inappropriate people for support in times of crisis (Andrews & Brown, 1988b), although this of course could be interpreted as a form of avoidance. Women who adopted this strategy (referred to as 'non-optimal' confiding) had a particularly high rate of low self-esteem prior to the crisis, and a particularly high rate of depression subsequently. Many of the women were confiding in spouses and other close contacts whom they had described in a previous interview as being unsympathetic and unsupportive, and it is not surprising that they again received negative responses from them. Other women with non-optimal confiding were telling intimate details of their current crisis to acquaintances and others whom they hardly knew, or whom they saw very infrequently. There appeared to be a certain naivety or romanticism in these women about the amount of trust or confidence it was appropriate to place in would-be supportive relationships. It seemed clear that a woman often needed to believe, in spite of contrary evidence, that those closest to her were helpful and supportive. For example, a woman described a well-nigh perfect relationship with her husband. Yet later in the follow-up year it came to light that he had been carrying on an open affair which had been well known to most of her relatives and friends.

It is also surprising that many of the women perceived the support to be helpful, even when objectively negative responses from others had been reported. One previously divorced woman who had lost her first child had married again very soon after meeting her prospective husband. She soon became pregnant, but tragically lost the baby due to pregnancy complications. There had been a number of signs of her husband's unreliability and possible infidelity while she was pregnant. When she poured out her feelings to him while still in hospital after the pregnancy was terminated he told her that he might as well leave her then. She became depressed at this time, bur reported that she had found his support helpful, and that he did not really mean what he said, it was just his way.

Given the low self-esteem of the majority of the women with inadequate parenting and non-optimal confiding, their perception of the support might be reflecting a feeling that what they had was all they could expect to get. In addition there was a propensity to romanticise and deny problems in relationships, although at some deeper unconscious level it is possible that the lack of any real support was felt, as the majority of these women became depressed.

It is important to underline that early adversity was by no means always associated with a raised rate of depression, or with an unusual attachment style. Women with inadequate parenting who received good crisis support from someone close had a low rate of depression. There was also a further small group of women with inadequate parenting who received no crisis support, but who did not seek help from inappropriate or unreliable contacts. Their rate of depression was also relatively low. Why these women should be less vulnerable without support is a matter for conjecture. The difference in rates may be due to a certain resonance with the past among those who sought help but received none from close ties. The more self-reliant women may have been protecting themselves effectively from repeated disappointment.

EARLY ADVERSITY AND MEANINGS ARISING FROM CURRENT SELF-ATTITUDES

As already illustrated, women with adverse childhoods often display negative self-attitudes. Low self-esteem, self-blame or self-criticism, and shame have all been mentioned in the literature. The links between past experiences and negative self-attitudes, and their impact on current meaning via the perception of the context and features of current events and situations are discussed in this section.

Low Self-esteem

Many severe life events have the propensity to crush carefully constructed plans and goals. A common reaction is disappointment and dejection, followed by a period of consolidation and reformulation. Plans are more likely to be abandoned completely, however, and are less likely to be effectively modified when there is little or no sense of personal effectiveness. Most contemporary psychological theories of depression are based on the notion that long-term negative attitudes towards the self and the environment confer vulnerability in this way in the face of adversity (e.g. Abramson, Seligman & Teasdale, 1978; Alloy et al., 1988; Beck, 1983).

In Beck's theory of cognitive vulnerability to depression he notes that the origins of negative cognitive schemas are likely to lie in childhood experiences. This strand has not generally been pursued by researchers, who have focused on attempting to confirm the role of negative cognitions in depression to the neglect of their origins. While research has burgeoned, success in predicting onset of clinical depression has been elusive in the main. The most convincing evidence is from the longitudinal study of Islington women already referred to. We adopted an in-depth approach involving interview measures to assess self-esteem before any provoking crisis (Brown et al., 1986). When prior symptoms were controlled, low self-esteem was shown to act as a vulnerability factor by doubling the risk of depression during a one-year follow-up period once a provoking crisis had occurred.

The basis for this research came from the findings of earlier cross-sectional studies (Brown & Harris, 1978; Harris, Brown & Bifulco, 1987) where it had been speculated that vulnerability factors such as low intimacy with close ties and adverse childhood experiences would lower self-esteem and thereby increase the risk of depression in the presence of a severely threatening life event. Findings from the Islington study confirmed the relationship between low self-esteem and reports of inadequate parenting in childhood (Andrews & Brown, 1988b). The key experiences associated with low self-esteem were parental neglect and maternal antipathy. The relationship has since been replicated in a sample of early adult daughters and their mothers who were a subset of the Islington women, but here early experiences of sexual and physical abuse were also included and shown to be related to low self-esteem (Andrews & Brown, 1993). In this replication, depression was controlled to rule out the possibility that negative mood was affecting the women's accounts of their childhoods. It should also be added that considerable effort was made when developing the measures to distinguish feelings and behaviour. Ratings of childhood adversity were made by the investigator and were based on detailed descriptions of actual parental behaviour.

This research forms part of a growing body of evidence of an association between negative self-attitudes and early adversity. Other evidence comes from (mostly) questionnaire studies investigating self-blame or self-criticism and poor parenting, including parental coldness and lack of affection, harshness and strict control (e.g. Andrews & Brewin, 1990; Blatt et al., 1979; Firth-Cozens, 1992). Following Bowlby's model, it seems plausible that childhood experiences affect the degree to which individuals feel confident in dealing with stressful life events. Low self-esteem is likely to be associated with feelings of reduced personal effectiveness in influencing outcomes, and self-blame and self-criticism may relate to feelings of not being entitled to hold on to plans and goals that have been threatened. Self-blame is considered in further depth below, in particular in connection with features of events and situations involving humiliation.

Self-blame

In considering life difficulties and social support, we have seen how elements of loss and rejection surrounding current events might have a severe and resounding impact on people whose childhoods have been typified by such experiences. But other features of current events involving humiliation and entrapment have recently been shown to be associated with a far greater risk of depression than events involving loss and danger without humiliation and entrapment (Brown, Harris & Hepworth, 1995). Marital violence and rape are situations typified by humiliation and entrapment, and women in Islington reporting maritally violent relationships, either currently or in the past, showed double the rate of depression over a three-year period than other women (Andrews & Brown, 1988a). The highest rate by far, however, was among those who had experienced abuse (either physical or sexual) in both childhood and adulthood (Andrews, 1995).

I set about investigating the reasons for this by considering specific cognitive and affective factors that might be involved. Because of the known association between negative self-attitudes and childhood adversity, the role of self-blame was considered in a subsample of 70 Islington women who had reported marital violence (Andrews & Brewin, 1990). We distinguished behavioural from characterological self-blame, as there was evidence that the latter but not the former was involved in depression (Janoff-Bulman, 1979). In a study of rape victims Janoff-Bulman had demonstrated that on the whole the women involved did not see themselves as deserving or provoking the rape. Rather they blamed the attack on some modifiable aspect of their behaviour. For example, they judged that they could have been more careful, or not have been out so late at night. This was seen as a healthy response as survivors would have retained some feeling of control over the risk of future attacks. In contrast, it had been suggested that those who are repeatedly assaulted or mistreated may be more likely to blame their character; they may feel that there must be something wrong with them if such an event happens more than once (Silver & Wortman, 1980).

Abused children are often told by their parents that they are bad and unlovable (Herbruck, 1979), and we thought this would be an additional reason for those abused in childhood to be more likely than others to respond to later abuse by blaming their character. In fact there was already evidence of greater characterological self-blame (CSB) for hypothetical bad events in people who have been sexually victimised in childhood (Gold, 1986). As expected, we found that self-blame for marital violence was common, but women who had experienced either physical or sexual childhood abuse were more likely to blame their character, whereas women with no such experiences were more likely to blame their behaviour. Furthermore, we found that women with CSB were more likely than the other women survivors to have suffered persistent depression after the violent relationship had ended.

It appears that even in extreme situations involving humiliation and entrapment, typically experienced in abusive adult relationships, the impact on mental health may depend on the meaning attached to the experience. This meaning is likely to be shaped by past experiences of the same kind. This is clearly illustrated in the following accounts. Both women experienced severe violence from their husbands, and although neither was still in the relationship they had both experienced persistent depression in the years that followed. The first woman had been severely beaten by her father as a child. When talking about her past marriage she said:

> I thought it was all my fault because he told me it was. I believed everything he said—that I was bad, not fit to be a mother.

The other woman, who had been sexually abused by her father as a child, said of her former husband:

> Years of the time I was with him I felt if only I could be different then I wouldn't cause him to be like this. I blamed a lot of it on myself. I thought he was a really sensitive musician who had been harmed by society and I was going to save him, and somehow if I loved him enough it would be all right. I couldn't believe it could happen to me when I was pregnant. I must have done something to provoke it. I must be a certain way with people. I had this real image of myself as a ball-breaking heavy lady.

Shame

The insights gained from this study of self-blame in the marital violence survivors were taken forward in the design of a subsequent study of a subset of the whole sample of Islington women that were followed over a further period. Overall these 100 women were investigated over an eight-year period with four contacts, and at the last contact their daughters were also interviewed. A number of authors had noted the similarity of CSB to the experience of shame, with its focus on stable negative characteristics of the self (e.g. Lewis, 1986; Tangney, Wagner & Gramzow, 1992; Weiner, 1986), and two groups had demonstrated an association between shame and internal stable attributions for negative events in undergraduate samples (Tangney, Wagner & Gramzow, 1992; Weiner, 1986).

The evidence for an association between CSB and early abusive experiences, and between CSB and general shame proneness, prompted this study. Because shame has been consistently noted in the literature to involve self-conscious feelings about the body (e.g. Gilbert, 1989; Mollon, 1984; Sartre, 1956), and because I wanted a measure that would provide a common and salient real-life focus for all the women, I chose to measure feelings of bodily shame. The women were asked direct questions about whether they had ever felt ashamed of their bodies and the onset and duration of such feelings, where they existed.

Bodily shame was associated with early experiences of both sexual and physical abuse in both the Islington women and their daughters. The relationship held when low self-esteem and body dissatisfaction were taken into account, suggesting that it was the specific shame element that was important in the association. In the Islington mothers, bodily shame mediated the relationship between early abuse and episodes of chronic or recurrent depression in the eight-year period of the study (Andrews, 1995). In the absence of bodily shame, the relationship between early abuse and depression was lost. In the daughters, early abuse was associated with disordered eating and bulimia (Andrews, Valentine & Valentine, 1995), and bodily shame also appeared to mediate that relationship (Andrews, in press).

It was surprising, given the humiliation involved in marital violence and rape, that neither of these abusive adult experiences was related to this type of shame in the absence of abusive childhood experiences. However, it was found that adult abuse increased the rate of chronic and recurrent depression among those with earlier abuse, and this might be explained by its propensity to provoke intense shame among women already prone to such feelings. In a similar manner, it seems possible that non-physically abusive life events, or chronic problems involving humiliating experiences, such as hostile reactions and rejection in intimate sexual relationships, are more likely than other stressors to provoke or exacerbate bodily shame in already vulnerable individuals.

Shame was not a fleeting experience for those women reporting it, but a chronic state pervading their adult lives. The two main themes in the content of the accounts involved individual concerns about bodily appearance in the eyes of others, and behaviour involving concealment of the body. One woman recalled that she would not get into the communal shower when she was at school unless she was wearing her underwear. Another reported how she would not go anywhere without a jacket to cover her arms, even in hot weather. Several women spontaneously reported feeling so ashamed of their bodies that they would not let their husbands see them undressed. The accounts illustrate how bodily shame may differ from bodily dissatisfaction and low self-esteem. Both these factors involve not living up to one's own standards (which may reflect societal and cultural values), but they do not necessarily involve concealment of supposed deficiencies, and inordinate concern about how one appears to others.

The research on shame has continued with a pilot study of depressed patients (Andrews & Hunter, in press). Preliminary findings suggest that non-bodily forms of shame involving character, but not behaviour, are also related to early abusive experiences in both female and male patients. In this small depressed sample, shame feelings also appear to be related to a chronic or recurrent course of the disorder.

These results on characterological self-blame and shame suggest that women (and perhaps men) who have suffered severe and humiliating abusive experiences in childhood are at an increased risk of feeling bad about themselves at the very core of their being. It seems likely from the evidence that, when faced with events involving subsequent humiliation in adulthood, these feelings would be reactivated or exacerbated.

CONCLUSIONS

Adverse experiences in childhood appear to shape the future context of people's lives, setting them up for further misfortune. Moreover, on top of the probability of experiencing more stressful life events and difficulties and poorer social relationships, those with adverse childhoods are further handicapped by the way they construe these problems. The meaning attached to current life stressors is to some extent influenced by the specific features of the events themselves, and the context in which they occur, but early experience adds an extra dimension to current meaning.

I have focused on particular aspects of early adversity that appear to play a role in the creation of meaning. Both invasive abusive experiences and non-invasive experiences seem to be involved. Non-invasive early experiences such as lack of care and maternal antipathy involve poor mothering in the main, and are associated with a greater risk of early physical and sexual abuse, usually by male family members, but also by people outside the immediate family (Andrews, Brown & Creasey, 1990; Andrews, 1994). In addition there is evidence that early lack of care rather than early abuse best predicts later abusive relationships (Andrews & Brown, 1988a). People who have experienced poor mothering have not been adequately protected, and have not had their natural childhood needs for attachment adequately met. I have argued that this leads to a greater need for attachment, and a feeling of not being worthy of being loved. The evidence and examples I have presented suggest that the combination of unmet needs and low self-esteem results in a tendency to engage in ill-judged relationships and to cling on to the belief that such relationships are worthwhile and supportive. When things go wrong, the initial experience of having been inadequately nurtured may be reactivated, and the meaning attached to the current experience is of repeated disappointment and desolation followed by depression. The tendency to deny relationship problems may be so great, however, that no negative meaning at all is consciously attached to situations that are objectively threatening, and the individual has no insight into what is making her depressed.

The additional experience of early physical or sexual abuse is related to a focus on stable negative characteristics of the self involving self-blame and shame. Additional analyses on the shame data suggest that early invasive abusive experiences are more important than non-invasive poor mothering in predicting shame. It may well be that current events involving humiliation and entrapment provide cues that colour meaning by activating prior early memories of abuse and the feelings that surrounded them. Intense self-blame and exacerbation of shame feelings may ensue. Partial support for such a process comes from a recent study reporting that among currently depressed women patients who had experienced childhood sexual abuse, there was a very high rate of intrusive thoughts about the abuse (Kuyken & Brewin, 1994). Whether these thoughts were triggered by specific events preceding or accompanying the depression, or by the episode itself, however, remains to be investigated.

A recurring theme concerns the way current adversity appears to resonate with experiences from the past, possibly through the triggering of specific autobiographical memories and more general cognitive/affective schemas. From the existing evidence, a tentative model is that people who have experienced poor mothering have a tendency to be susceptible to events involving loss and rejection, and those who have experienced early physical or sexual abuse have an additional tendency to be sensitive to events and situations involving humiliation and entrapment. The examples I have presented suggest that these sensitivities are mediated both by conscious and unconscious processes (see Power, this volume, Chapter 4). What seems clear is that childhood adversity is a potent source of meaning and has considerable power to explain differing reactions to stressful events experienced in adulthood.

To end on an optimistic note, throughout this chapter I have made clear that there is by no means an inevitable path between early adversity and a maladaptive view of self and the external world. The evidence shows that through planning, or sometimes through simple good fortune, people with poor childhoods often experience events that compensate for earlier experiences of neglect and abuse. Establishing secure relationships and gaining worthwhile employment in early adulthood are two ways in which personal meaning can be transformed at this critical lifestage. Compensatory experiences can, however, occur throughout the life-course, and there is also evidence that an increase in job status and positive changes in close personal relationships are strongly associated with a significant decrease in negative self-attitudes in mid-life women (Andrews & Brown, 1995). Positive life changes often involved leaving behind bad relationships and unfulfilling work conditions as well as developing better ones. The research suggests that bad patterns can be broken. In this context therapists can encourage and help clients with poor childhoods to sustain change through sometimes difficult and painful transitions, and encourage awareness and understanding of the conscious and unconscious processes related to their particular sensitivities when facing life crises.

REFERENCES

Abramson, L.Y., Seligman, M.E.P. & Teasdale, J.D. (1978). Learned helplessness in humans: Critique and reformulation. *Journal of Abnormal Psychology*, **87**, 49–74.

Alloway, R. & Bebbington, P. (1987). The buffer theory of social support—a review of the literature. *Psychological Medicine*, **17**, 91–108.

Alloy, L.B., Abramson, L.Y., Metalsky, G.I. & Hartlage, S. (1988). The hopelessness theory of depression: Attributional aspects. *British Journal of Clinical Psychology*, **27**, 5–21.

Andrews, B. (1994). Family violence in a social context: why men abuse children. In J. Archer (ed.), *Male Violence*. London: Routledge.

Andrews, B. (1995). Bodily shame as a mediator between abusive experiences and depression. *Journal of Abnormal Psychology*, **104**, 277–285.

Andrews, B. (1997). Bodily shame in relation to abuse in childhood and bulimia. *British Journal of Clinical Psychology*, **36**, 41–50.

Andrews, B. & Brewin, C.R. (1990). Attributions for marital violence: a study of antecedents and consequences. *Journal of Marriage and the Family*, **52**, 757–767.

Andrews, B. & Brown, G.W. (1988a). Marital violence in the community: a biographical approach. *British Journal of Psychiatry*, **153**, 305–312.

Andrews, B. & Brown, G.W. (1988b). Social support, onset of depression and personality: An exploratory analysis. *Social Psychiatry & Psychiatric Epidemiology*, **23**, 99–108.

Andrews, B. & Brown, G.W. (1993). Self-esteem and vulnerability to depression: the concurrent validity of interview and questionnaire measures. *Journal of Abnormal Psychology*, **102**, 565–572.

Andrews, B. & Brown, G.W. (1995). Stability and change in self-esteem: the role of psychosocial factors. *Psychological Medicine*, **25**, 23–31.

Andrews, B. & Hunter, E. (1997). Shame, early abuse and course of depression in a clinical sample: A preliminary study. *Cognition and Emotion* (in press).

Andrews, B., Brown, G.W. & Creasey, L. (1990). Intergenerational links between psychiatric disorder in mothers and daughters: the role of parenting experiences. *Journal of Child Psychology & Psychiatry*, **31**, 1115–1129.

Andrews, B., Valentine, E.R. & Valentine, J.D. (1995). Depression and eating disorders following abuse in childhood in two generations of women. *British Journal of Clinical Psychology*, **34**, 37–52.

Beck, A.T. (1983). Cognitive therapy of depression: New perspectives. In P.J. Clayton & J.E. Barrett (eds), *Treatment of Depression: Old Controversies and New Approaches* (pp. 265–290). New York: Raven.

Blatt, S.J., Wein, S.J., Chevron, E. & Quinlan, D.M. (1979). Parental representations and depression in normal young adults. *Journal of Abnormal Psychology*, **88**, 388–397.

Bowlby, J. (1973). *Attachment and Loss: Vol 2. Separation*. London: Hogarth Press.

Bowlby, J. (1980). *Loss: Sadness and Depression. Attachment and Loss*, Volume 3. London: Hogarth Press.

Brown, G.W. (1989). Life events and measurement. In G.W. Brown & T.O. Harris (eds), *Life Events and Illness*. New York: Guilford Press.

Brown, G.W. & Harris, T.O. (1978). *Social Origins of Depression: A Study of Psychiatric Disorder in Women*. London: Tavistock.

Brown, G.W. & Harris, T.O. (1989). *Life Events and Illness*. New York: Guilford Press.

Brown, G.W., Bifulco, A. & Harris, T.O. (1987). Life events, vulnerability and onset of depression: some refinements. *British Journal of Psychiatry*, **150**, 30–42.

Brown, G.W., Harris, T.O. & Hepworth, C. (1995). Loss, humiliation and entrapment among women developing depression: A patient and non-patient comparison. *Psychological Medicine*, **25**, 7–21.

Brown, G.W., Andrews, B., Harris, T., Adler, Z. & Bridge, L. (1986). Social support, self-esteem and depression. *Psychological Medicine*, **16**, 813–831.

Cohen, S. & Wills, T.A. (1985). Stress, social support and the buffering hypothesis. *Psychological Bulletin*, **98**, 310–357.

Egeland, B., Jacobvitz, D. & Paptola, K. (1984). Intergenerational continuity of abuse. Paper given at the Conference on Child Abuse and Neglect, Maine, USA.

Firth-Cozens, J. (1992). The role of early family experiences in the perception of organisational stress: Fusing clinical and organisational perspectives. *Journal of Occupational and Organizational Psychology*, **65**, 61–75.

Gilbert, P. (1989). *Human Nature and Suffering*. London: Lawrence Erlbaum.

Gold, E.R. (1986). Long-term effects of sexual victimization in childhood: An attributional approach. *Journal of Consulting & Clinical Psychology*, **54**, 471–475.

Harris, T., Brown, G.W. & Bifulco, A. (1987). Loss of parent in childhood and adult psychiatric disorder: the role of social class position and premarital pregnancy. *Psychological Medicine*, **17**, 163–183.

Herbruck, C. (1979). *Breaking the Cycle of Child Abuse*. Minneapolis: Winston Press.

Janoff-Bulman, R. (1979). Characterological versus behavioral self-blame: Inquiries into depression and rape. *Journal of Personality & Social Psychology*, **37**, 1798–1809.

Kuyken, W. & Brewin, C.R. (1994). Intrusive memories of childhood abuse during depressive episodes. *Behaviour Research and Therapy*, **32**, 525–528.

Lewis, H.B. (1986). The role of shame in depression. In M. Rutter, C.E. Izard & P.B. Read (eds), *Depression in Young People: Developmental and Clinical Perspectives*. New York: Guilford.

Mollon, P. (1984). Shame in relation to narcissistic disturbance. *British Journal of Medical Psychology*, **57**, 207–214.

Oatley, K. & Bolton, W. (1985). A social-cognitive theory of depression in reaction to life events. *Psychological Review*, **92**, 372–388.

Quinton, D., Rutter, M. & Liddle, C. (1984). Institutional rearing, parenting difficulties and marital support. *Psychological Medicine*, **14**, 107–124.

Rutter, M., Quinton, D. & Hill, J. (1990). Adult outcomes of institution-reared children: Males and females compared. In L. Robins & M. Rutter (eds), *Straight and Devious Pathways from Childhood to Adulthood*. Cambridge: Cambridge University Press.

Sartre, J.P. (1956). *Being and Nothingness*. New York: Philosophical Library.

Silver, R.L. & Wortman, C.B. (1980). Coping with undesirable life events. In J. Garber & M.E.P. Seligman (eds), *Human Helplessness: Theory and Applications*. New York: Academic Press.

Tangney, J.P., Wagner, P. & Gramzow, R. (1992). Proneness to shame, proneness to guilt and psychopathology. *Journal of Abnormal Psychology*, **101**, 469–478.

Weiner, B. (1986). *An Attributional Theory of Motivation and Emotion*. New York: Springer.

Wolfe, D.A. (1987). *Child Abuse: Implications for Child Development and Psychopathology*. London: Sage.

Chapter 6

THE IMPACT OF TRAUMA ON MEANING: FROM MEANINGLESS WORLD TO MEANINGFUL LIFE

Ronnie Janoff-Bulman* and Cynthia McPherson Frantz*

Traumatic life events force survivors to confront questions of meaning in their lives. These questions are posed with an intensity and immediacy that reflect the overwhelming power of meaning-related concerns in the aftermath of extreme negative events. Survivors are struck by the extent to which meaning, in its many guises, had typically been assumed and taken for granted in their lives. Now their traumatic experience compels them to re-examine these earlier, easy assumptions.

Meaning can be defined in numerous ways, including purpose, intent, order, sense, interpretation, signification and denotation. Certainly, considerable work has been devoted to understanding 'meaning' in the field of linguistics. Based on two decades of work with victims, however, there appear to be two primary understandings of meaning that help inform survivors' crises and coping post-trauma: meaning as comprehensibility and meaning as significance. The first involves questions regarding whether something 'makes sense'; in other words, whether it fits with a system of accepted rules or theories. The second involves questions regarding whether something is of value or worth.

In addition to these two different constructions of meaning, there are two levels of concern that should be distinguished in exploring survivors' reactions post-trauma. These are questions about the world, or life in general, versus questions about one's own life in particular. As will be discussed below, the questions of meaning and meaninglessness that

*University of Massachusetts, Amherst, USA

The Transformation of Meaning in Psychological Therapies.
Edited by Mick Power and Chris R. Brewin. © 1997 John Wiley & Sons Ltd.

initially confront the survivor are those concerning the comprehensibility of the world and life in general. Do events and outcomes in our world make sense? The survivor's crisis is an existential one about the meaninglessness of the universe.

Over time, and this may involve a very long time for many, most survivors are able to minimize this crisis, and their success is largely dependent on their ability to shift their meaning concerns to questions of significance and value in their own lives. In successfully responding to their traumatic experience, survivors make the remarkable transition from the terror of a meaningless universe to the gratification of a personal life of value and worth. Although they remain aware that dread dwells next door and could strike at any time, they derive deep satisfactions from the realization of value and meaning in their own lives. In the aftermath of traumatic victimization, survivors ultimately change their appraisal of the traumatic event itself and move from 'life is meaningless' to 'my life is full of meaning'. This journey in meaning from terror to fulfilment forms the substance of this chapter.

THE INITIAL CONFRONTATION WITH MEANING

In the immediate aftermath of traumatic life events, survivors come face-to-face with their own fragility. Experiences such as rape, life-threatening illness, off-time death of a loved one, physical assault, debilitating accidents and natural disasters throw the victim into a crisis that is both psychological and existential; the comfortable assumptions that had previously been valuable guides to daily living can no longer be trusted, and the world now seems unpredictable and incomprehensible.

The depth of this crisis can better be appreciated by realizing the extent to which we generally operate on the basis of fundamental assumptions that typically go unchallenged and unquestioned. The phrase heard most often during 20 years of work with victims was 'I never thought it could happen to me'. After intensive victimization survivors recognize the extent to which they had taken for granted their own sense of protection and invulnerability, their own beliefs in the continuity of a secure existence. After intense victimization we are forced to recognize and examine our most basic assumptions about the world and our existence.

The World is Meaningful: A Fundamental Assumption

At the core of our inner world, at the very foundation of our cognitive-emotional systems, are theories or working models that are built over years of experience and guide our interactions in the world (e.g. Bowlby, 1969; Epstein, 1973, 1984; Janoff-Bulman, 1985, 1992; Parkes, 1975). According to Janoff-Bulman (1992), three of these core assumptions are: generalized beliefs about ourselves, the external world, and the relationships between the two. More specifically, at the deepest levels of our psyche, we assume not only that we are worthy and the world is benevolent, but that the world makes sense. We believe that the nature of the relationship between ourselves and the world is neither random nor unpredictable, but meaningful.

When viewed from the perspective of our fundamental assumptions, a 'meaningful' world is one in which there is a relationship between a person and what happens to him or her. In other words, there is a person–outcome contingency that makes sense, or can be understood. Just as in science phenomena are comprehensible if they fit certain accepted physical laws or theories of events, so in our daily lives outcomes make sense if they fit certain accepted social laws or theories. In Western culture, our most accepted theories used to explain person–outcome contingencies are those of justice and control (Janoff-Bulman, 1992). Justice accounts for the contingency through a consideration of the person's nature and moral attributes, whereas control accounts for the contingency through a consideration of the person's actions and behaviors.

As the just world theory (Lerner, 1980) suggests, we believe people get what they deserve and deserve what they get. Justice entails judgments about deservingness. Thus, a moral, good, decent person should be protected from misfortune. Negative events are not distributed randomly, but rather are most apt to strike those who are morally corrupt; personal outcomes are essentially viewed as punishments or rewards. Theories of deservingness generally encompass many religious perspectives, which enable believers to perceive meaning through the expectations of rewards and punishments that may be considerably delayed, such as one's fate after death (see, for example, Pargament et al., 1990).

In addition to considering people's character in our attempts to discover or impose a contingency between people and their outcomes, we also attend a great deal to actions and behaviors. We assume that we are able to control our outcomes. There is considerable psychological research demonstrating that we tend to minimize randomness and overestimate our control over events (see, for example, Henslin, 1967; Langer, 1975; Seligman, 1975; Wortman, 1975; also see Gilovich, 1991). From this perspective, auto accidents happen to those who do not drive carefully, diseases strike those who do not eat right or exercise properly, and assaults happen to those who do not take the proper precautions on our city streets.

Our theories of justice and control typically afford us the means to make sense of outcomes, particularly negative outcomes. Essentially, they allow us to account for the selective incidence of events—why they happen to particular people. In other words, questions of meaning are not about why rape or cancer occurs, but why they happen to specific people. These questions of 'Why me?' or 'Why him or her?' can be answered by turning to deservingness and/or control.

Although theories of justice and control are the most common means of making sense of events in Western culture, they are by no means the sole possibilities available. For example, people can engage some implicit compensatory model of outcomes, by which a past filled with positive outcomes is perceived as appropriately balanced by an extreme negative outcome, and vice versa (see Brickman, Coates & Janoff-Bulman, 1978). In other cultures there are other explanatory theories that provide meaningful responses to questions about the selective incidence of events. Among the Azande of the Sudan, for example, the parent whose son died when his boat was overturned by a hippo knows that the cause of death was drowning; yet, the 'Why him?' question requires another type of explanation. Among the Azande, witchcraft provides a meaningful explanation; a witch or sorcerer brought together the paths of the boat and the angry hippo (Gluckman, 1944). Regardless of culture, people strive to maintain a belief in a meaningful world by making sense of the relationship between people and their outcomes. Individuals are not harmed arbitrarily, bad events are not distributed randomly, and malevolence is not haphazard.

These beliefs afford considerable comfort. In assuming that our world is meaningful, we are able to believe that we are safe and secure. As long as we are good people who engage in the right behaviours, we will be protected from misfortune. We can maintain an illusion of invulnerability (Janoff-Bulman, Madden & Timko, 1983; Perloff, 1983) and unrealistic optimism about the future (Taylor, 1990; Weinstein, 1980, 1989).

The Terror of Meaninglessness

Traumatic events shatter these fundamental assumptions, and survivors experience the terror of their own vulnerability (Janoff-Bulman, 1992; also see Epstein, 1991; McCann & Pearlman, 1990). They are plagued by a double dose of fear and anxiety, for both their internal and external worlds are assaulted. Internally, they experience the disintegration of basic assumptions, which had provided psychological stability and coherence in a complex world. The survivor's inner world is now in a state of dramatic upheaval, no longer able to provide a trustworthy road map for negotiating daily life.

As a result, the external world is now perceived as frightening; survivors realize all too vividly the possibility of their own annihilation.

They can no longer assume that their own self-worth and precautionary behaviors will protect them, for randomness and arbitrariness now characterize the workings of the universe. Old certainties and securities are gone. They suddenly confront the world described by the Existentialists, a world that appears absurd, with no end to suffering, no cure for anxiety, and no hope for universal safety (Sartre, 1964, 1966; see also Barratt, 1962). They are intensely aware that bad things can happen to them. The world no longer makes sense, and this realization is devastating. As Ernest Becker writes in *The Denial of Death*, it is terrifying 'to see the world as it really is . . . it makes *routine, automatic, secure, self-confident activity impossible* . . . It places a trembling animal at the mercy of the entire cosmos and the problem of the meaning of it' (1973, p. 26). Trauma survivors see the world as it really is, stripped of the meaning and order we all too readily assume to exist.

INITIAL EFFORTS TO MINIMIZE MEANINGLESSNESS

The horror of a meaningless universe and shattered assumptions creates a state of disequilibrium, dread and hyperarousal for survivors. Danger and threat appear everywhere. It is, perhaps, no small wonder that a very marked initial response to victimization is an attempt to validate one's earlier assumptions and minimize the perceived randomness of the world by re-evaluating one's role in the extreme event. Survivors engage in a search for meaning (e.g. Dollinger, 1986; Frankl, 1963; Lifton, 1967; Silver, Boon & Stones, 1983; Silver & Wortman, 1980; (Janoff-)Bulman & Wortman, 1977; Taylor, 1983; Thompson, 1991). If some person–outcome contingency can be discovered or imposed, then the survivors' assumptions about meaning can be maintained and the world can once again appear orderly and safe.

It is true that some people can account for their negative experience by invoking the 'inscrutability of God', a view that entails a willingness to accept whatever happens because it is God's will. These survivors maintain a very fatalistic outlook and minimize the extent to which the traumatic event is perceived as meaningless and problematic (see, for example, McIntosh, Silver & Wortman, 1993; Pargament et al., 1990; Wuthnow, Christiano & Kuzlowski, 1980). Most survivors, however, engage in intense efforts to find meaning in the immediate aftermath of their victimization, and initially they generally do so by searching for their own possible contribution to the outcome.

The search for meaning typically involves questions about one's own 'goodness' as a person or one's own careless actions or inactions. Survivors try to come up with answers to 'Why me?' It is not surprising, then, that self-blame is an extremely common response to all sorts of traumatic events (for a review, see Janoff-Bulman, 1992), for it reflects the survivor's profound struggle over meaning in the early aftermath of trauma.

Based on past research with survivors, Janoff-Bulman (1979) distinguished between two types of self-blame, which correspond to the two major types of self-attributions that satisfy the search for person–outcome contingency. Characterological self-blame focuses on the person's character or enduring qualities, reflecting assessments about the 'goodness' of the person. Behavioral self-blame focuses on the person's behaviors, the acts or omissions that may have contributed to the victimization. Thus, a rape victim who speaks of being a bad person or the kind of person who cannot be trusted is engaging in characterological self-blame, which is esteem-related. A rape victim who says that she should not have gone back to her date's apartment or she should not have hitch-hiked is engaging in behavioral self-blame, which is control-related (Janoff-Bulman, 1979).

Although either type of attribution would respond to the 'Why me?' question and provide a basis for re-establishing a sense of meaning, characterological self-blame clearly has more costs associated with it. It involves more global negative assessments, decreases in self-esteem, and, potentially, the view of oneself as a chronic victim. Behavioral self-blame, with its specific, narrower attributions, protects against self-esteem loss, for it is a particular behavior, rather than the nature of the individual, that is deemed responsible. Further, behavioral self-blame also provides a more optimistic picture for protection against future victimization; survivors can believe that by altering their behaviors—far easier than altering their basic character—they can avoid future misfortune. For reasons of maintaining self-esteem and bolstering perceived invulnerability, behavioral self-blame attributions are particularly common following traumatic life events (for a review, see Janoff-Bulman & Lang-Gunn, 1989).

Based on their work with crime victims, Bard & Sangrey (1979) note that these victims often seem eager to take responsibility and point to specific behaviors, such as leaving a window open or walking in a particular neighborhood, for which they fault themselves. As Hursch (1977) writes, 'If you have been raped and are still alive, you will forever ask yourself why you didn't fight harder, why you didn't think of some trick to break away, or why you didn't engage in some act—obvious to you now—which would have prevented rape' (p. 95; also see Medea & Thompson, 1974). Parents of children who are terminally ill look for something they did or failed to do that could have been responsible for their child's illness (e.g. Chodoff, Friedman & Hamburg, 1964). Victims of life-threatening diseases often blame themselves for working too hard, not eating the right foods, not taking good enough care of themselves, or other behaviors that are believed to have contributed to their illness (e.g. Bard & Dyk, 1956; Taylor, 1983). Survivors play and replay their victimization, looking for ways their own behaviors might have contributed to the traumatic event.

The self-blame of survivors does not reflect a need for accuracy in evaluating the victimization, but rather a need for making sense of the event. If victims blame themselves, this clearly does not give others the right to blame them. Their self-blame reflects positive coping impulses, and in no way does this imply that survivors are, in fact, responsible for their victimization. It is as if they want to believe that there is something they could have done, for they can then minimize or eliminate the threatening, meaningless implications of their traumatic experience.

TURNING TO QUESTIONS OF VALUE IN SURVIVORS' LIVES

Self-blame, with its emphasis on questions of deservingness and control, is an early response to victimization. For many, it provides a means of modulating the terror of the traumatic event, of minimizing the panic and paralysis produced by the sudden realization of a meaningless universe and invalid internal guides and assumptions. Over time, however, for most survivors this search for person–outcome contingency and contributory behaviors dissipates, although unanswered questions about meaning linger. Perceiving some personal contribution may minimize meaninglessness somewhat, but ultimately it appears to be unsatisfactory in resolving these questions entirely.

Perhaps survivors recognize, over time, that they truly are not to blame, or that even if they believe they contributed somewhat, it is not enough to account for their horrible experience. The 'smallness' of their action or omission does not seem equal to the psychological immensity of the victimization. When perceived meaningfulness of the world is tapped via questions about person–outcome contingencies, research has found that even years after the traumatic event, survivors believe the world is significantly less meaningful, in this sense, than do comparison non-victims (e.g. Janoff-Bulman, 1992; Schwartzberg & Janoff-Bulman, 1991).

Ultimately the attempt to find meaning via person–outcome contingencies and the distribution of good and bad events in our world gives way to another type of meaning-making. Now meaning begins to revolve around questions of value and significance. For the trauma survivor, the primary meaning-related concern is no longer whether the world makes sense, but rather whether his or her life is meaningful—whether it is of value (see Frankl, 1963, on people's ability to find meaning by choosing an attitude with which to face the future; also see Klinger, 1977, on meaning, goals, and value).

Traumatic events lead to a 'value'-ation, or rather re-evaluation, of one's life. Meaning-making occurs through a process of recognizing or creating significance and worth in one's daily existence. Survivors reconsider their lives and what is important, for life has been stripped to its essentials. Meaning is embraced as survivors' lives move from the superficial to the profound (Janoff-Bulman, 1992). Generally, this entails a reordering of priorities, as life, or at least aspects of one's life, is now regarded as precious and valuable (see, for example, Collins, Taylor & Skokan, 1990; Silver & Wortman, 1980; Taylor, 1983; Taylor, Lichtman & Wood, 1984; Thompson, 1985; Thompson & Janigian, 1988). Survivors report a new-found appreciation for 'what really matters'. Statements such as the following are frequently expressed:

> 'I live my life more fully now.'
> 'Before I was just existing; now I'm alive.'
> 'I spend more time on the important things in life. There's been a real shift in my priorities.'
> 'I never before really appreciated what I had.'

Why do survivors now recognize or attribute value to their lives? One might instead expect a very different turn of events. The utter insignificance—rather than significance—of the human condition is a conclusion that might be expected to follow traumatic victimization. Our 'creatureliness', our fragility as physical beings, might preclude seeing great value in human life. Yet survivors see beyond this biological basis of our being to the more symbolic aspects of existence. Perhaps it is precisely the new, jarring awareness of our physical mortality and finiteness that provides the impetus for seeking value. Because life cannot be taken for granted, for it can end at any time, because negative outcomes can occur when least expected, people must make choices and decide what matters. In the face of absurdity and dread, people must create their own values out of nothingness (Sartre, 1964, 1966). Our choices are the basis for actions (e.g. devoting time and effort to the chosen aspects of one's life) and commitments (see Brickman, 1987). It is here that meaning and fulfilment lie.

For survivors, the traumatic victimization is never far away. It resides in their minds, accessible and easily imagined (see Kahneman & Tversky, 1973, on the availability heuristic). It is always there to remind them of alternatives—the pain of shattered assumptions and the possibility of even greater loss. Their daily experiences are now perceived and evaluated within the context of a new framework, one that includes their own past victimization. Whether considered from the perspective of adaptation level (e.g. Helson, 1964; Brickman, Coates & Janoff-Bulman, 1978), norm theory (Kahneman & Miller, 1986; Miller, Turnbull & McFarland, 1990), simulation processes (Kahneman & Tversky, 1982; Taylor & Schneider, 1989), or anchoring and adjustment (Kahneman & Tversky, 1973; Greenberg, Williams & O'Brien, 1986), the traumatic victimization provides a powerful painful contrast with which to compare aspects of the survivor's daily existence. With this salient event always available, previously underappreciated elements of the survivor's life now appear positive, pleasurable and worthy of considerable investment.

Although meaning can be found or established in any number of realms, there are a few areas that are chosen particularly often by survivors. Close relationships and altruistic social causes are two domains that are often 'chosen' for their value and meaning, perhaps because they enable survivors to establish a connection with others, to look beyond the self in their relation with the world. Thus, victims of disease, accidents, disasters and crime often report how important family and friends are to them now; spending time with loved ones is now seen as a priority and a gift. Others choose to engage in altruistic actions: rape victims may work at rape crisis centers; Vietnam veterans may work through outreach projects to help other veterans or to inform the public about the evils of war; AIDS victims may help others diagnosed with the disease. Both Mothers Against Drunk Driving (MADD) and the Stop the Madness campaign were begun by mothers whose children were killed, respectively, by a drunk driver and a gunshot in a parking lot. By engaging in behaviors to promote social causes and help others, survivors of traumatic events transform their lives into meaningful, valuable existences.

Similarly, others turn to some form of spirituality in an attempt to make meaning by connecting to something greater than themselves, again going beyond the boundaries of the self. Some survivors speak of their newfound devotion to God, or their commitment to particular religious practices, often within the context of a larger community. Some establish a spiritual connection to something greater through a new-found appreciation of nature and its beauty.

Through these new commitments survivors engage in powerful forms of meaning-making and discover value and significance in their lives. They begin to look like Kobasa's (1979; Kobasa, Maddi & Kahn, 1982) 'hardy' individuals, who are able to handle stress because of a sense of commitment in their lives—a feeling that the tasks they are engaged in are meaningful and important. Survivors know to devote less time and energy to unimportant tasks, and many note how unfortunate it is that something so dire—their victimization—was needed to shake them from their complacency. Nevertheless, survivors are very aware that their victimization, though wholly unchosen, has had its unexpected and deeply felt benefits (Janoff-Bulman, 1992; (Janoff-)Bulman & Wortman, 1977; Taylor, 1983; Thompson, 1991).

Survivors now notice and attend to aspects of their lives in new ways. In social psychology, dual-process models of person perception and social cognition have become very popular (for a review, see Fiske, 1993). There is much that we do automatically, in the interests of conserving mental resources; but we are all also motivated tacticians who engage in effortful or thoughtful processing when we are sufficiently interested in the outcome or interaction (Fiske & Taylor, 1991). Applied to victimization, survivors are motivated to perceive their lives differently, to find meaning where it was not noticed before. They examine their lives and seem to engage in much more effortful processing than non-victims regarding the way they live. They are motivated to live more meaningful lives, to discover value in their day-to-day existence, to live as if each day counts. They pay attention and do not simply drift on the surface; they create their lives thoughtfully.

IMPLICATIONS FOR THERAPY

In the immediate aftermath of victimization, the traumatic event is understandably perceived as wholly negative, unchosen, unwanted. It certainly has no redeeming qualities; it is associated with fear and anxiety. Over time, however, the meaning-making process moves from a concern with the randomness of the universe to the recognition of value in one's life. The terror of a meaningless world dissipates as survivors create meaning and value in their lives.

Not all survivors are so successful. A small minority experience chronic post-traumatic stress and remain overwhelmed by the terrors of a dangerous world years after their traumatic experience. Yet, as research has moved from clinical case studies to large community samples, there is an increasing recognition that coping successes rather than failures are the norm. Unfortunately, the specific predictors of success and failure remain largely elusive, no doubt in part because the process of adaptation is complex and multidetermined. Such pervasive positive factors as self-esteem and secure attachment are often presented as important predictors of successful coping (e.g. Basic Behavioral Science Task Force of the National Advisory Mental Health Council, 1996), but do relatively little to further our understanding of adjustment processes in the aftermath of victimization.

Rather than search for particular personality factors that might facilitate or impede successful coping, it may be useful to focus on the way therapy and therapists can facilitate the coping tasks that confront survivors on the road to successful adaptation. From the present perspective, a central concern of victims is meaning, and there are two meaning-related tasks that survivors address: minimizing the terror of a meaningless world and maximizing value in their lives. The creation of value can only occur once the anxiety and fear are resolved, and thus the nature of therapeutic interventions should depend largely on where the survivor is located at a given time in this adaptation process.

Certainly, therapists can move the process along more quickly, for throughout the therapeutic endeavor they offer the survivor the real possibility of social support, interpersonal connection and a safe environment. More specifically, however, work with trauma survivors requires a particularly eclectic approach, involving, early on, strategies to help the survivor minimize terror and anxiety, and, later, strategies that maximize the creative construction of meaning in people's lives.

Given the terror of a random, meaningless world during the early phase of coping, it is helpful to recognize the importance of actions by survivors. By making choices and engaging in behaviors, even minor ones, survivors can slowly perceive a contingency between actions and outcomes, evidence that the world is not wholly random. By encouraging and empowering the survivor to act and make choices, therapists can help survivors move beyond the experience of helplessness in a meaningless universe (see Herman, 1992).

Equally important in the early stages of survivors' coping, however, are therapists' efforts to teach strategies to avoid the painful experience of terror. Too often the affective load is overwhelming for the survivor. Although denial and numbing often 'naturally' take over as means of modulating the hyperanxiety, these avoidance states are typically soon interrupted by intrusive thoughts and images, again reminding the survivor of the intensity of the terror associated with the traumatic event (see Horowitz, 1976, 1982, on the alternation of denial and intrusions). Survivors who seek therapy are often those who are unable to modulate the terror and anxiety on their own, individuals who remain unable, over time, to confront their victimization without being overwhelmed. In many ways, the therapist functions as a 'container' for the survivor's intense, painful affect (see McCann & Pearlman, 1990). During this first stage of the coping process, however, cognitive-behavioral therapies that focus on stress management—including such techniques as thought-stopping, systematic desensitization, imaginal flooding and progressive relaxation—can provide survivors with some control over their anxiety and intrusive re-experiencing of the trauma (e.g. Dye & Roth, 1991; Keane & Kaloupek, 1982; Ochberg, 1988). Pharmacological treatments that minimize arousal may prove helpful as well (e.g. Friedman, 1988).

Insight-oriented therapies and other dynamic approaches are likely to be particularly appropriate and helpful as survivors' terror decreases and they are willing to confront the victimization. During this second phase, therapeutic work that facilitates coping is more apt to focus on interpretations and meaning-making, examinations and appraisals not only of the traumatic event but of the survivor's life choices and possibilities. It is during this period of adjustment that survivors, optimally, begin to create meaning and value in their own lives, and effective therapists can facilitate this process by providing both a creative voice and an empathic ear.

CONCLUDING THOUGHTS

Over time, on their own or with the help of a therapist, survivors successfully shift from a concern with the meaning of life to questions of meaning in life, and the victimization itself may take on new, unexpected qualities. The negative experience is now often perceived as being of instrumental value—a powerful teacher of lessons about the self and the world. Suffering now seems to have had a purpose.

Survivors often say that they would not have chosen their negative outcome, but that the experience has had its profound gifts. These gifts include a new-found appreciation of life and the significance and value of their own existence, as discussed above, as well as lessons about themselves. Trauma survivors often see themselves as stronger people for having survived their victimization. They recognize their own coping abilities and strengths; they see that they have been able to survive and rebuild, or begin to rebuild, their lives. These realizations are empowering, for survivors can now believe that they will be able to cope with future misfortune. In the words of survivors:

> 'Somehow I was able to get over this; I'm much more confident that I could cope with anything now.'
> 'The world is more dangerous to me now, but I am less vulnerable. I am stronger, able to handle anything . . .'

It is as if the survivors are living the adage, 'What doesn't kill you will make you stronger.' Despite their recognition that their safety is not guaranteed in a random, meaningless world, they are nevertheless able to maintain a belief in their ability to handle life's future trials. In essence, they have established a sort of secondary control (see, for example, Rothbaum, Weisz & Snyder, 1982) over future victimization, a belief that they will be able to cope with whatever comes their way. This secondary control, or belief in their own personal strengths, serves to minimize their earlier over-concern with the meaninglessness of the world, and coupled with their newfound creation and/or recognition of value in their lives, provides survivors with a new sense of confidence and satisfaction.

In the literature on extreme negative events, there are studies that emphasize the negative changes following traumatic experiences, and others that discuss more positive changes; these differences have sometimes been regarded as contradictory, or are attributed to differences in the impact of distinct victimizations or in survivors' coping abilities. Yet, in recent studies, researchers have noted that these positive and negative changes are typically reported by the same survivors; that is, victimization has both a positive and negative impact on the same survivors (see, for example, Collins, Taylor & Skokan, 1990; Lehman et al., 1993). Such findings are consistent with the present perspective, which argues that survivors experience the pain of shattered assumptions and increased awareness of their own vulnerability; they know human outcomes can be random and meaningless. Yet they also experience the pleasure of a newfound appreciation of life and sense of value and meaning in their daily existence.

Survivors seem to possess a special sort of wisdom in acknowledging the worst and best of human existence. At the deepest levels of their psyche, they know we are all vulnerable; their vision has been stripped of illusions and they understand the essential meaninglessness of the world in relation to human outcomes. Survivors feel they know what the world is really like, yet they also are powerfully aware of what is important in their lives. Such is the terror, wonder, and ultimately the wisdom of surviving traumatic events. Against the backdrop of a meaningless world, survivors create a life of meaning.

REFERENCES

Bard, M. & Dyk, R.B. (1956). The psychodynamic significance of beliefs regarding the cause of serious illness. *Psychoanalytic Review*, **43**, 146–162.

Bard, M. & Sangrey, D. (1979). *The Crime Victim's Book*. New York: Basic Books.

Barret, W. (1962). *Irrational Man: A Study in Existential Philosophy*. Garden City, NY: Doubleday.

Basic Behavioral Science Task Force of the National Advisory Mental Health Council (1996). Basic behavioral science research for mental health: Vulnerability and resilience. *American Psychologist*, **51**, 22–28.

Becker, E. (1973). *The Denial of Death*. New York: Free Press.

Bowlby, J. (1969). *Attachment and Loss*, Vol. 1: Attachment. London: Hogarth.

Brickman, P. (1987). *Commitment, Conflict, and Caring*. Englewood Cliffs, NJ: Prentice-Hall.

Brickman, P., Coates, D. & Janoff-Bulman, R. (1978). Lottery winners and accident victims: Is happiness relative? *Journal of Personality and Social Psychology*, **36**, 917–927.

Chodoff, P., Friedman, S.B. & Hamburg, D.A. (1964). Stress, defense, and coping behavior: Observations in parents of children with malignant disease. *American Journal of Psychiatry*, **120**, 743–749.

Collins, R.L., Taylor, S.E. & Skokan, L.A. (1990). A better world or a shattered vision: Changes in life perspectives following victimization. *Social Cognition*, **8**, 263–285.

Dollinger, S.J. (1986). The need for meaning following disaster: Attributions and emotional upset. *Personality and Social Psychology Bulletin*, **12**, 300–310.

Dye, E. & Roth, S. (1991). Psychotherapy with Vietnam veterans and rape and incest survivors. *Psychotherapy*, **28**, 103–120.

Epstein, S. (1973). The self-concept revisited, or a theory of a theory. *American Psychologist*, **28**, 404–416.

Epstein, S. (1984). Controversial issues in emotion theory. In P. Shaver (ed.), *Review of Personality and Social Psychology: Emotions, Relationships, and Health*. Beverly Hills, CA: Sage.

Epstein, S. (1991). The self-concept, the traumatic neurosis, and the structure of personality. In D. Ozer, J.M. Healy, Jr & A.J. Stewart (eds), *Perspectives on Personality*, Vol. 3. London: Jessica Kingsley.

Fiske, S.T. (1993). Social cognition and social perception. *Annual Review of Psychology*, **44**, 155–194.

Fiske, S.T. & Taylor, S.E. (1991). *Social Cognition*. New York: McGraw-Hill.

Frankl, V.E. (1963). *Man's Search for Meaning: An Introduction to Logotherapy*. New York: Washington Square Press.

Friedman, M.J. (1988). Toward rational pharmacotherapy for post-traumatic stress disorders: An interim report. *American Journal of Psychiatry*, **145**, 281–285.

Gilovich, T. (1991). *How We Know What Isn't So: The Fallibility of Human Reason in Everyday Life*. New York: Free Press.

Gluckman, M. (1944). The logic of African science and witchcraft: An appreciation of Evans-Pritchard's 'Witchcraft Oracles and Magic among the Azande' of the Sudan. *The Rhodes-Livingstone Institute Journal*, **June**, 61–71.

Greenberg, J., Williams, K.D. & O'Brien, M.K. (1986). Considering the harshest verdict first: Biasing effects on mock juror verdicts. *Personality and Social Psychology Bulletin*, **12**, 41–60.

Helson, H. (1964). *Adaptation Level Theory: An Experimental and Systematic Approach to Behavior*. New York: Harper.

Henslin, J.M. (1967). Craps and magic. *American Journal of Sociology*, **73**, 316–330.

Herman, J.L. (1992). *Trauma and Recovery*. New York: Basic Books.

Horowitz, M. (1976). *Stress Response Syndromes*. New York: Aronson.

Horowitz, M. (1982). Stress response syndromes and their treatment. In L. Goldberger & S. Bresnitz (eds), *Handbook of Stress*. New York: Free Press.

Hursch, C.J. (1977). *The Trouble with Rape*. Chicago: Nelson-Hall.

Janoff-Bulman, R. (1979). Characterological versus behavioral self-blame: Inquiries into depression and rape. *Journal of Personality and Social Psychology*, **37**, 1798–1809.

Janoff-Bulman, R. (1985). The aftermath of victimization: Rebuilding shattered assumptions. In C. Figley (ed.), *Trauma and its Wake: The Study and Treatment of Post-traumatic Stress Disorder*. New York: Brunner/Mazel.

Janoff-Bulman, R. (1992). *Shattered Assumptions: Towards a New Psychology of Trauma*. New York: Free Press.

Janoff-Bulman, R. & Lang-Gunn, L. (1989). Coping with disease and accidents: The role of self-blame attributions. In L.Y. Abramson (ed.), *Social–personal Inference in Clinical Psychology*. New York: Guilford.

(Janoff-)Bulman, R. & Wortman, C.B. (1977). Attributions of blame and coping in the 'real world': Severe accident victims react to their lot. *Journal of Personality and Social Psychology*, **35**, 351–363.

Janoff-Bulman, R., Madden, M. & Timko, C. (1983). Victims' reactions to aid: The role of perceived vulnerability. In A. Nadler, J.D. Fisher & B. DePaulo (eds), *New Directions in Helping*, Vol. 3. New York: Academic Press.

Kahneman, D. & Miller, D.T. (1986). Norm theory: Comparing reality to its alternatives. *Psychological Review*, **93**, 136–153.

Kahneman, D. & Tversky, A. (1973). On the psychology of prediction. *Psychological Review*, **80**, 237–251.

Kahneman, D. & Tversky, A. (1982). The simulation heuristic. In D. Kahneman, P. Slovic & A. Tversky (eds), *Judgment under Uncertainty: Heuristics and Biases*. New York: Cambridge University Press.

Keane, T.M. & Kaloupek, D. (1982). Imaginal flooding in the treatment of a post-traumatic stress disorder. *Journal of Consulting and Clinical Psychology*, **50**, 138–140.

Klinger, E. (1977). *Meaning and Void: Inner Experience and the Incentive in People's Lives*. Minneapolis, MN: University of Minnesota Press.

Kobasa, S.C. (1979). Stressful life events, personality, and health: An inquiry into hardiness. *Journal of Personality and Social Psychology*, **37**, 1–11.

Kobasa, S.C., Maddi, S.R. & Kahn, S. (1982). Hardiness and health: A prospective study. *Journal of Personality and Social Psychology*, **42**, 168–177.

Langer, E.J. (1975). The illusion of control. *Journal of Personality and Social Psychology*, **32**, 311–328.

Lehman, D.R., Davis, C.G., DeLongis, A., Wortman, C.B., Bluck, S., Mandel, D.R. & Ellard, J. (1993). Positive and negative life changes following bereavement and their relations to adjustment. *Journal of Social and Clinical Psychology*, **12**, 90–112.

Lerner, M.J. (1980). *The Belief in a Just World*. New York: Plenum.

Lifton, R.J. (1967). *Death in Life: Survivors of Hiroshima*. New York: Simon and Schuster.

McCann, I.L. & Pearlman, L.A. (1990). *Psychological Trauma and the Adult Survivor: Theory, Therapy, and Transformation*. New York: Brunner/Mazel.

McIntosh, D.N., Silver, R.C. & Wortman, C.B. (1993). Religion's role in adjustment to a negative life event: Coping with the loss of a child. *Journal of Personality and Social Psychology*, **65**, 812–821.

Medea, A. & Thompson, K. (1974). *Against Rape*. New York: Farrar, Straus, & Giroux.

Miller, D.T., Turnbull, W. & McFarland, C. (1990). Counterfactual thinking and social perception: Thinking about what might have been. In M.P. Zanna (ed.), *Advances in Experimental Social Psychology*, Vol. 23. New York: Academic Press.

Ochberg, F.M. (ed.) (1988). *Post-traumatic Therapy and Victims of Violence*. New York: Brunner/Mazel.

Parkes, C.M. (1975). What becomes of redundant world models? A contribution to the study of adaptation to change. *British Journal of Medical Psychology*, **48**, 131–137.

Pargament, K.I., Ensing, D.S., Falgout, K., Olsen, H., Reilly, B., Van Haitsma, K. & Warren, R. (1990). God help me: I. Religious coping efforts as predictors of outcomes to significant negative life events. *American Journal of Community Psychology*, **18**, 793–824.

Perloff, L.S. (1983). Perceptions of vulnerability to victimization. *Journal of Social Issues*, **39**, 41–62.

Rothbaum, F., Weisz, J.R. & Snyder, S.S. (1982). Changing the world and changing the self: A two-process model of perceived control. *Journal of Personality and Social Psychology*, **42**, 5–37.

Sartre, J.P. (1964). *Nausea*. Norfolk, CT: New Directions.

Sartre, J.P. (1966). *Being and Nothingness: A Phenomenological Study of Ontology*. New York: Washington Square Press.

Schwartzberg, S.S. & Janoff-Bulman, R. (1991). Grief and the search for meaning: Exploring the assumptive worlds of bereaved college students. *Journal of Social and Clinical Psychology*, **10**, 270–288.

Seligman, M.E.P. (1975). *Helplessness: On Depression, Development, and Death*. San Francisco: W.H. Freeman.

Silver, R.L. & Wortman, C.B. (1980). Coping with undesirable life events. In J. Garber & M.E.P. Seligman (eds), *Human Helplessness: Theory and Application*. New York: Academic Press.

Silver, R.L., Boon, C. & Stones, M.L. (1983). Searching for meaning in misfortune: Making sense of incest. *Journal of Social Issues*, **39**, 81–101.

Taylor, S.E. (1983). Adjustment to threatening events: A theory of cognitive adaptation. *American Psychologist*, **38**, 1161–1173.

Taylor, S.E. (1990). *Positive Illusions: Creative Self-Deception and the Healthy Mind*. New York: Basic Books.

Taylor, S.E. & Schneider, S.K. (1989). Coping and the simulation of events. *Social Cognition*, **7**, 176–196.

Taylor, S.E., Lichtman, R.R. & Wood, J.V. (1984). Attributions, beliefs about control, and adjustment to breast cancer. *Journal of Personality and Social Psychology*, **46**, 489–502.

Thompson, S.C. (1985). Finding positive meaning in a stressful event and coping. *Basic and Applied Social Psychology*, **6**, 279–295.

Thompson, S.C. (1991). The search for meaning following a stroke. *Basic and Applied Social Psychology*, **12**, 81–96.

Thompson, S.C. & Janigian, A.S. (1988). Life schemes: A framework for understanding the search for meaning. *Journal of Social and Clinical Psychology*, **7**, 260–280.

Weinstein, N.D. (1980). Unrealistic optimism about future life events. *Journal of Personality and Social Psychology*, **39**, 806–820.

Weinstein, N.D. (1989). Optimistic biases about personal risks. *Science*, **246**, 1232–1233.

Wortman, C.B. (1975). Some determinants of perceived control. *Journal of Personality and Social Psychology*, **31**, 282–294.

Wuthnow, R., Christiano, K. & Kuzlowski, J. (1980). Religion and bereavement: A conceptual framework. *Journal for the Scientific Study of Religion*, **19**, 408–422.

Chapter 7

PSYCHOLOGICAL DEFENCES AND THE DISTORTION OF MEANING

*Chris R. Brewin**

If external stressors cannot be physically avoided, the possibility remains that they can be made less threatening by distorting their meaning. Similarly, the impact of upsetting thoughts and memories may be much reduced by mental operations that suppress or transform them. These operations have generally been attributed to psychological defences.

For many years the focus on mechanisms of psychological defence was one of the characteristics that divided psychoanalytic theory and therapy from behavioural and cognitive therapies. For psychoanalysts, symptoms were usually seen as an indication of a hidden meaning, either in the form of a disguised conflict or of unacceptable feelings, and resistance to the exploration of this hidden material was an expected, if not inevitable, element of therapy (Wachtel, 1982). Behaviour therapists were able largely to sidestep these observations because they tended to treat the presenting symptom rather than being interested in its underlying cause or in their clients' more obscure thought processes. As behaviour therapists predicted, however, paying attention to clients' cognitions has slowly but unavoidably led to renewed interest in theories and observations previously the main preserve of psychoanalysis and some humanistic therapies.

Freud identified 17 types of psychological defence (Vaillant, 1992), and at least 37 different defences have now been distinguished by various authors (Cramer, 1991). All defences represent ways in which meaning can be distorted, either by denying, avoiding or transforming threatening ideas or their associated affect. However, not too much is known about

*Royal Holloway, University of London, UK

The Transformation of Meaning in Psychological Therapies.
Edited by Mick Power and Chris R. Brewin. © 1997 John Wiley & Sons Ltd.

how different defences are related to one another, or to underlying psychological mechanisms, and there is only scope in this chapter to discuss a few of them.

A frequently discussed defence is *denial*. This takes the form of a continuum, with clients at one extreme withdrawing attention from and denying the evidence of their senses in a refusal to recognise reality that may border on or involve actual psychosis. This primitive form of perceptual denial may be distinguished from a more common, cognitive variant (sometimes called *disavowal*) in which the client constructs a personal fantasy and interprets the available evidence in a way that is more consistent with this fantasy than with the facts. In other words, the client is aware of an event but may fail to accept it or to appreciate its implications. For example, he may fall ill and be admitted to a cancer hospital but refuse to believe in the possibility that he has cancer or that his life is in danger. Similarly, denial of the loss is recognised as a common stage in initial reactions to bereavement. Cramer (1991) suggested that in both these categories of denial the reality of events may be negated, minimised, exaggerated or reversed.

Moreover, people may differ in the extent to which they are aware of their denial. For some it may be a largely conscious strategy that they can report on. Trauma survivors, for example, sometimes speak of pretending that the trauma never happened, and resist attempts to persuade them to talk about the event for fear of having to accept its reality. For others the denial may be completely unconscious. Still others may switch between states in which they accept and deny reality at different times, or appear to do both simultaneously. Clinically this can manifest itself in a client appearing to agree with a statement but then forgetting it or contradicting it a few minutes later without being aware of the contradiction. A large number of clinicians from Freud on have noted the ability of some clients to hold two contradictory views at the same time. Freud (1893, p. 117) referred to this as 'the blindness of the seeing eye' in which 'one knows and does not know a thing at the same time'. Turkel (1994) suggested that this particular form of disavowal should be called 'doublethink'.

Suppression describes the conscious avoidance of threatening thoughts or memories by redirecting attention elsewhere. The term *repression* may be applied both to ideas or memories and their accompanying emotions, and is used in two main ways: first, when the process of suppression has been repeated so often that it has become automatic and the person is no longer aware that certain material is being excluded from consciousness (what Freud termed 'repression proper' or 'after-expulsion'); second, when the painful material has never reached consciousness in the first place (i.e. a fully unconscious process, termed 'primary repression' by Freud).

Whereas repression is characterised by a unitary consciousness from which certain thoughts or feelings are excluded, *dissociation* refers to a whole class of mental states in which consciousness is separated or divided. For example, the client may go into a trance or relive a traumatic memory and lose touch with their surroundings, becoming unaware of the sights and sounds that are currently present. More extreme examples include fugue states, in which the person temporarily loses their identity despite being fully conscious, and dissociative identity disorder, in which a number of more or less fully formed personalities appear to coexist, some being unaware of the presence of others or of information available to other subpersonalities. Finally, to conclude this brief survey, *projection* involves the attribution to others of thoughts or feelings that clients are unable to recognise in themselves. It is a central feature of Kleinian psychoanalytic theory. *Intellectualisation* refers to the description of highly emotionally charged events in excessively controlled or rational terms, enabling the emotional experience to be avoided.

Despite their observations concerning the importance of behavioural avoidance of feared situations, behaviour therapists were reluctant for some time to concede that mental avoidance of feared thoughts and memories might also be taking place. Two developments have contributed to a widespread change in professional opinion. The first has been the growing numbers of people coming forward to be helped overcome the effects of trauma, particularly abuse in childhood or adulthood. Rather than necessarily associating hidden feelings with psychoanalytic theories such as the existence of Oedipal conflict, therapists of all theoretical backgrounds are now far more aware of the fact that many clients have memories of real and horrible events that have happened to them. It is no longer hard to believe that they might go to great lengths to suppress these memories, especially when clients will often give detailed descriptions of the strategies they use to do so. With this new focus on trauma, the existence of and necessity of dealing with psychological defences has become much more apparent, as the difficulty in accepting the reality of the traumatic events often lies at the heart of the problem (Briere, 1992; Herman, 1992).

The second development is the recognition by cognitive-behaviour therapists that the effects of exposure to a feared stimulus may be blocked by distraction or cognitive avoidance (e.g. Rachman, 1980). Considerable efforts are now made to diagnose and prevent cognitive avoidance at an early stage. Moreover, influential cognitive-behavioural theories now explicitly contain the idea that mental activity can be used to block feared images or thoughts. Borkovec, Shadick & Hopkins' (1990) theory of generalised anxiety disorder suggested that worrying blocks access to feared thoughts and images. There is experimental evidence to show that the cardiovascular response to a phobic image is reduced by concurrent distracting mental activity such as worry (Borkovec & Hu, 1990; Borkovec et al., 1993), and that worry is associated with reduced levels of imagery (Borkovec & Inz, 1990; East & Watts, 1994).

What has so far received little empirical investigation is the nature of the feared thoughts and images. Salkovskis' (1985) theory of obsessive-compulsive disorder suggested that the use of neutralising thoughts or actions serves to avoid automatic negative thoughts of personal responsibility for harm. This is closely akin to Freud's description of the defence of 'undoing' or reversing hostile wishes: 'Compulsive acts like this, in two successive stages, of which the second neutralises the first, are a typical occurrence in obsessional neurosis' (Freud, 1909, p. 192).

The similarities between the observations of cognitive avoidance described above and psychoanalytic observations of defences mobilised to protect the person from a hidden idea or feeling are striking, and represent another example of the potential rapprochement between psychodynamic theory and cognitive science (e.g. Power & Brewin, 1991; Westen, 1991). The term 'cognitive avoidance' is neutral, however, regarding the extent to which individuals are aware of what they are avoiding or of the fact that they are avoiding something at all. Descriptions in the literature suggest that there are likely to be varying degrees of awareness. Like the term 'psychological defence', it can thus be applied both to deliberate avoidance and avoidance of which the person is not aware.

EVIDENCE FOR DEFENSIVE PROCESSES

Denial

As indicated above, denial refers to a process in which a person fails to acknowledge the existence or extent of actual or potential threat in the external world. It appears to be a ubiquitous response to threatening situations. Not only has it been noted by hundreds of medical and psychological practitioners (e.g. Shedler, Mayman & Manis, 1993), but it is a core construct in research on stress and coping. Lazarus (1966), for example, cited denial as one of the major forms of defensive reappraisal, and in a series of experiments showed that denial functioned to reduce autonomic arousal generated by a threatening film.

More recently Taylor & Brown (1988) have argued that positive illusions such as inflated self-evaluations, exaggerated perceptions of control, and unrealistic optimism are normative and promote mental health. Although some of these illusions do involve a distortion of objective reality, Taylor et al. (1989) argued that positive illusions are distinct from psychological defences on four grounds: (a) defences alter reality whereas illusions simply interpret it in the best possible light; (b) positive illusions are associated with mental health and defences with ill-health; (c) defences, but not illusions, interfere with social competence and creative, productive work; (d) defensive reactions are exacerbated by threat whereas people with positive illusions respond adaptively. In rebuttal it should be pointed out that many psychoanalysts, including Freud, have argued that defences have adaptive as well as maladaptive functions (e.g. Vaillant, 1986) and, as we have seen, some forms of denial involve the reinterpretation rather than the alteration of reality. At this point the evidence for Taylor et al.'s other proposed distinctions is also quite weak. Moreover, some of their positive illusions have been found not to be normative but to exist in certain subgroups such as repressors (Myers & Brewin, 1996) or people with a narcissistic personality (John & Robins, 1994). Thus it seems reasonable to accept the data on positive illusions as evidence for psychological defences of a mild, and possibly adaptive, kind.

Medical settings have been a fruitful arena for denial, and various examples of dangerous, bizarre or strikingly illogical behaviour have been provided (Ness & Ende, 1994). Many of these involve a failure to recognise or take action in the face of clear signs of pathology, or of bodily changes such as pregnancy. Scales have been devised for assessing denial in alcoholics, patients with breast cancer, psychiatric patients, and cardiac patients. Denial is also frequently encountered in the context of intimate relationships. One example is the belief that a violent partner will fulfil his promise not to be violent in the future, despite having made many failed promised in the past. Main & Goldwyn (1984) also described several patterns of recall of parenting indicative of denial, including downplaying the significance of attachment experiences, and making globally positive judgements about parenting that could not be substantiated by specific memories. Main & Goldwyn found that mothers reporting their childhoods in these ways were more likely to be rejecting towards their own children. Subjects displaying these same indicators of denial showed increased skin conductance levels when asked about their attachment experiences with parents (Dozier & Kobak, 1992).

Complexity in the definition of denial may account for the inconsistency in the way it is operationalised and for the conflicting results when the relationship of denial to adjustment is studied. Denial, along with avoidant coping in general, has been found to predict higher levels of distress in prospective studies (Carver et al., 1993; Carver & Scheier, 1994). However, there is also evidence that denial can be associated with positive health outcomes (e.g. Havik & Maeland, 1988; Levenson et al., 1989).

Repression

Unlike denial, which has always played a role in mainstream psychological theory, repression has been and remains a controversial construct. This is probably due to its focus on internal rather than external threat. After a long period of neglect, however, it has recently become the focus of a renewed research effort.

Studies of clients in therapy

Although experimental psychologists have laboured in vain to demonstrate convincingly repression for material consisting largely of sexual, aggressive or other generally threatening words, clinical psychologists and psychiatrists working with the survivors of major trauma have reported this phenomenon for years. Some of the earliest accounts come from Freud's (1896a) description of patients with early sexual trauma, and from British psychologists working with 'shell-shocked' soldiers in the First World War (e.g. Myers, 1921). They described soldiers as having psychogenic amnesia for some of their combat experiences, and linked recovery from 'shell-shock' to the return of memories with abreaction therapy.

More recently, several retrospective studies have found that a substantial proportion of clients in therapy for the effects of child sexual abuse (somewhere between 20 and 60%) report having periods in their lives (often lasting for several years) when they could not remember that the abuse had taken place. Moreover, forgetting has been associated in several studies with a higher incidence of violence accompanying the abuse. Although the rates vary between studies, broadly similar findings have been obtained by clinical psychologists (Briere & Conte, 1993), psychiatrists (Herman & Schatzow, 1987), and cognitive psychologists (Loftus, Polonsky & Fullilove, 1994). A national survey of American psychologists (Feldman-Summers & K.S. Pope, 1994) also found that, of those reporting abuse, 40% said they had had periods of forgetting some or all of the abuse. Both sexual and non-sexual abuse were subject to forgetting.

Prospective studies

Considerable scepticism has been expressed about the accuracy of retrospective reports of childhood, particularly when made by psychiatric patients (e.g. Lewinsohn & Rosenbaum, 1987). In fact, appraisal of the evidence suggests that recall of salient autobiographical facts from childhood is often surprisingly good and offers no support for recall, whether by psychiatric patients or people with no psychiatric history, being systematically biased in a positive or negative direction (Brewin, Andrews & Gotlib, 1993; Fromholt, Larsen & Larsen, 1995).

Nevertheless, evidence from prospective community surveys of individuals with documented histories of child sexual abuse is of great interest. Bagley (1995), for example, reported a study of women aged 18–24 years who had been removed from home 10 years previously by social services and had been separated from their natural mothers for at least one year. Prior to leaving home there had been intrafamilial sexual abuse according to the girl's own report and the report of an adult familiar with the household. Of 19 women for whom there was evidence for serious sexual abuse, 14 remembered events corresponding to the original records. Two remembered that abuse had taken place but could recall no details. Three did not report abuse when specifically asked whether they had been sexually abused as children. Of these three, two described long blank periods for their memory of childhood corresponding to the age when abuse had taken place.

Williams (1994a) reported a 17-year follow-up of women referred to hospital as children and diagnosed as having been sexually abused. Of 129 women interviewed, 38% failed to report anything resembling the abuse experience documented in the hospital records, and 12% reported no abuse experience of any kind. Inability to remember the trauma was associated with the perpetrator being a family member rather than a stranger, and with younger age. These associations held good even after excluding children who were three years of age or younger at the time of the abuse, and hence would not be expected to retain any conscious memories of it. In her paper Williams explored several alternative explanations of her data, for example that respondents deliberately withheld information about the abuse, and concluded that these were unlikely.

Corroboration

Interpretation of these data is hampered by a number of issues, of which one of the most important concerns the corroboration of facts apparently recalled after a period of amnesia. Some authors (e.g. H.G. Pope & Hudson, 1995) demand stringent evidence of the authenticity of a memory before they are willing to concede that it has been recovered after a period of amnesia. Feldman-Summers & K.S. Pope (1994) asked their respondents for any corroborative evidence for recovered memories of abuse; 47% reported some corroboration, for example the abuser acknowledged some or all of the remembered abuse, someone who knew about the abuse told the respondent, or someone else reported abuse by the same perpetrator.

Despite the problems arising from the relatively recent appreciation of the extent and importance of child sexual abuse, and the fact that such events often occur in secret, Pope & Hudson do not accept such evidence as adequate, arguing that independent, documented evidence is required. Such evidence is available from Williams' (1994a) study reported above. In her sample, approximately one in six of the women who recalled the abuse at interview said that there had been a period when they had completely forgotten the abuse. When current accounts of the abuse and the original records were compared, Williams (1995) found that women with recovered memories had no more discrepancies in their accounts than women who had always remembered the abuse.

It has not been doubted that individuals with fugue states subsequently recall reasonably accurately the details of their identity and autobiography, as many of these facts are easily checked. It is far more difficult to collect convincing evidence relevant to childhood experiences that may have taken place with nobody else present. The available data suggest that recovered memories are sometimes correct, but this of course does not mean that they are always correct.

Psychological mechanisms

How can reports of amnesia for childhood sexual abuse best be explained? One suggestion (Loftus, 1993) is that some of the reports are not veridical, but are false memories 'implanted' by therapists who have prematurely decided that the client is an abuse victim and who use inappropriate therapeutic techniques to persuade the client to recover corresponding 'memories'. The American False Memory Syndrome Foundation and the British False Memory Society have claimed that there are many cases known to them in which previously happy families have been disrupted by accusations of abuse that were only triggered by an adult child entering therapy with a poorly trained or 'fringe' practitioner. Loftus (1993) and Lindsay & Read (1994) have marshalled evidence to suggest that this is a possibility that must be taken seriously. For example, they review studies concerning the fallibility and malleability of memory, note the potential for inaccurate recall involved in techniques like hypnosis, and report evidence that some therapists adopt beliefs and methods that run counter to generally accepted notions of good practice.

These warnings, although largely based on indirect evidence, deserve to be taken seriously and are a reminder to practitioners to be scrupulous about the methods they use and the inferences they draw from therapeutic material. Nevertheless, the hypothesised implantation of false memories cannot account for more than a subset of recovered memories (and at present it is unclear how large or small this subset is). Apart from the evidence for the accuracy of recovered memories reviewed above, recent surveys indicate that recovered memories do not always concern sexual abuse, are sometimes recovered prior to entering therapy, and are reported routinely by well qualified psychologists who are alive to the possibility of false memories (Andrews et al., 1995; Poole et al., 1995).

Loftus, Garry & Feldman (1994) acknowledge that the view that traumas cannot be forgotten has now been disproved. They argue, however, that the mechanism involved is ordinary forgetting, and that there is no need to posit a special mechanism such as 'repression'. None of the studies discussed above offers any direct evidence about the mechanism involved, but trauma researchers argue that Loftus et al.'s argument is implausible. In rebuttal they point to several characteristics often associated with recovered memories, namely the extreme emotions that accompany them, the clients' reluctance to discuss them, and clients' accounts of deliberate attempts to avoid the memories intruding after the trauma. Williams (1994b) offers several examples of dramatic and personally meaningful events that on the face of it would be extremely hard simply to forget.

What is needed to support the concept of repression is evidence that there is an active inhibitory process that is keeping memories out of consciousness, not simply a passive failure to remember. Although there is as yet little direct evidence from the trauma field, there are numerous indications that such a process is possible. For example, given instructions to forget certain words and remember others, so-called 'directed forgetting', ordinary people appear to lose the ability to free recall the to-be-forgotten words, although they are perfectly well able to recognise them. Summarising a series of experiments on this effect, Bjork (1989) concluded that the most plausible explanation is an active inhibitory process that functions to exclude the to-be-forgotten words from consciousness.

Other research has been conducted with individuals who demonstrate a 'repressive coping style', defined as a tendency to score low on measures of trait anxiety and high on measures of social desirability. These are individuals who subjectively report little anxiety, although they are highly physiologically reactive to stress (Weinberger, Schwartz & Davidson, 1979). They appear genuinely to believe that they feel little anxiety, anger, jealousy, greed, or other antisocial impulses (Weinberger, 1990). They take longer to recall negative (but not positive) autobiographical memories (Davis, 1987; Myers & Brewin, 1994), and have impaired memory for negative (but not positive or neutral) story material (Myers & Brewin, 1995). With these characteristics one would expect them to report very happy childhoods with lots of positive and few negative experiences. What is interesting about the female 'repressors' that have been studied so far is that in fact they report significantly worse relationships with their fathers than matched controls (Myers & Brewin, 1994). These kinds of data suggest that there may well be inhibitory processes in memory that could account for clinical hypotheses concerning repression, although much more research is clearly needed.

Projection

In 1896 Freud wrote 'In paranoia, the self-reproach is repressed in a manner which may be described as *projection*. It is repressed by erecting the defensive symptom of *distrust of other people*. In this way the subject withdraws his acknowledgement of the self-reproach . . .' (1896b, p. 184). Recent research by Bentall and colleagues has supported this formulation. When explicit tasks were used that allowed subjects to deploy self-presentational strategies, paranoid patients showed extreme positive self-serving biases on tests of attributional style (Kaney & Bentall, 1988) or perception of control (Kaney & Bentall, 1992). However, when tested with an implicit, non-obvious measure of attributional style, paranoid patients showed a pattern much more characteristic of depression, i.e. high levels of self-blame for negative outcomes (Lyon, Kaney & Bentall, 1994). The authors interpreted their data as evidence for a defensive view of paranoid ideation.

IMPLICATIONS FOR COGNITIVE THERAPY

According to cognitive theory (e.g. Beck et al., 1979), meaning is derived from schemas in long-term memory that function to select and organise incoming information. In anxiety or depression normal patterns of meaning are altered because latent negative schemas have been activated by current stressors. Any resistance to a change in meaning is thought to arise from the fact that a schema, once activated, tends to assimilate information in such a way as to maintain a consistent view of the world. This process of fitting new information to prior expectations is considered to be an adequate explanation of cognitive distortions such as selective abstraction, magnification, minimisation, personalisation, and so on.

The implication that patients' thought processes reflect the activation of a single generalised self- or other-schema does not account for various aspects of depressive cognition. For example, autobiographical information is represented in the form of individual episodic memories as well as summary schematic memories (e.g. Klein & Loftus, 1990). The majority of depressed clients in fact experience intrusive memories of specific upsetting incidents such as childhood assaults and devote considerable effort to blocking these out (Brewin et al., 1996; Kuyken & Brewin, 1994). It cannot be assumed that all the traumatic experiences that commonly feature in the histories of anxious and depressed clients (or all aspects of these experiences) have been incorporated into the currently dominant self-schemas.

Cognitive psychologists such as Power & Champion (1986; Champion & Power, 1995; Power, this volume, Chapter 4) and Teasdale & Barnard (1993; Teasdale, this volume, Chapter 9) have also argued that Beck's schema model is too inflexible to account for depressive thinking. Empirically, there is evidence that depressed people can discriminate their current views of themselves, their perception of how they are generally, and their perception of how they have ever been (Brewin et al., 1992). Social psychologists have emphasised the likelihood of multiple self-representations, of which some will contain undesired or aversive wishes, emotions and traits (Ogilvie, 1987; Westen, 1991). Horowitz (1991) similarly proposed that people have a variety of internal role-relationship models in memory that represent a synthesis of past experience with attachment figures. These internal models, which may be activated in current relationships and contribute to the meaning placed on interpersonal events, contain representations of both desired outcomes and feared outcomes that have to be 'warded off'. In this way ordinary events may come to be invested with unrealistically positive or negative meanings.

The existence of complex representations of self and others suggests that cognitive distortions cannot simply be explained in terms of a drive for cognitive consistency with a single negative self-schema. From a psychological defence perspective, negative thoughts and logical errors may be maintained because they enable the individual to avoid confronting other specific unwanted thoughts, emotions or memories. Resistance thus arises because there are real feared consequences of thinking or acting in a different way. Individuals will vary in the extent to which they are aware of these feared consequences. Such ideas are of course commonplace to psychoanalytically trained therapists, although much discussion of defences has been in the context of forbidden drives and impulses rather than traumatic memories. Three examples will be given to illustrate this perspective.

The first example is taken from a case described by Brewin (1988). The client was a 35-year-old self-employed man who complained of constant headaches, irritability and sleep disturbance. Although his business appeared to be successful, he felt under continual pressure at work and even when at home worried about whether what he was doing was cost-effective. He typically felt inefficient and dissatisfied with himself, had a history of anxiety in childhood, and had never had many friends. In view of the obvious signs of tension, the first step was to introduce relaxation training. This was effective in eliminating his headache during the consultation, but he did not persevere with the exercises over the following weeks and made little progress.

Repertory grid analysis suggested that in his system of beliefs, relaxation was associated with a number of negative qualities such as being slapdash, unambitious and self-satisfied—characteristics exemplified by his disliked father. When questioned, the client confirmed that he did see his father in this way, and that he regarded his father as having let down the family badly by not working and by providing inadequate financial support. This was something the client was determined to avoid where his own family were concerned. It seems likely, therefore, that he was experiencing conflict between the goal of becoming more relaxed, which he consciously recognised as a desirable one, and the goal of not becoming more similar to his father on this important dimension. Although negative perceptions of himself as inefficient and ineffective were active in consciousness, the conflict had remained unresolved because the fear of perceiving himself as similar to his father had been disavowed.

A second example is the frequently encountered lack of assertiveness arising from excessive concern with the possibility of hurting others. This is likely to be approached by the cognitive therapist by having the client appraise the real risk of others being hurt through assertive behaviour. Past episodes of assertion will be reviewed, appropriate assertiveness modelled, anticipated consequences such as losing control investigated, and prospective data collected, in order to correct misperceptions of risk and thereby alter behaviour. Not every cognitive therapist will consider, however, that the fear of assertion may represent a defensive exclusion of alternative self-representations containing anger, violent thoughts, and the wish to cause hurt. In some individuals such feelings may be unacceptable because of personal experience of domestic violence, and negative self-perceptions as weak, put-upon and helpless, although aversive, are nevertheless preferable. In both the cases discussed therapeutic progress may be facilitated by identifying the denied self-perceptions and using standard cognitive techniques to analyse the feared consequences for the client's self-concept.

In other cases clients may have lost contact with autobiographical memories that are relevant to the origin of negative thoughts and feelings about themselves. Cognitive features of depression such as shame, dysfunctional attributions, characterological self-blame, and the inability to recall specific memories are empirically associated with childhood adversity, particularly assault and abuse (Andrews, 1995; this volume, Chapter 5; Andrews & Brewin, 1990; Kuyken & Brewin, 1995; Rose et al., 1994). Clinically it appears that negative cognitions can frequently be traced to specific experiences, or to actual words or criticisms spoken by significant others, that constitute part of the evidence supporting them (see also Hackmann, this volume, Chapter 8). Socratic dialogue may fail to make a lasting impact if it concentrates on current experiences and ignores important data from the past.

In the absence of any autobiographical support for negative cognitions, and client resistance to change, the therapist may consider whether relevant episodic memories have been forgotten or repressed, and whether important data supporting the beliefs are unavailable to consciousness. Evidence of blank periods in memory for childhood, internally inconsistent accounts of relationships with caregivers, and cognitive avoidance of trauma-related issues would be consistent with, but not diagnostic of, this possibility. Active attempts to recover memories or to express specific expectations to clients are, however, fraught with danger (Lindsay & Read, 1994). Exploration of hypothesised repressed memories should only be undertaken, if at all, with extreme caution, and with due recognition of the power of suggestion and of the fallibility of memory.

CONCLUSIONS

In some ways it is surprising that cognitive therapy for anxiety and depression has not addressed explicitly the issue of psychological defences and their role in the treatment process. There are now substantial theoretical and empirical grounds for regarding defensive mental operations as important contributors to clients' perceptions of themselves and others, to their errors and distortions in thinking, and to the strategies they adopt to control external and internal sources of threat. Westen (1991) has provided a detailed account of the contribution that this perspective and the cognitive approach to psychopathology could make to each other. It seems likely that the next decade will lead to a much greater appreciation of the mechanisms underlying psychological defences and to their incorporation within mainstream cognitive therapy.

REFERENCES

Andrews, B. (1995). Bodily shame as a mediator between abusive experiences and depression. *Journal of Abnormal Psychology,* **104**, 277–285.

Andrews, B. & Brewin, C.R. (1990). Attributions of blame for marital violence: A study of antecedents and consequences. *Journal of Marriage and the Family,* **52**, 757–767.

Andrews, B., Morton, J., Bekerian, D., Brewin, C.R., Davies, G.M. & Mollon, P. (1995). The recovery of memories in clinical practice. *The Psychologist,* **8**, 209–214.

Bagley, C. (1995). *Child Sexual Abuse and Mental Health in Adolescents and Adults.* Aldershot: Avebury.

Bjork, R.A. (1989). Retrieval inhibition as an adaptive mechanism in human memory. In H.L. Roediger III & F.I.M. Craik (eds), *Varieties of Memory and Consciousness*, pp. 309–330. Hillsdale, NJ: Erlbaum.

Borkovec, T.D. & Hu, S. (1990). The effect of worry on cardiovascular response to phobic imagery. *Behaviour Research and Therapy,* **28,** 69–73.

Borkovec, T.D. & Inz, J. (1990). The nature of worry in generalized anxiety disorder: A predominance of thought activity. *Behaviour Research and Therapy,* **28,** 153–158.

Borkovec, T.D., Shadick, R. & Hopkins, M. (1990). The nature of normal and pathological worry. In R. Rapee & D.H. Barlow (eds), *Chronic Anxiety and Generalized Anxiety Disorder.* New York: Plenum.

Borkovec, T.D., Lyonfields, J.D., Wiser, S.L. & Deihl, L. (1993). The role of worrisome thinking in the suppression of cardiovascular response to phobic imagery. *Behaviour Research and Therapy,* **31,** 321–324.

Brewin, C.R. (1988). *Cognitive Foundations of Clinical Psychology.* London and Hove: Lawrence Erlbaum.

Brewin, C.R., Andrews, B. & Gotlib, I.H. (1993). Psychopathology and early experience: A reappraisal of retrospective reports. *Psychological Bulletin,* **113,** 82–98.

Brewin, C.R., Smith, A.J., Power, M. & Furnham, A. (1992). State and trait differences in depressive self-perceptions. *Behaviour Research and Therapy,* **30,** 555–557.

Brewin, C.R., Hunter, E., Carroll, F. & Tata, P. (1996). Intrusive memories in depression. *Psychological Medicine,* **26,** 1271–1276.

Briere, J.N. (1992). *Child Abuse Trauma.* Newbury Park, CA: Sage.

Briere, J. & Conte, J. (1993). Self-reported amnesia for abuse in adults molested as children. *Journal of Traumatic Stress,* **6,** 21–31.

Carver, C.S. & Scheier, M.F. (1994). Situational coping and coping dispositions in a stressful transaction. *Journal of Personality and Social Psychology,* **66,** 184–195.

Carver, C.S., Pozo, C., Harris, S.D., Noriega, V., Scheier, M.F., Robinson, D.S., Ketcham, A.S., Moffat, F.L. & Clark, K.S. (1993). How coping mediates the effect of optimism on distress: A study of women with early stage breast cancer. *Journal of Personality and Social Psychology,* **65,** 375–390.

Champion, L.A. & Power, M.J. (1995). Social and cognitive approaches to depression: Towards a new synthesis. *British Journal of Clinical Psychology,* **34,** 485–503.

Cramer, P. (1991). *The Development of Defense Mechanisms.* New York: Springer-Verlag.

Davis, P.J. (1987). Repression and the inaccessibility of affective memories. *Journal of Personality and Social Psychology,* **53,** 585–593.

Dozier, M. & Kobak, R.R. (1992). Psychophysiology in attachment interviews: Converging evidence for deactivating strategies. *Child Development,* **63,** 1473–1480.

East, M.P. & Watts, F.N. (1994). Worry and the expression of imagery. *Behaviour Research and Therapy,* **32,** 851–855.

Feldman-Summers, S. & Pope, K.S. (1994). The experience of 'forgetting' childhood abuse: a national survey of psychologists. *Journal of Consulting and Clinical Psychology,* **62,** 636–639.

Freud, S. (1893). Studies on hysteria. *Standard Edition,* vol. 2. London: Hogarth Press.

Freud, S. (1896a). The aetiology of hysteria. *Standard Edition,* Vol. 3. London: Hogarth Press.

Freud, S. (1896b). Further remarks on the neuropsychoses of defence. *Standard Edition*, vol. 3. London: Hogarth Press.

Freud, S. (1909). Notes upon a case of obsessional neurosis. *Standard Edition*, vol. 10. London: Hogarth Press.

Fromholt, P., Larsen, P. & Larsen, S.F. (1995). Effects of late onset depression and recovery of autobiographical memory. *Journal of Gerontology: Psychological Sciences*, **50B**, 74–81.

Havik, O.E. & Maeland, J.G. (1988). Verbal denial and outcome in myocardial infarction patients. *Journal of Psychosomatic Research*, **32**, 145–157.

Herman, J.L. (1992). *Trauma and Recovery*. New York: Basic Books.

Herman, J.L. & Schatzow, E. (1987). Recovery and verification of memories of childhood sexual trauma. *Psychoanalytic Psychology*, **4**, 1–14.

Horowitz, M.J. (ed.) (1991). *Person Schemas and Maladaptive Interpersonal Patterns*. Chicago: University of Chicago Press.

John, O.P. & Robins, R.W. (1994). Accuracy and bias in self-perception: Individual differences in self-enhancement and the role of narcissism. *Journal of Personality and Social Psychology*, **66**, 206–219.

Kaney, S. & Bentall, R.P. (1988). Persecutory delusions and attributional style. *British Journal of Medical Psychology*, **62**, 191–198.

Kaney, S. & Bentall, R.P. (1992). Persecutory delusions and the self-serving bias: Evidence from a contingency judgement task. *Journal of Nervous and Mental Disease*, **180**, 773–780.

Klein, S.B. & Loftus, J. (1990). The role of abstract and exemplar-based knowledge in self-judgements: Implications for a cognitive model of the self. In T.K. Srull & R.S. Wyer (eds), *Advances in Social Cognition*, vol. 3, pp. 131–139. Hillsdale, NJ: Erlbaum.

Kuyken, W. & Brewin, C.R. (1994). Intrusive memories of childhood abuse during depressive episodes. *Behaviour Research and Therapy*, **32**, 525–528.

Kuyken, W. & Brewin, C.R. (1995). Autobiographical memory functioning in depression: The role of early adverse experiences. *Journal of Abnormal Psychology*, **104**, 585–591.

Lazarus, R.S. (1966). *Psychological Stress and the Coping Process*, New York: McGraw-Hill.

Levenson, J.L., Mishra, A., Hamer, R.M. & Hastillo, A. (1989). Denial and medical outcome in unstable angina. *Psychosomatic Medicine*, **51**, 27–35.

Lewinsohn, P.M. & Rosenbaum, M. (1987). Recall of parental behavior by acute depressives, remitted depressives and nondepressives. *Journal of Personality and Social Psychology*, **52**, 611–619.

Lindsay, D.S. & Read, J.D. (1994). Psychotherapy and memories of childhood sexual abuse. *Applied Cognitive Psychology*, **8**, 281–338.

Loftus, E.F. (1993). The reality of repressed memories. *American Psychologist*, **48**, 518–537.

Loftus, E.F., Garry, M. & Feldman, J. (1994). Forgetting sexual trauma: What does it mean when 38% forget? *Journal of Consulting and Clinical Psychology*, **62**, 1177–1181.

Loftus, E.F., Polonsky, S. & Fullilove, M. (1994). Memories of childhood sexual abuse: remembering and repressing. *Psychology of Women Quarterly*, **18**, 67–84.

Lyon, H.M., Kaney, S. & Bentall, R.P. (1994). The defensive function of persecutory delusions: Evidence from attribution tasks. *British Journal of Psychiatry*, **164**, 637–646.

Main, M. & Goldwyn, R. (1984). Predicting rejection of her infant from mother's representation of her own experiences. *Child Abuse and Neglect*, **8**, 203–217.

Myers, C.S. (1921). The revival of emotional memories and its therapeutic value. *British Journal of Medical Psychology*, **1**, 20–22.

Myers, L.B. & Brewin, C.R. (1994). Recall of early experience and the repressive coping style. *Journal of Abnormal Psychology*, **103**, 288–292.

Myers, L.B. & Brewin, C.R. (1995). Repressive coping and the recall of emotional material. *Cognition and Emotion*, **9**, 637–642.

Myers, L.B. & Brewin, C.R. (1996). Illusions of well-being and the repressive coping style. *British Journal of Social Psychology*, **35**, 443–457.

Ness, D.E. & Ende, J. (1994). Denial in the medical interview: Recognition and management. *Journal of the American Medical Association*, **272**, 1777–1781.

Ogilvie, D.M. (1987). The undesired self: A neglected variable in personality research. *Journal of Personality and Social Psychology*, **52**, 379–385.

Poole, D.A., Lindsay, D.S., Memon, A. & Bull, R. (1995). Psychotherapy and the recovery of memories of childhood sexual abuse: U.S. and British practitioners' opinions, practices and experiences. *Journal of Consulting and Clinical Psychology*, **63**, 426–437.

Pope, H.G. & Hudson, J.I. (1995). Can memories of childhood abuse be repressed? *Psychological Medicine*, **25**, 121–126.

Power, M.J. & Brewin, C.R. (1991). From Freud to cognitive science: A contemporary account of the unconscious. *British Journal of Clinical Psychology*, **30**, 289–310.

Power, M.J. & Champion, L.A. (1986). Cognitive approaches to depression: A theoretical critique. *British Journal of Clinical Psychology*, **25**, 201–212.

Rachman, S. (1980). Emotional processing. *Behaviour Research and Therapy*, **18**, 51–60.

Rose, D.T., Abramson, L.Y., Hodulik, C.J., Halberstadt, L. & Leff, G. (1994). Heterogeneity of cognitive style among depressed inpatients. *Journal of Abnormal Psychology*, **103**, 419–429.

Salkovskis, P.M. (1985). Obsessional-compulsive problems: A cognitive-behavioural analysis. *Behaviour Research and Therapy*, **23**, 571–583.

Shedler, J., Mayman, M. & Manis, M. (1993). The *illusion* of mental health. *American Psychologist*, **48**, 1117–1131.

Taylor, S.E. & Brown, J.D. (1988). Illusion and well-being: A social psychological perspective on mental health. *Psychological Bulletin*, **103**, 193–210.

Taylor, S.E., Collins, R.L., Skokan, L.A. & Aspinwall, L.G. (1989). Maintaining positive illusions in the face of negative information: Getting the facts without letting them get to you. *Journal of Social and Clinical Psychology*, **8**, 114–129.

Teasdale, J.D. & Barnard, P.J. (1993). *Affect, Cognition and Change*. Hove: Lawrence Erlbaum.

Turkel, J. (1994). Disavowal and defensive alterations of cognitive style as a consequence of childhood trauma. *Issues in Psychoanalytic Psychology*, **16**, 191–209.

Vaillant, G.E. (1992). The historical origins and future potential of Sigmund Freud's concept of the mechanisms of defence. *International Review of Psycho-Analysis*, **19**, 35–50.

Vaillant, G.E. (1986). *Empirical Studies of Ego Mechanisms of Defence*. Washington, DC: American Psychiatric Press.

Wachtel, P.L. (ed.) (1982). *Resistance: Psychodynamic and Behavioral Approaches*. New York: Plenum.

Weinberger, D.A. (1990). The construct validity of the repressive coping style. In J.L. Singer (ed.), *Repression and Dissociation*, pp. 337–386. Chicago: University of Chicago Press.

Weinberger, D.A., Schwartz, G.E. & Davidson, R.J. (1979). Low-anxious, high-anxious and repressive coping styles: Psychometric patterns and behavioral responses to stress. *Journal of Abnormal Psychology*, **88**, 369–380.

Westen, D. (1991). Social cognition and object relations. *Psychological Bulletin,* **109,** 429–455.
Williams, L.M. (1994a). Recall of childhood trauma: A prospective study of women's memories of child sexual abuse. *Journal of Consulting and Clinical Psychology,* **62,** 1167–1176.
Williams, L.M. (1994b). What does it mean to forget child sexual abuse? A reply to Loftus, Garry, & Feldman (1994). *Journal of Consulting and Clinical Psychology,* **62,** 1182–1186.
Williams, L.M. (1995). Recovered memories of abuse in women with documented child sexual victimization histories. *Journal of Traumatic Stress,* **8,** 649–673.

Chapter 8

THE TRANSFORMATION OF MEANING IN COGNITIVE THERAPY

Ann Hackmann*

ELICITING MEANING IN COGNITIVE THERAPY

It is well known that the basic tenet of cognitive therapy is that 'Men are not moved by things, but by the views they take of them' (Epictetus). A.T. Beck (1976) writes about the ways in which responses to events are coloured by thoughts, feelings and ideas. These are accessible to consciousness, but not necessarily in full awareness or reported spontaneously. Using conscious experience as the 'working-space' in therapy differentiates the cognitive from the behavioural, psychoanalytic and neuropsychiatric approaches.

A.T. Beck (1976) suggests that internal reality is made up of 'meanings, significances and imagery', and Greenberger & Padesky (1995) add that in order to understand our strong emotions we need to study the 'words, images and memories' which accompany them. This is important, as merely focusing on the first thoughts that come up may miss much of the meaning of an upsetting event. Thus eliciting meaning when reviewing a distressing incident involves thoughtful reflection. Greenberger & Padesky (1995) pose a series of useful questions, such as 'What does this mean about me, my life, other people, the future? What am I afraid of? What might happen? What images or memories do I have in this situation?' They recommend staying with such questions until words, images

*University Department of Psychiatry, Warneford Hospital, Oxford.

The Transformation of Meaning in Psychological Therapies.
Edited by Mick Power and Chris R. Brewin. © 1997 John Wiley & Sons Ltd.

or memories come to mind which are sufficient to account for the strength and type of emotion experienced. This is very similar to the process of allowing oneself to reflect on the 'felt sense' of a situation, and to get a 'handle' on what it is that is upsetting about it, as described by Gendlin (1988).

An individual's internal reality incorporates several aspects of meaning which the cognitive therapist may choose to explore or transform at different times. The first aspect of meaning lies in the conscious thoughts, visual images and images in other sensory modalities which an individual has at a particular moment (e.g. having the image of the sound of people talking about one, or the sense that one suddenly feels very small in stature). The second type of meaning is concerned with the general themes which arise as this type of material is repeatedly examined over time. An overview begins to suggest that there are a set of underlying beliefs and assumptions about the self, other people and the world, which vary from individual to individual, but which are relatively stable in each person. Some may be functional or positive, whilst others may be dysfunctional or negative.

The cognitive model proposes that all individuals have underlying beliefs, often based on early experience. Some of these beliefs are unconditional, and some are conditional. An example of a negative unconditional belief would be 'I am unlovable', and an example of a negative conditional belief (or dysfunctional assumption) would be 'I will be rejected if I make mistakes'. Conditional beliefs (or assumptions) suggest strategies or rules for managing life. People's characteristic underlying beliefs and assumptions (some of which will usually be positive) are a function of their experience, and need not be problematic, unless triggered by specific 'critical incidents', which then give rise to particular interpretations of events and strategies for dealing with them, which may not in fact be appropriate at the present time. In therapy we need to tackle both the surface 'weeds' (negative automatic thoughts, images, etc.) and the deeper 'roots' (underlying beliefs and assumptions) of the meanings we give to events (Greenberger & Padesky, 1995).

A full cognitive conceptualisation involves linking: early experience; underlying beliefs and assumptions; critical incidents; automatic thoughts, images and memories in various modalities; emotions; physiological reactions; and behaviour, as shown in Figure 8.1. Some of the links between the last four categories may be made in different directions for different people or at different times. The section of the diagram linking the last four items is similar to that used by Padesky & Mooney (1991). At any one time only part of the conceptualisation may need to be shared with the client, and not all the possible links shown will be relevant. Individualised maintenance vicious circles will need to be

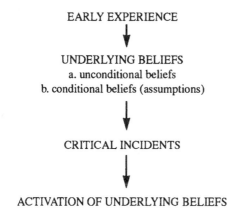

EARLY EXPERIENCE

UNDERLYING BELIEFS
a. unconditional beliefs
b. conditional beliefs (assumptions)

CRITICAL INCIDENTS

ACTIVATION OF UNDERLYING BELIEFS

Gives rise to reactions outlined below, and
links between them:

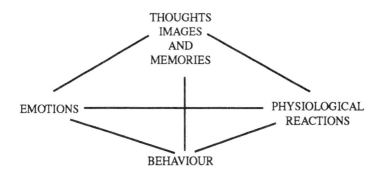

THOUGHTS
IMAGES
AND
MEMORIES

EMOTIONS   PHYSIOLOGICAL
                                  REACTIONS

BEHAVIOUR

Figure 8.1   The cognitive model

drawn out, based on clients' accounts of their reactions in specific situations. In many disorders a typical vicious circle can be drawn out. A classic example would be the cognitive model of panic (Clark, 1986), which simply links thoughts, emotions and physiological sensations of anxiety.

A person's underlying beliefs and assumptions can often be elicited by use of the 'downward arrow technique' (e.g. Burns, 1980; Greenberger & Padesky, 1995). This involves focusing on an automatic thought, and asking 'What does this mean about me (or other people, or the world)?' repeatedly, until an *absolute*, generalised statement is arrived at. For example, a social phobic who was afraid of her mind going blank was asked what this would mean to her. She replied that people would think her stupid and inferior, which would mean that they would reject her. Two of her underlying beliefs were that she was inferior, and that people reject others who appear stupid. Underlying beliefs can be elicited in other ways (J. Beck, 1995), including the use of belief questionnaires such as the Dysfunctional Attitude Scale (Weissman, 1979), the Schema Questionnaire (Young, 1990), and the Schema Checklist (A.T. Beck et al., 1990). More simply, Padesky (1994) suggests that underlying beliefs can often be elicited by asking people to complete the sentences: 'I am . . .', 'People are . . .', 'The world is . . .'. A.T. Beck (1967) postulates that affect is closely linked to underlying beliefs, and also suggests that these can often be identified following an upsetting incident by asking what the event seemed to mean about the self, the world and other people.

The fleeting visual or other sensory images people get when distressed can often be particularly valuable in gathering information concerning underlying beliefs. An image may pass rapidly through awareness amongst a string of negative automatic thoughts. Slowly reviewing the contents of this image may enable its full significance to be unpacked. Questions like 'What did that mean to you? What led up to the event in the image? What was the worst thing about it?' may be used, revealing the depth of meaning given to an event. For example, an agoraphobic reported having a fear of collapsing. He had an image of this happening in public, him being taken to hospital and kept there against his will, and never being visited or discharged. This suggested important interpersonal issues, such as a fear that no one would care about him or help him, in addition to his purely physical concerns. Each of these meanings had to be tackled during therapy. An account of the underlying beliefs elicited from the images of a group of hypochondriacs has been given by Wells & Hackmann (1993).

It is possible when reviewing the whole 'felt sense' of a situation to build a bridge back to particularly salient early experiences, during which underlying beliefs may have been formed or strengthened. It has already been mentioned that in a given situation memories themselves may pass through awareness and produce emotional changes. For example, Kuyken & Brewin (1994) studied a group of people who had been sexually or physically abused during childhood, and found that during periods of depression memories of this abuse frequently came to mind. Furthermore, careful questioning about emotions, bodily sensations, images and thoughts in a specific situation followed by the question 'And when in your life do you remember feeling like this? When was the first time?' can often be used to elicit important childhood memories. Such memories may involve sensory content and interpersonal themes similar to those in images occurring in the current situation (Hackmann, 1995), and this raises interesting questions about the relationships between images and memory, since 'memories' may be distorted, and 'images' contain chunks of input from memory.

The meaning of the original traumatic memories can be elicited by asking the person to relive the memory in the imagination, giving an account of the thoughts they had at that time, and the conclusions they drew about the self, the world and other people, and their own lovability, competence and control (Layden et al., 1993). What we know about memory suggests that such an account is very unlikely to be accurate, although it could accurately reflect internalised meanings, or current meanings of past events. These traumatic 'memories' may be restructured later in therapy, to give them new meanings (see page 137).

A particularly interesting connection seems to exist between images triggered in upsetting situations, and early traumatic memories. For example, a client frequently had images or impressions during panic attacks of being cramped up in a barrel at the bottom of the sea. He had been put there by the Devil, as an eternal punishment. When reviewing this image (and having been asked when in his life he could remember having such sensations and thoughts), he recalled that as a small boy he had often been shut in a small, dark cupboard by his brothers, and wrestled to the floor and held in a claustrophobic grip. He had also received severe punishments from his father, and at school. From this he had concluded that he was the sort of person who deserved punishment (an underlying, unconditional belief), and that he should strive to get everything right to avoid it (a dysfunctional assumption). He had also frequently observed flamboyant funerals at around the same age (four or five years old), whilst living abroad. When he had seen bodies buried he had assumed that the dead were still aware of what was happening to them. Since he believed that he deserved punishment, he came to believe that after death this could take the form of hateful claustrophobic experiences like those his brothers had inflicted on him. All this meaning could be understood as being expressed in his current panic attacks, through the images of the barrel. These images were proprioceptive rather than visual.

The third type of meaning that cognitive therapists work on is that reflected in memories of traumatic incidents (such as those described above) around which underlying beliefs were formed or strengthened, either in childhood, or in the face of extremely distressing experiences in adult life, such as those in post-traumatic stress disorder (PTSD). At times these memories can persist and colour current experience. For example, a woman client suffered from brief intrusive memories of looking at her shattered leg after a car accident and thinking that she would never walk again. This memory made her sad, even though she had recovered the use of her leg. Another client experienced memories of a time when (as a small child) she had been forced into a swimming pool by an adult who thought this would be good for her. This memory would flash through her mind whenever she felt a situation was being taken out of her control, and would make her feel tearful, even when faced with what was supposed to be a nice surprise.

Ways of transforming meaning in each of the three categories described above (i.e. negative automatic thoughts, images and impressions; unconditional and conditional underlying beliefs; and traumatic memories themselves) will now be discussed.

TRANSFORMING MEANING IN COGNITIVE THERAPY

Working with Negative Automatic Thoughts and Images

Cognitive therapy usually begins with work at this level. Since it has been noted that this material is not necessarily in full awareness, the first task is to help clients to notice, identify and record the thoughts and images that accompany the emotion (A.T. Beck, 1976). A recent or forthcoming event, a shift of mood in the session, or an imagery or role-play exercise can be used to elicit thoughts and images which are then examined using the questions above to ensure that the meanings elicited would be sufficient to account for the emotion experienced.

The most familiar techniques for transforming meaning in cognitive therapy are verbal discussion of negative automatic thoughts and behavioural experiments to test their validity. The style of communication between therapist and client is known as 'collaborative empiricism', and involves the therapist posing a careful series of questions, to foster guided discovery. Socratic questioning is used, and can be defined as asking questions which clients have the knowledge to answer, and which draw their attention to relevant information which may be outside their current focus; these generally move from the concrete to the more abstract so that the client can apply this information to re-evaluate a previous conclusion, or construct a new idea. The guided discovery process consists of asking informational questions, then summarising meanings for clients using their own words, then asking synthesising and analytical questions which encourage a shift in perspective, or suggest ways of testing reality. The therapist aims at true guided discovery, in which clients draw their own conclusions, rather than merely changing clients' minds in a predetermined direction, by lecturing them, or relying on debate, persuasion or cross-examination (Padesky, 1993a).

Useful verbal techniques for changing the meanings of automatic thoughts include the following: evaluating the evidence for and against the thought; eliciting alternative perspectives; and looking for evidence of distorted thinking. Evidence for and against a thought can be evaluated in a therapy session, or by the client on a Dysfunctional Thought Record (A. T. Beck et al., 1979; Greenberger & Padesky, 1995). Clients learn to spot particular types of cognitive distortion, such as all-or-nothing thinking, or jumping to conclusions (Burns, 1989).

Images can also be evaluated by using such verbal discussion techniques. A single image can contain many cognitive distortions. For example, a father was worried about his son's performance in a baseball match and had images of his son growing up (thanks to his father) to be *either* the most successful, happiest, best adjusted graduate in the world *or* a homicidal maniac. He was overgeneralising, fortune telling, catastrophising, thinking in a black and white way, and magnifying the importance of his own efforts, and the significance of that particular day, on which the son might catch (or drop) a ball at the match.

As well as using verbal discussion techniques to evaluate thoughts and images, behavioural experiments can be carried out to test their validity. For example, in panic disorder the true causes and consequences of the frightening bodily sensations can be investigated through experiments (Clark et al., 1994). A client could be encouraged to breathe rapidly as if having a panic attack, in order to discover that the rapid breathing causes dizziness. Then this could be extended by asking the client to breathe like that for a longer time, to test the prediction that this will cause fainting. In social phobia clients can be videoed whilst anxious, and can then watch and rate the video to discover that although they feel terrible, this does not correspond with what others see (Clark & Wells, 1995).

Behavioural experiments can also be done to check the reactions of others to feared catastrophes. For example, a social phobic might be asked to spill wine deliberately in a restaurant, or an agoraphobic might watch the therapist pretend to faint in a shopping centre, in order to check whether anyone notices the spilling or shaking, or whether a huge, embarrassing crowd gathers.

The degree to which images are realistic can be tested in a variety of ingenious ways. In social phobia it appears that clients get a clear and often vivid sense of how they come across to others. The raw material for this appears to be their bodily sensations, but this is translated into a felt sense of how they appear, sometimes experienced as a visual image of the self, seen from an observer perspective (Clark & Wells, 1995). Examples include having an image of the self looking as red as a jelly-baby or covered in rivers of sweat, or having the impression of stumbling terribly over words. Video and auditory tape feedback of a situation in which the client believes they appeared in these ways can have a very useful therapeutic effect, and correct the distorted image.

Many anxious patients use 'safety behaviours' to protect them from imagined feared consequences (Salkovskis, 1991). Thus, instead of learning from experience that the feared outcome does not occur, they conclude that what they did kept them safe or protected them. In therapy they can be encouraged to enter situations without using safety behaviours, to discover what really happens. Agoraphobics entering a phobic situation for a short time, first using safety behaviours and then without them, discover that anxiety decays much more quickly on the second occasion, as they discover that nothing bad will happen (Salkovskis, 1995). Social phobics discover that not only do they feel less anxious if they drop their safety behaviours, they also feel less self-conscious and as if they are coming across better to others (Wells et al., 1995).

The meanings encapsulated in an image can also be changed by directly altering the image in the modality (or modalities) in which it is experienced, having first established that it is unrealistic. This may be much more effective than using verbal techniques alone to challenge the meaning. For example, despite having fully understood that his images were echoes of early memories, rather than manifestations of what might happen in the future, the client who imagined himself trapped in a barrel by the Devil was much relieved by imaging moving backwards in time, so that the barrel moved up, out of the sea and onto the deck of a ship, and lost its lid, so that he could move and see out. This was accompanied by a further shift in meaning, to the effect that he no longer believed that any horrific or bad experiences could go on for ever.

Another client was extremely upset by images of her own gravestone, and the cheerful faces of her husband and children as they walked away from it. She believed that her images were revelations of what would really happen in the future. Verbal discussion produced an intellectual appreciation that this was probably not true, but this intellectual insight did not lessen her distress. In order to change the emotional meaning of the images she was asked to evoke the image, and then frame it on a television screen. In the new image she placed herself, alive and well, on the sofa with her husband and children, watching the horrible images on television. She was then able to imagine switching it off. This gave her tremendous relief, not only from distressing images, but from nightmares as well. This transformation brought about change not only in the content of the image, but also at a metacognitive level (Wells, 1995), since she no longer held the view that her images would reflect the actual future.

Often, as well as working on the actual contents of internal reality, the cognitive therapist is striving to bring about changes in metacognition, i.e. in the beliefs the person has about their own mental processes. The first task for clients is to learn that thoughts and images do not necessarily reflect reality, and that there may be other possible perspectives on events.

Secondly, they may need to work on more specific beliefs, such as the idea that worry is a useful activity or that it can, in itself, prevent catastrophes.

Working at the level of metacognition can be very useful, since it would be extremely time-consuming (and probably counterproductive) to focus on every negative thought or image, as this might cause an escalation in unpleasant rumination. For example, social phobics often engage in an extensive post-mortem after a social event, about everything that went wrong. In therapy, as well as challenging the *general* content of the thoughts a few times, clients are guided towards evaluating the effects of the actual process at a metacognitive level, i.e. to see that the post-mortem has a negative effect on mood and keeps the problem going, even though it does not reflect reality. Thus clients are encouraged to move towards banning it entirely (Clark & Wells, 1995). However, when using tactics like these the work still needs to arise out of a cognitive conceptualisation of the problem and what keeps it going. It is important to find out whether the upsetting thoughts are unrealistic, and/or establish that dwelling on them does indeed cause a worsening mood. Pure avoidance and distraction are not being advocated here.

Wells (1995) has also written about meta-beliefs in Generalised Anxiety Disorder. The main themes of these beliefs are that worry is harmful and must be controlled, but also that it serves a useful purpose in helping one plan how to cope with possible catastrophes. Treatment implications include the idea that patients should be aware of these contradictory beliefs, and should then be encouraged to experiment and discover what will happen if they do not control the worries (for example, testing the prediction that they might go mad). They should also be encouraged to experiment with reducing the amount of time spent worrying, and finding out whether this impairs or improves their ability to cope. Wells & Hackmann (1993) have also noted that in hypochondriasis there are many superstitious beliefs about worrying, such as that thinking in a positive way about their health could tempt providence and make them ill. These beliefs, too, can be evaluated in therapy, using discussion and behavioural experiments.

To summarise, when working at the level of meaning that is reflected by thoughts, images and impressions, clients are taught to tune in to their internal reality in the here and now, and to evaluate its validity and arrive at a balanced view, using verbal discussion techniques, behavioural experiments and imagery modification. They are also taught to understand certain features of their mental processes, and how these keep the problem going. The overall aim is to teach generalisable skills for managing internal reality.

Working with Unconditional and Conditional Underlying Beliefs

As discussed above, the cognitive model suggests that we all have a set of underlying beliefs formed early in life, about ourselves, other people and the world. Some of these beliefs may be positive, and some negative. Some are unconditional, and some conditional. Assumptions are usually conditional rules for behaviour, which suggest ways to manage the world in the light of the individual's underlying beliefs. These beliefs determine why one individual will react differently to another in the same situation. Such beliefs often need to be addressed in therapy, since the model suggests that they are the source of the negative automatic thoughts, which could continually be generated unless the beliefs are evaluated and modified. Once the cognitive therapist has helped clients to challenge negative automatic thoughts and images their next task is to work on underlying beliefs so that they will not be as vulnerable in the face of further critical incidents.

The first step is to help the client to make his or her underlying beliefs explicit, using techniques like those described in the introduction. This may take some time, since one is moving towards deeper and often previously unarticulated ideas or understandings. However, repeated examination of themes will usually indicate that a few major beliefs underlie a wide range of upsetting thoughts. In order to focus therapy most efficiently the most important beliefs (those held most strongly, and affecting life most) are worked on first (Safran et al., 1986).

Plenty of time is needed for this work, as underlying beliefs may be harder to shift than negative automatic thoughts, and working on them may elicit more intense affect. An important objective is to get the client to explore the idea that, like thoughts, beliefs are not facts and thus are open to change. This needs sensitive handling, since it can be distressing to discover that one has made many decisions in life which have been based on false premises. The advantages and disadvantages of holding such beliefs, or of having particular rules for behaviour, can be evaluated (Burns, 1980). If the client feels that the belief or rule is somewhat problematic, he or she may feel motivated to work on it, and rewrite it in a less rigid, absolutist way.

Dismantling old beliefs, and reframing them in new ways, can be done using many of the discussion techniques and behavioural experiments which are used to challenge automatic thoughts (see J. Beck (1995), for example). Another useful set of techniques involves the use of continua, recommended as being helpful in breaking down the primitive, global, black and white thinking characteristic of negative underlying beliefs (Burns, 1980; Pretzer, 1983). For example, a client held the belief that if she made a mistake others would think she was totally unintelligent.

Drawing a graph, and plotting many people known to her, on these two supposedly orthogonal dimensions (intelligence, and tendency to make mistakes) quickly revealed that in fact these two qualities did not correlate very well. This weakened the idea that if she made a mistake others would think she was unintelligent. This work was then followed by observing just how often others actually did make mistakes, and how little attention was given to them.

Having rewritten some of the key beliefs and rules for behaviour, the client is encouraged to experiment with new behaviour in real life in line with these changes. The therapist may need to offer skill building, and rehearse new behaviours in role-plays if they are missing from the client's repertoire. An example here would be assertiveness training.

As described above, underlying conditional and unconditional beliefs may be relatively easy to shift, provided that they are not too negative, rigid or inflexible, and that the person also has some alternative, positive beliefs. However, some people with very long-term psychological difficulties may have extremely negative underlying beliefs which are hard to shift and have a powerful maintaining function, as they have a strong effect on what they notice, remember or attend to of their experiences. They can also be maintained in the face of contradictory information through processes of distorting, discounting and ignoring counter evidence (see A. T. Beck, Freeman & Associates, 1990). Work on such very negative underlying beliefs (sometimes called schemas: see Young (1990); Layden et al. (1993)) forms the main thrust of cognitive therapy for personality disorders (A. T. Beck, Freeman & Associates, 1990; Young, 1990; Layden et al. 1993).

Having identified the schemas as described above, the next step is to put them into the client's own words: the client is invited to consider how each one works in his life, and whether there are any images or memories associated with it. The next task is to begin to identify a positive, alternative schema, once again in the client's own words. The new schema will not necessarily be the polar opposite of the old, and will possibly, although absolute, be less extreme than the negative schema. This is because negative implies total absence (I am unlovable) whilst positive implies presence, which may nevertheless be less than perfect (I am lovable, i.e. to some people some of the time) (Padesky, 1994).

Before starting work on this type of belief it is important that the client has had practice in identifying thoughts and emotions, and evaluating negative automatic thoughts and images. Often some work is done on an Axis I problem, such as panic or social anxiety, before work commences on more deep-seated underlying issues. This also helps to instil hope, and some trust in the therapist. The client may make considerable progress in areas not linked to pathological schemas, but may be harder to work with once work commences in this area.

Layden et al. (1993) describe the ways in which developmental issues can affect those with maladaptive schemas underlying personality disorders. If they had traumatic experiences very early in life, then these memories may have been stored in the form of visual images or as more disorganised cognitions which the authors refer to as 'the cloud'. This 'cloud' is said to consist of information taken in from touch, body position, tone of voice and unformed visual inputs. This type of material is often more difficult to work with than that stored in verbal memory. Also, if schemas are formed very early, the client's cognitive processing when these schemas are active can be extremely immature and maladaptive, compared with their ability to solve problems at other times. Layden et al. (1993) have shown that in borderline personality disorder cognitive development, schemas can be operating at a very early Piagetian level of development characterised by egocentricity, emotional reasoning, dichotomous thinking and a lack of metathought, or ability to see alternatives or to understand hypotheticals. Thus a great deal of client education is required before much progress can be made. It is also likely that the therapy relationship will activate underlying beliefs about the self, the world and other people, and will thus provide plenty of useful material to be used in a 'schema laboratory'.

Once clients begin to accept that their beliefs are not necessarily facts, continua techniques can be very useful in the schema change process (Padesky, 1994). Clients can learn through guided discovery that schemas can operate like prejudices and are just as hard to change (Padesky, 1993b). A positive data log can be used over long periods to readjust the filtering process by recording evidence from current everyday life which even weakly supports an alternative, positive schema (such as 'I am just as competent as other people').

Another method of evaluating schemas is Young's Historical Test of Schema (Young, 1984). Since schemas are formed and held over long periods of life, a lifetime of data needs to be evaluated. The therapist and client work together to make lists of confirming and disconfirming evidence for the belief being examined, in each period of the client's life in the past. Written summaries are produced, usually over a number of sessions.

Another useful tool is the Core Belief Worksheet (J. Beck, 1995), designed for use fairly far on in therapy. On it the client writes the old, negative core belief, and the new belief. Then evidence can be accumulated which either contradicts the old belief and supports the new belief, or supports the old belief *with a reframe* so that it will *also* strengthen the new belief.

This type of work can seem intellectual and arid to the client, and it is useful to develop metaphors which support it. Fairy tales and novels with particular themes can be used to help clients conceptualise their problems, and devise new coping strategies. For example, one patient compared herself to Gretel in Hansel and Gretel, all alone in the wood, and in great danger unless she could get home to people who would take care of her. She was encouraged instead to think of herself as like Vasalisa, whose mother had died, but who had left Vasalisa with a little doll to guide her through life. The client compared the little doll to her own developing intuition and ability to look after herself, without needing to cling to others who might in any case let her down. She found this more useful than telling herself that she needed to learn to stand on her own feet, and manage without other people, which had previously felt rather stark, unfair and lonely.

Working with Memories in Cognitive Therapy

If upsetting memories or fragments of them enter awareness in certain trigger situations, or if links are made between other current contents of internal reality and traumatic memories, then it is possible to work on the meanings carried by these memories. In many cases these meanings can be elicited and evaluated using the usual range of verbal techniques and behavioural experiments. However, such techniques may bring about intellectual shifts without a change in affect. Experiential techniques can then be brought into play, including the use of role-plays and reverse role-plays with important figures from the past, and the use of imagery modification techniques.

When memories of the past are particularly traumatic the best course of action may be to attempt to repair the memories directly (see below), in order to change the meaning given to these events. This may be indicated in therapy when a situation triggers a strong and distinctive emotion and related behaviour, without an easily accessible thought, and inappropriate in the present situation. An example would be an incident during which a client threw a present her daughter had given her into the girl's face, whilst experiencing a strong feeling of abandonment. It transpired that as a little child she had been left in Care by her mother, who had then vanished but sent her a present at Christmas. The gift was then removed by the matron, who announced that no one was allowed personal presents. This had triggered a terrible feeling of aloneness and abandonment in the child, which was triggered again by the present from her daughter. It appeared that a cognitive affective behavioural structure laid down as a result of traumatic experience had been activated. This has close parallels with the flashbacks experienced in PTSD, in which the techniques described below may also be applicable.

Layden et al. (1993) have given a particularly clear account of how to work directly on memories. The client is encouraged to evoke the memory, and relive it giving an account of its perceived meanings about himself, other people and the world. These are then evaluated using verbal discussion techniques. The memory is then restructured to incorporate the new elements from the discussion, in a way which makes the fresh perspective vividly real in the reconstructed memory.

For example, the agoraphobic who feared being kept in hospital against his will had actually had this experience as a small boy. He had been taken to hospital, and then his parents had disappeared unexpectedly. As he was an unwanted child in a poor family, and had often been told that it was a pity he had ever been born, he decided that he had probably been abandoned by his parents, and they would not want him back. He was able to reframe this experience in therapy, by imagining his adult self going into the past to warn his parents that they should explain to him that they did love him, and would come back for him. He had plenty of evidence that they did care for him from later in his childhood. Simply reliving this memory with this new twist led to a great reduction in anxiety and panic attacks, and a lessening of the conviction that it would be possible for him to be separated permanently from people to whom he felt really close.

Similar techniques can be used effectively with those who have experienced sexual abuse, or other types of PTSD. This type of work can be very time-consuming and stressful for the client and the therapist, so it is important to plan for sessions which are long enough for the material to be worked on adequately before the client has to leave the office, and for a rest after the session before daily life must be resumed. It may also be important to give the client some practice in distancing themselves from the image, or switching it on and off, before tackling the content, to prevent it from seeming overwhelming.

CONCLUSION

This chapter outlines methods used by cognitive therapists to elicit and transform meaning as represented in automatic thoughts and images, in underlying unconditional and conditional beliefs and in traumatic memories. Verbal and imagery modification techniques and behavioural experiments have been described, for changing the current contents of internal reality, underlying beliefs (including metacognitive beliefs), and the meanings of experiences which gave rise to all of these. Links have been made between visual images (and those in other modalities) and traumatic memories. The cognitive model provides a useful framework for expanding and refining our understanding of current experience and its links with the past. It also provides a basis for developing new methods of transforming meaning in subtle and increasingly effective ways.

ACKNOWLEDGEMENT

The author is supported in this work by the Wellcome Trust.

REFERENCES

Beck, A.T. (1967). *Depression: Clinical, Experimental and Theoretical Aspects.* New York: Hoeber.

Beck, A.T. (1976). *Cognitive Therapy and the Emotional Disorders.* New York: International Universities Press.

Beck, A.T. (1979). *Cognitive Therapy of Depression.* New York: Guilford Press.

Beck, A.T., Rush, A.J., Shaw, B.F. & Emery, G. (1979). *Cognitive Therapy of Depression,* New York: Guilford.

Beck, A.T., Freeman, A. & Associates (1990). *Cognitive Therapy of Personality Disorders.* New York: Guilford Press.

Beck, J. (1995). *Cognitive Therapy: Basics and Beyond.* New York: Guilford Press.

Burns, D. (1980). *Feeling Good: The New Mood Therapy.* New York: Avon Books.

Burns, D. (1989). *The Feeling Good Handbook.* New York: Morrow.

Clark, D.M. (1986). A cognitive approach to panic. *Behaviour Research and Therapy,* **24**, 461–470.

Clark, D.M. & Wells, A. (1995). A cognitive model of social phobia. In: R. Heimberg, M. Liebowitz, D.A. Hope & F.R. Schneier (eds), *Social Phobia: Diagnosis, Assessment and Treatment.* New York: Guilford Press.

Clark, D.M., Salkovskis, P.M., Hackmann, A., Middleton, H., Anastasiades, P. & Gelder, M.G. (1994). A comparison of cognitive therapy, applied relaxation and imipramine in the treatment of panic disorder. *British Journal of Psychiatry,* **164**, 759–769.

Gendlin, E. (1988). *Focussing.* USA: Bantam Books.

Greenberger, D. & Padesky, C. (1995). *Mind over Mood: A Cognitive Therapy Treatment Manual for Clients.* New York: Guilford Press.

Hackmann, A. (1995). Image, memory, metaphor and meaning: Some case material. Paper presented at the World Congress of Behavioural and Cognitive Therapies, Copenhagen (unpublished).

Kuyken, W. & Brewin, C.R. (1994). Intrusive memories of childhood abuse during depressive episodes. *Behaviour Research and Therapy,* **32**, 525–528.

Layden, M., Newman, C., Freeman, A. & Morse, S.B. (1993). *Cognitive Therapy of Borderline Personality Disorder.* USA: Allyn & Bacon.

Padesky, C. (1993a). Socratic questioning: Changing minds or guiding discovery? Keynote address presented at the meeting of the European Congress of Behavioural and Cognitive Psychotherapies, London (unpublished).

Padesky, C. (1993b). Schema as self-prejudice. *International Cognitive Therapy Newsletter,* **5/6**, 16–17.

Padesky, C. (1994). Schema change processes in cognitive therapy. *Clinical Psychology and Psychotherapy*, **5**, 267–278.

Padesky, C. & Mooney, K. (1991). Clinical tip: Presenting the cognitive model to clients. *International Cognitive Therapy Newsletter*, **5/6**, 3–4.

Pretzer, J.L. (1983). *Borderline personality disorder: Too complex for cognitive-behavioural approaches? Paper presented at the meeting of the American Psychological Association, Anaheim, CA.* ERIC Document Reproduction Service No. ED 243007.

Safran, J., Vallis, T., Segal, Z. & Shaw, B. (1986). Assessment of core cognitive processes in cognitive therapy. *Cognitive Therapy and Research*, **10**, 509–526.

Salkovskis, P.M. (1991). The importance of behaviour in the maintenance of anxiety and panic: a cognitive account. *Behavioural Psychotherapy*, **19**, 6–19.

Salkovskis, P.M. (1995). Cognitive approaches to health anxiety and obsessional problems: some unqiue features and how this affects treatment. Paper presented at the World Congress of Behavioural and Cognitive Therapies, Copenhagen, Denmark, 10–15 July.

Weissman, A. (1979). The Dysfunctional Attitude Scale: A validation study. *Dissertation Abstracts International*, **40**, 1389–1390B.

Wells, A. (1995). Meta-cognition and worry: A cognitive model of Generalised Anxiety Disorder. *Behavioural and Cognitive Psychotherapy*, **23**, 265–280.

Wells, A. & Hackmann, A. (1993). Imagery and core beliefs in health anxiety: Content and origins. *Behavioural and Cognitive Psychotherapy*, **21**, 265–273.

Wells, A., Clark, D.M., Salkovskis, P.M., Ludgate, J., Hackmann, A. & Gelder, M.G. (1995). Social phobia: The role of in-situation safety behaviours in maintaining anxiety and negative beliefs. *Behaviour Therapy*, **26**, 153–161.

Young, J. (1984). *Cognitive therapy with difficult patients*. Philadelphia, PA: Workshop presented at the meeting of the Association for Advancement of Behaviour Therapy.

Young, J. (1990). *Cognitive Therapy for Personality Disorders: A Schema-focussed Approach*. USA: Professional Resource Exchange.

Chapter 9

THE TRANSFORMATION OF MEANING: THE INTERACTING COGNITIVE SUBSYSTEMS APPROACH

John D. Teasdale*

Cognitive therapy is based on the assumption that emotional reactions are mediated through the interpretations, or meanings, given to experience. It is assumed that such meanings are available in consciously accessible thoughts and images. The goal of cognitive therapy is to alter maladaptive emotional responses by transforming dysfunctional meanings to more functional meanings.

In this chapter I shall describe the Interacting Cognitive Subsystems (ICS) approach to understanding meaning in emotional disorders and in cognitive therapy. ICS is a complex approach, so I shall anchor my discussion by focusing on two related clinical issues that have emerged in the practice of cognitive therapy, particularly of depression. The first issue is the contrast between 'intellectual' and 'emotional' belief, or meaning; the second issue is the distinction, made by Chris Padesky (1993), between using the cognitive therapy procedure of Socratic dialogue to 'change minds' as compared with using it to 'guide discovery'.

I shall first describe each of these clinical issues in more detail. Then I shall summarise the ICS approach, focusing on a distinction between two, qualitatively different, kinds of meaning that are recognised within this framework. Recognition of these different forms of meaning, each playing a different role in the production, maintenance and modification of emotional states, casts light on the distinctions between 'intellectual' and 'emotional' belief, and between 'changing minds' and 'guiding

*MRC Applied Psychology Unit, Cambridge, UK

The Transformation of Meaning in Psychological Therapies.
Edited by Mick Power and Chris R. Brewin. © 1997 John Wiley & Sons Ltd.

discovery', in the transformation of meaning. I shall also consider some of the wider implications of the ICS analysis for our understanding of the ways in which cognitive therapy, and related treatments, may lead to lasting therapeutic gains.

'INTELLECTUAL' AND 'EMOTIONAL' BELIEF

Within cognitive therapy, 'rational' argument or 'corrective' information is frequently ineffective in changing emotional response, even when the client acknowledges 'intellectually' the logical power of the evidence. For example, with a client who expresses the belief that she or he is a 'total failure', the therapist might review evidence of recent successes or achievements that are incompatible with that belief. The response from the client to such a review is often something along the lines 'I know, intellectually, that I am not a total failure, but I don't believe it emotionally'.

This contrast between 'intellectual' and 'emotional' belief in cognitive therapy is one aspect of a wider recognition of a distinction otherwise referred to as 'knowing with the head' versus 'knowing with the heart', or 'cold' versus 'hot' cognition.

Within cognitive therapy, the classic response to such contrasts has been to suggest that there is no essential difference between intellectual and emotional belief—they are simply *quantitative* variations in degree of one basic kind of belief. So, the basic text on cognitive therapy for depression, in specifically considering this issue, suggests:

> Patients often confuse the terms "thinking" and "feeling". This semantic problem is most obvious when the patient mistakenly uses the word "feel" for "believe", for example, "I feel you're wrong". The therapist can tell the patient that a person cannot believe anything "emotionally". Emotions include feelings, sensations; thoughts and beliefs lead to emotions. When the patient says he believes or does not believe something emotionally, he is talking about *degree of belief*. (Beck, et al., 1979, p. 302, original italics.)

In practice, many clinicians have found this analysis unconvincing, regarding 'emotional' belief as qualitatively distinct from 'intellectual' belief, and functionally more important.

'CHANGING MINDS' AND 'GUIDING DISCOVERY'

Within cognitive therapy, Socratic dialogue represents one of the main vehicles through which the therapist, by skilful questioning, attempts to help the client recognise and modify the dysfunctional negative thinking that, it is assumed, contributes to the production and maintenance of depression. As such, Socratic dialogue is regarded as a central procedure for the transformation of meaning.

In a very thoughtful discussion, Chris Padesky (1993) has recently made a number of suggestions and distinctions concerning the use of Socratic questioning in cognitive therapy. Padesky distinguishes between two ways in which Socratic dialogue can be used: 'changing minds' and 'guiding discovery'.

'Changing minds' uses questioning to produce evidence that will invalidate belief in a specific negative thought that has been identified. In changing minds, the therapist appears to know exactly where he or she is headed: '. . . the therapist would ask a series of factual questions "one-two-three" and then say to the client (almost triumphantly) "well, then how can you think thus and so?" The client . . . would invariably say, "Oh, I see what you mean."' (Padesky, 1993, p. 5). For example, a client who regarded himself as a 'total failure' would be questioned in a way that would reveal that he had, in fact, recently achieved a number of goals and completed a number of useful tasks. He would then be asked if it was wholly accurate to describe himself as a complete failure in every way, and would have to acknowledge that it was not.

In 'guiding discovery', by contrast, the therapist, rather than focusing on demonstrating the illogicality or erroneousness of a specific belief, asks questions that lead clients to discover new, alternative, wider views of situations that the therapist may not actually know in advance. For example, a client expressing the view that he was a complete failure in every way might be questioned in a way that would open the possibility of his taking constructive action in a problem area that had contributed to his sense of being a total failure.

Padesky expresses a firm conviction of the superiority of the guided discovery approach, a view apparently shared by the overwhelming majority of experienced cognitive therapists. And yet, as Padesky points out, there are many clinical vignettes in the literature (even in Beck et al., 1979!) that imply that cognitive therapy consists primarily of changing minds; a therapist and client working to reveal logical flaws in the client's thought process: One-two-three-aha!

The clinical cognitive model underlying cognitive therapy suggests that belief in the meaning of negative depressive thoughts leads to depression. Bearing this in mind, the fact that the authors of cognitive therapy texts include many vignettes of 'changing mind' questioning to invalidate specific beliefs is hardly surprising. And yet, there is a considerable consensus for Padesky's views on the limited value of this approach.

As if this were not curious enough, Padesky (1993, p. 6) goes on to say: 'Theoretically, I can't accept that the goal of Socratic questioning is to change client's beliefs.' Anticipating the puzzled reaction to this assertion, she continues: 'Why not? Isn't change in beliefs one of the primary goals of cognitive therapy?' and responds to her own question: 'Yes . . . and no.'

It is clear that the transformation of meaning in cognitive therapy may involve something more than the invalidation of specific negative beliefs. Equally, it seems that change in 'intellectual' belief may be insufficient, and that therapeutic change may require shifts at the 'gut level' of 'emotional' belief.

I shall suggest that the inadequacies of 'changing minds' and of failing to make a *qualitative* distinction between intellectual and emotional belief are linked, and that a more formal level of analysis of the cognitive change processes involved may help clarify some of the apparently puzzling features of clinically derived cognitive accounts. In order to elaborate these suggestions, it is first necessary to describe a framework within which a more formal analysis can be developed, Interacting Cognitive Subsystems (ICS).

INTERACTING COGNITIVE SUBSYSTEMS (ICS)

ICS is a comprehensive information-processing framework that provides a vehicle for developing accounts of a wide range of phenomena. Originally developed within mainstream cognitive science by Barnard, he and I have collaborated to develop this approach and to apply it to understanding depression. ICS is a complex approach, described in detail in a book (Teasdale & Barnard, 1993) and a number of papers (Barnard & Teasdale, 1991; Teasdale, 1993; Teasdale, Segal & Williams, 1995; Teasdale, 1996). Here, I shall only sketch out aspects of direct relevance to the current topic.

ICS is based on four essentially simple ideas. The first is that we have to recognise the existence of qualitatively different kinds of information or mental codes. Each of these codes represents a distinct aspect of experience. Amongst these different kinds of information, ICS distinguishes codes related to two kinds of meaning, a relatively specific and a more generic. This distinction is central to our present discussion and will be considered in greater detail shortly.

The second basic idea is that there are processes that transform information from one kind of code to another. These transformations are learned on the basis of regularities and co-variations in the patterns of information codes encountered in an individual's experience. Information processing consists of sequences of these transformation operations.

The third idea is that each kind of information has its own memory store, there being separate memory systems for each of the different mental codes. For example, following a conversation, multiple memories of the same event will exist. In the speech-level memory store there will be representations corresponding to the actual words uttered during the conversation. In the store for specific meanings will be representations corresponding to the specific meanings derived from those words. And in the high-level meaning store there will be representations corresponding to the high-level interpretations created in relation to the total conversation experience, for example, of threat, attraction or hidden agendas.

Finally, ICS involves a cognitive architecture in which the transformation processes and the different memory stores are arranged in nine cognitive subsystems. Each subsystem is specialised for processing input in a given information code. The total architecture works according to a limited number of defined principles of operation.

MEANING IN ICS

ICS recognises two levels of meaning, a specific and a more generic level. Patterns of Propositional code represent specific meanings in terms of discrete concepts and the relationships between them, for example, the specific meaning behind the speech form 'Roger has brown hair'. Meaning at this level can be grasped relatively easily as there is a fairly direct relationship between language and concepts at this level. Propositional meanings have a truth value that can be assessed. That is, they convey information about specific states of the world that can be verified by reference to evidence.

Patterns of Implicational code represent a more generic, holistic, level of meaning. Meaning at this level is difficult to convey because it does not map directly onto language. Traditionally, attempts to convey such holistic meanings by language have taken the form of poems, parables and stories. Meanings at this level represent deep regularities, themes, interrelationships, and prototypical features extracted from the patterns of specific meanings and sensory features that recur across experiences that share deep similarities, even though they may be superficially different. ICS proposes that only this generic level of meaning is directly linked to emotion. Implicational meanings cannot be evaluated as simply true or false in the same way that more specific Propositional meanings can.

Coherent patterns of implicational code represent schematic mental models of experience. Mental models, in general, represent interrelationships between semantic elements (Johnson-Laird, 1983; Power & Champion, 1986). Schematic models represent inter-relationships between generic features of experience, capturing, as implicit knowledge, high-level recurring regularities in the world, the body and 'the mind'. From such knowledge, schematic models produce outputs reflecting the implications derived from the state of the information that they have taken as input.

ICS suggests that, subjectively, synthesis of generic meanings is marked by experience of particular holistic 'senses' or 'feelings' with implicit meaning content: 'something wrong', 'confidence', 'on the right track', 'hopelessness'. For example, a sense of confidence marks the creation of schematic models associated with themes of competence, worth, optimism and positive expectancy.

In relation to the self, Propositional meanings refer to aspects of the self-as-object, whereas Implicational meanings are associated with different experiences of self-as-subject. From this perspective, the same words 'I am worthless' can refer to two, qualitatively distinct meanings; at the specific Propositional level the meaning is 'there is nothing of worth about me as an object'; at the Implicational level, the feeling 'I am worthless' marks the processing of a much more generic representation related to themes extracted from experiences in which an individual has been humiliated or rejected.

Reflecting the fact that patterns of Implicational code represent recurring patterns extracted across all other codes, sensory features, such as tone of voice or proprioceptive feedback from facial expression or bodily arousal, make a direct contribution to Implicational meanings, together with patterns of specific meanings. So, the higher-order meanings we derive from the specific meanings conveyed in what someone is telling us may be directly influenced by the actual sounds of the words, whether the speaker's voice tone is tense and strained, rather than warm and relaxed, and whether, at a bodily level, we are calm and alert rather than tired and uncomfortable.

Some 'feel' for representations at the Implicational level can be gained by considering the analogy between a sentence and a poem. A sentence conveys one or more specific meanings by appropriate arrangements of letters or words in the appropriate sequence. A poem conveys 'holistic' meanings, that cannot be conveyed by single sentences, by arranging sentences in appropriate sequences, together, very importantly, with appropriate direct sensory contributions from the sounds of the words, the rhythms and metres of the whole, and from the visual imagery elicited.

The total meaning conveyed by a poem is *qualitatively* different from the sum of the separate specific meanings, just as the meaning of a sentence is qualitatively different from that of its component letters or words. This is illustrated in Figure 9.1, where an extract of a poem is presented. The holistic meaning created by the poetry is marked by a 'sense' of melancholy and abandonment. Figure 9.1 also includes (italicised) a 'prose' version which retains the same sequence of specific level

'Oh what can ail thee, knight-at-arms

Alone and palely loitering?

The sedge has wither'd from the lake

And no birds sing.'

'What is the matter, armed old-fashioned soldier,

standing by yourself and doing nothing with a pallid expression?

The reed-like plants have decomposed by the lake

and there are not any birds singing.'

Figure 9.1   Poetry as Implicational meaning. The original poem in the upper part of the table and the alternative version in the lower part have the same sequence of Propositional meanings. However, only the original version conveys a coherent Implicational 'sense' (from Teasdale & Barnard, 1993)

meanings, but the ways in which they are expressed lack the coherence, evocative sound qualities and imagery of the poem. The total effect of the prose version is quite different.

Figure 9.1 can also be used to illustrate the 'implicit' knowledge inherent in the schematic models created by the poem. If one reads the poetry aloud, gets the 'sense' that it conveys, and then answers the question: 'Would he be fun to meet at a party?', one can answer the question very directly and immediately by consulting the implicit knowledge of the schematic model constructed. By contrast, if one reads the 'prose' version and then answers the question, most likely one will have to do this piecemeal, considering each of the propositions in turn and arriving at a judgement more slowly and 'rationally'.

ICS AND EMOTION

According to ICS, affect-related schematic models play a central role in the production and maintenance of emotional states. In the same way that Implicational schematic models, in general, encode features extracted as prototypical from classes of experience, emotion-related schematic models encode features extracted as prototypical of previous situations eliciting a given emotion. When, subsequently, patterns of Implicational code corresponding to such models are synthesised, the corresponding emotion is produced. So, for example, synthesis of schematic models encoding themes extracted as prototypical of previous depressing situations, such as ['globally negative view of self'] or ['hopeless, highly aversive, uncontrollable situation that will persist indefinitely'], will lead to production of a current depressed emotional state.

Within ICS, the ability to elicit directly an emotional response is restricted to affect-related schematic models; emotion-related representations in other information codes only contribute to emotion production to the extent that they feed the production of such models. Relatedly, ICS restricts the capacity to elicit emotion to generic level meanings; more specific meanings, even if they have emotionally relevant content, cannot, themselves, elicit emotion (Teasdale, 1993).

Consistent with the ICS analysis, reviews of existing experimental studies of mood-related biases in memory and judgement suggest that such biases are more easily explained by accounts that link affect to generic levels of representation than by accounts that link affect to more specific levels of representation, e.g. to changes in construct accessibility (Teasdale & Barnard, 1993). Empirical studies of depressive thinking directly investigating this issue have also supported the ICS position (Teasdale et al., 1995; Sheppard & Teasdale, 1996).

ICS AND THE TRANSFORMATION OF MEANING IN PSYCHOLOGICAL THERAPIES

The ICS analysis suggests that synthesis of an affect-related Implicational schematic model is the immediate antecedent to the production of an emotional response. It follows that the primary task of psychological treatments is to create, in situations that might otherwise elicit maladaptive emotions, alternative schematic models (generic, implicit meanings) that do not produce dysfunctional emotional reactions. A number of aspects of this process can be distinguished.

Changing Affect-related Schematic Models

Affect-evoking schematic models can be thought of as coherent patterns of elements of Implicational code. These elements will reflect both patterns of specific meanings (derived from current environmental events, and from 'internal' processing), and direct contributions from patterns of internal and external sensory input. In the case of depression, an important sensory source will be internal, proprioceptive sensory input related to posture, facial expression, psychomotor retardation, etc.

The production of alternative schematic models (holistic meanings) involves creating new patterns of Implicational code by changes to the elements that contribute to the total pattern. As with changing the meaning of a sentence, this could be achieved by rearranging existing elements (letters/words), adding new elements, and/or replacing old elements. The synthesis of alternative meanings (models) in therapy depends on creating new patterns of Implicational elements that *cohere* together, on the basis of a history of past co-occurrences. Simply assembling a new, arbitrary, pattern of Implicational elements may produce something more like the italicised version of the poem in Figure 9.1, that will not act as an alternative model, or meaning, that will be of much therapeutic benefit. In other words, the task of the therapist is more like that of the poet than of the prose writer. That may be why it is not easy to be a good therapist.

Making small changes to the sequence of letters making up a sentence can radically alter the specific meaning it represents (e.g. 'the man said "go on"' *versus* 'the man said "no go"'). In the same way, changing just a small portion of a total pattern of Implicational code may be sufficient to alter radically the high-level meaning represented, and change emotional response. The ICS analysis suggests that it may well be therapeutically useful to make changes to one or more specific meanings if they alter the total pattern of Implicational code sufficiently to create a new higher-level meaning. For example, for someone who has synthesised the high-level meaning ['self-as-a-total-failure'] following failure in an examination, helping them discover that 95% of other candidates also failed may create changes in the related parts of the total Implicational pattern that, although limited, are sufficient to create a radically different higher-order meaning.

Equally, the ICS analysis suggests that high-level meanings can be altered by modifying purely sensory elements. The higher-order meaning that I create following a failure experience may be quite different if I combine the specific failure-related meanings with the elements related to the sensory feedback from a smiling facial expression rather than a frown, or from high bodily arousal and an erect posture rather than from a sluggish body-state and bowed, stooped posture. The ICS analysis suggests a very useful place for purely physical interventions, such as training in maintaining a half-smiling expression, or vigorous physical exercise, in the cognitive therapy of depression.

More often, it may be necessary to alter more than single elements of depression-related Implicational code patterns in order to transform depressogenic patterns into those related to more adaptive high-order meanings. Interventions may be needed that create alternative, coherent, 'packages' of semantically and sensorily derived elements. Guided imagery can be seen as such an intervention. For example, in the treatment of victims of early sexual abuse, clients relive, in imagery, scenes of childhood abuse but introduce into the images the elements of control and power that they now have as adults but lacked as children, at the time of the abuse. Such imagery clearly has no worth as evidence for refuting specific Propositional meanings. However, from the ICS perspective, it can be seen as potentially a very powerful way of introducing new elements into a pattern of Implicational code to create new coherent higher-order meanings that allow clients to free themselves from the domination of dysfunctional childhood schematic models.

The ICS analysis suggests that, in order to achieve change at the level of schematic models, it may not be sufficient simply to gather data *about* experience and to evaluate beliefs against this evidence. Rather, it may be necessary to arrange for actual experiences in which new or modified models are created. As far as self-related models are concerned, this would mean changes in the patient's actual way of *being*, rather than the detached consideration of evidence for or against beliefs related to self-as-object, described in some accounts of schema change procedures in cognitive therapy.

For example, although dispassionately reviewing evidence of previous successes might be an appropriate way to invalidate the specific propositional belief 'I am a total failure as a person', this would probably not be an effective way to create alternative self-related schematic models. The recall of previous success experiences that might be involved in such reviews might achieve change in affect-related models, but only if recall was associated with re-experience of success-related positive affect, marking access to the related positive self-models stored in memory. Alternatively, enactive procedures could be used to create, on-line, success- or mastery-related schematic models. On the other hand, it might also be important to help clients, at times when they feel that they are total failures, to relate to themselves more gently and kindly, in that way creating a store of alternative models related to failure.

Lasting Effects of Treatment

I have outlined ways in which the pattern of elements comprising affect-related schematic models may be changed so that more adaptive models are synthesised and dysfunctional emotional responses are altered. I have focused on strategies that might be used in therapy sessions in the consulting room or in 'the real world'. How do the changes in models achieved in therapy sessions generalise to other situations, and how are enduring effects of treatment mediated?

According to the ICS analysis, lasting effects of therapy will depend on clients synthesising alternative, adaptive, schematic models in emotive situations, long after therapy sessions are over. How is this to be achieved? The ICS analysis suggests that such lasting effects depend on accessing representations of adaptive schematic models stored in Implicational memory.

For example, the treatment of depression involves arranging situations in which patients approach symptoms of depression, and related experiences, with a different 'mind-set', e.g. when depressed feelings arise, looking out for negative thoughts with a view to assessing their validity or usefulness; or approaching difficult situations as problems-to-be-investigated-and-solved. According to the present analysis, these procedures create a store of modified depression-related models. These alternative models can then be accessed, subsequently, in similar contexts, pre-empting access to depressogenic models and the re-establishment of depression.

This analysis suggests that structured psychological treatments for depression, both cognitive therapy and behavioural approaches, achieve their long-term effects through the creation of a store of memories of alternative depression-related models (Teasdale & Barnard, 1993, Chapter 16; Teasdale, Segal & Williams, 1995). Homework assignments are important because they ensure that these modified models are created in association with a wide range of contexts. Consequently, the chances of these contexts subsequently accessing these alternative models are increased.

Clinical observation suggests that cognitive therapy often leads to a shift in perspective, sometimes referred to as 'decentring' or 'disidentification'; patients move to a wider perspective on their symptoms and problems in which, rather than simply 'being' their emotion, or identifying personally with negative thoughts and feelings, patients relate to negative experiences as mental events in a wider context or field of awareness. In terms of the present analysis, this shift involves the creation of alternative schematic models; patients create models related to themes such as: [depression-as-a-psychological-state-in-which-I-see-myself-as-worthless], in contrast to models related to depressogenic themes such as: [the-reality-of-my-worthlessness-and-the-hopelessness-of-the-current-situation].

On this view, an important aspect of answering negative automatic thoughts may not be the extent to which beliefs in specific thoughts are modified as much as the fact that the thought-answering exercise implicitly creates a modified mind-set or model. This alternative model embodies a different view and relationship to depressive experience in general: 'thoughts and feelings as mental events that can be considered and examined' rather than 'thoughts as self-evident facts'. Similarly, the important feature of behavioural experiments in cognitive therapy may

not be so much the actual 'evidence', in the shape of specific facts, tha
they yield, so much as the fact that they implicitly create a 'set' which
involves a different relationship to difficult experiences; 'problems to be
considered, approached, and investigated' rather than 'further evidence
of my inadequacy and the hopelessness of my position'.

'INTELLECTUAL' AND 'EMOTIONAL' BELIEF, 'CHANGING MINDS' AND 'GUIDING DISCOVERY' REVISITED

The ICS analysis suggests that 'intellectual' and 'emotional' beliefs refer
to *qualitatively* different kinds of meaning that stand in different relation
ships to emotion.

'Intellectual' beliefs are at the level of specific Propositional meaning
they have a truth value that can be assessed; they are not directly influ
enced by aspects of sensory level information (e.g. the voice tone in which
a verbal message is conveyed); and they have no direct link to emotion
production, any link being indirect through their contribution, as one of a
number of elements, to affect-related schematic models.

'Emotional' beliefs are at the level of generic Implicational meaning
corresponding to schematic models extracted from emotive experiences
they do not have a specific truth value that can be assessed; they can
reflect contributions from a wide variety of sources, including multiple
patterns of specific meanings, and patterns of direct sensory input; syn
thesis of schematic models with emotive themes and prototypical pat
terns is the immediate antecedent to emotion production. The suggestion
within the ICS analysis, that sensory inputs, particularly from the body
make a direct and important contribution to affect-related schematic
models is particularly interesting in relation to the predominance o
bodily terms in the language used to describe 'emotional' belief: 'gut
level' knowledge; knowing 'with the heart'; knowing 'in one's bones'
'feelings'; 'senses'; 'felt senses', etc.

In making this qualitative distinction between forms of meaning, or be
lief, the ICS analysis contrasts with the position of Beck et al. (1979), re
ferred to earlier. I believe the ICS analysis accords more closely with clinica
impression, and has direct implications for treatment strategies (Teasdale
1993). Among these is a clearer perspective on the ways in which Socratic
questioning can most usefully lead to lasting therapeutic change.

'Changing minds' involves reducing the patient's problem to agree
ment with a specific negative belief, and then, by using questioning to
conduct a focused review of directly relevant evidence, attempting to
change the truth value attached to that belief. This makes sense if the

therapist is operating from a cognitive model which views belief in such specific negative thoughts as the antecedent to the depressive emotional response ('thoughts and beliefs lead to emotion', as it was expressed, above (p. 142) in the quotation from Beck et al., 1979).

In ICS terms, 'changing minds' involves attempting to modify negative meanings at the specific, Propositional, level. As the ultimate goal, from the ICS perspective, is to effect change at the more generic, Implicational, level of meaning, related to schematic models of experience, 'changing minds' could be seen as directing one's therapeutic efforts to the wrong level of cognitive representation. In particular, it is possible that the patient may use words such as 'I am a total failure as a person' as a verbal tag to refer to the experience of processing schematic models related to that theme. If the therapist wrongly regards the patient's statement as an expression of a specific, Propositional, belief and then proceeds to evaluate its truth value against relevant evidence, therapeutic effort may simply be misapplied.

None the less, 'changing minds' may, sometimes, have beneficial effects. First, as already discussed, in some situations, changing only a small fragment of a total pattern of Implicational code, such as that related to a limited number of specific meanings, may be sufficient to create significant change in the wider pattern. Second, as we have also noted, the 'non-specific' effect of identifying and evaluating negative thoughts as mental events that can be considered and evaluated, rather than as self-evident truths, may be important. Frequently repeated, such 'thought-answering' may lead to a more general 'decentring' shift in the schematic models through which negative thinking is viewed; patients achieve the 'insights' that 'thoughts aren't facts' or that 'I am not my thoughts'.

Unfortunately, these ways in which 'changing minds' may be useful are offset by a potential for harmful effects which is inherent in this method. This is that the process of revealing the illogicality or invalidity of a specific negative belief may, through its effects on the wider pattern of specific meanings and sensory inputs created by the questioning process, simply add more fuel to support continued production of schematic models related to personal failure: 'Not only am I depressed, I can't even think straight, either'. Attention to the wider semantic context, which follows naturally from the ICS proposal that the key action is at the Implication level, is likely to maintain therapist's sensitivity to this possibility. By contrast, the narrow, 'laser beam', focus of semantic awareness that is naturally associated with therapeutic efforts concentrated exclusively on changing specific Propositional meanings, may mean that therapists are less sensitive to such possibilities.

'Guiding discovery' uses questioning to elicit information that allows the patient to 'reframe' her or his view of a problematic area. For example, in the detailed transcript of 'guided discovery' provided by Padesky (1993), the therapist uses questioning to take the patient from his initial statement 'I'm no good' to the actual situation that triggered that feeling (adverse comparison of his own fathering behaviour with that of his non-depressed brother); to specification of what better fathering might involve ('talk to the children more, encourage them'); to acceptance of the possibility that he might still be able to do some of these things, even when depressed; and, finally, to agreeing to engage in the experiment of trying to increase these behaviours for a week. In ICS terms, this would be seen as a progressive modification of the prevailing schematic mental model from one related to themes of global personal inadequacy to one related to themes of problem investigation and attempted solution.

The ICS analysis proposes that the key action, as far as affect generation is concerned, is at the level of generic schematic models, rather than the more specific level of Propositional meanings. From this perspective, the central effective process in psychological treatments is changing the pattern of Implicational code, so that the total pattern is re-configured from one corresponding to a schematic model engendering maladaptive emotion, to an alternative, more functional model. It is clear why, from this perspective, use of Socratic questioning to guide discovery is preferable to its use to change minds. Not only does the central 'action' of 'guided discovery' appear to be at the more appropriate level of meaning, but also this use of questioning emphasises the synthesis of *alternative*, adaptive models and meanings, rather than simply the invalidation of existing maladaptive specific meanings.

Finally, it is of interest to bring the ICS analysis to bear on Padesky's intriguing statement, already mentioned: 'Theoretically, I can't accept that the goal of Socratic questioning is to change client's beliefs. Why not? Isn't change in beliefs one of the primary goals of cognitive therapy? Yes . . . and no.' The full quotation continues: 'While changing beliefs is often very therapeutic, I worry about the therapeutic costs if belief change *by any means* is the goal. Our theoretical underpinnings in cognitive therapy are that we are to be collaboratively empirical' (Padesky, 1993, p. 6; original emphasis).

Why should collaborative empiricism be so important? First, we can note that it would, hopefully, reduce the possible adverse effects of questioning with a narrow, 'laser-beam' focus, which we have already discussed. These effects are, presumably, the 'therapeutic costs' to which Padesky refers.

The second virtue of collaborative empiricism may be less obvious. This is that, from the ICS perspective, the alternative patterns and models created at the Implicational level within therapy will be influenced by the total therapeutic situation. This situation will include both the relationship with the therapist, and the relationship to negative thinking that is enacted or 'modelled' between patient and therapist.

I have suggested that a very general 'decentring' shift from views that regard negative thoughts and feelings as 'realities', or identical with the 'self', to models that regard thoughts and feelings as 'mental events in the field of awareness' may be one of the most important and wide-ranging shifts in models that occurs in the course of therapy. In other words, the key shift may be in models to do with how to relate to unpleasant thoughts and feelings. The relationship to mental events modelled by the therapist as he or she deals with them in collaboration with the client is likely to be a powerful influence on such models. The type of relationship to such events that it would be most helpful to incorporate into alternative models is exactly the kind of friendly, interested, but 'unattached' approach to thoughts and feelings modelled in patient–therapist relationships characterised as 'collaborative and empirical'. This may be why these characteristics are afforded such importance in cognitive therapy.

CONCLUSION

Theoretical analyses cannot provide therapists with precise, detailed, 'prescriptions' for exactly what to do in any particular therapeutic encounter. Indeed, it is inherent in the theoretical analysis that has been presented that the quality of therapists' 'artistry', based on extended experience, and 'intuitive' skills, is of critical importance in assisting clients to synthesise the alternative, coherent, schematic mental models that are required for therapeutic change.

None the less, theoretical analyses that can articulate central change processes with some precision may provide invaluable strategic and tactical guidance to therapists on the ways in which they should use their skills. For example, it is possible that the kind of explicit analysis that has been presented will help therapists clarify, in their own minds, exactly what they are attempting to do when they use Socratic questioning.

Perhaps an even more important argument for more precise theoretical analyses is that, without them, it may not be possible to explicate our ideas on therapeutic change processes sufficiently clearly for them to be subjected to detailed empirical investigation. History suggests that, in the long term, this may be the most effective route through which to achieve further gains in therapeutic effectiveness and efficiency.

REFERENCES

Barnard, P.J. & Teasdale, J.D. (1991). Interacting cognitive subsystems: A systemic approach to cognitive–affective interaction and change. *Cognition and Emotion*, 5, 1–39.

Beck, A.T., Rush, A.J., Shaw, B.F. & Emery, G. (1979). *Cognitive Therapy of Depression*. New York: Guilford Press.

Johnson-Laird, P.N. (1983). *Mental Models*. Cambridge: Cambridge University Press.

Padesky, C.A. (1993). *Socratic questioning: changing minds or guiding discovery?* Keynote address to European Congress of Behavioural and Cognitive Therapies, London, 24 September, 1993.

Power, M.J. & Champion, L.A. (1986). Cognitive approaches to depression: A theoretical critique. *British Journal of Clinical Psychology*, 25, 201–212.

Sheppard, L.C. & Teasdale, J.D. (1996). Depressive thinking: changes in schematic mental models of self and world. *Psychological Medicine*, 1996, 26, 1043–1051.

Teasdale, J.D. (1993). Emotion and two kinds of meaning: Cognitive therapy and applied cognitive science. *Behaviour Research and Therapy*, 31, 339–354.

Teasdale, J.D. (1996). Clinically relevant theory: integrating clinical insight with cognitive science. In P. Salkovskis (ed), *Frontiers of Cognitive Therapy*, New York: Guilford.

Teasdale, J.D. & Barnard, P.J. (1993). *Affect, Cognition and Change: Remodelling Depressive Thought*. Hove: Lawrence Erlbaum Associates.

Teasdale, J.D., Segal, Z.V. & Williams, J.M.G. (1995). How does cognitive therapy prevent depressive relapse and why should attentional control (mindfulness) training help? *Behaviour Research and Therapy*, 33, 25–39.

Teasdale, J.D., Taylor, M.J., Cooper, Z., Hayhurst, H. & Paykel, E.S. (1995). Depressive thinking: shifts in construct accessibility or in schematic mental models? *Journal of Abnormal Psychology*, 104, 500–507.

Chapter 10

EMOTION IN THE CREATION OF PERSONAL MEANING

Leslie S. Greenberg* and Juan Pascual-Leone*

In this chapter we will argue that emotion serves an organizing role in human experience and that the creation of personal meaning involves an ongoing dialectic between two streams of consciousness: consciously mediated conceputalization on the one hand, and automatic, immediate emotional experiencing on the other—a dialectic between reason and emotion, explanation and direct experience (Gendlin, 1962; 1964; 1968; Greenberg & Safran, 1987; Greenberg, Rice & Elliott, 1993; Guidano, 1987; 1991; 1995; Mahoney, 1991). Therapy thus needs to help clients attend to their emotional experience in order to create new meaning.

Human beings are active processing organizations. They generate a unified stream of consciousness by the dynamic synthesis of a variety of levels of information processing and a variety of cognitive/affective schemes (Pascual-Leone, 1990a; Pascual-Leone & Irwin, 1994; Pascual-Leone & Johnson, 1991). Lower-level, sensory-motor, and higher-level, emotion schematic and conceptual structures process information outside awareness, and synthesize it into a unified whole to produce experience. Experience may then be consciously symbolized in language and finally explained by propositional reasoning in a coherent manner. This form of synthesized consciousness, where personal meaning is generated by an ordering of a person's internal experience, provides a person's lived sense of reality and is the target and goal of therapeutic discourse.

*York University, North York, Canada

The Transformation of Meaning in Psychological Therapies.
Edited by Mick Power and Chris R. Brewin. © 1997 John Wiley & Sons Ltd.

EMOTIONS: A PRIMARY MEANING SYSTEM

Affect is a neuropsychologically independent means of informing individuals, through visceral sensations and action tendencies, of their unconscious evaluative responses with regard to body, self and world. Emotion gives people feedback about what is important and meaningful, what is good or bad for them. It is a meaning system that informs people of the significance of events to their well-being. Dysfunction in the ability to access emotional information disconnects people from one of their most adaptive-meaning production and orienting systems (Greenberg & Safran, 1984; 1987; 1989). The emotion system is thus a crucial focus of attention and target of change. It needs to be attended to for its adaptive information, and evoked and restructured when maladaptive.

Recent developments in neuroscience suggest that the emotional processing of simple sensory features occurs extremely early in the processing sequence. This occurs as inputs to the emotional brain (the subcortical amygdala) are received from the thalamus. This information is processed prior to the construction of real-world objects and analysis of events from simple sensory stimuli by the cortex. The amygdala also receives inputs from the cortex, but this occurs only after information is first received from the thalamus. This suggests the operation of a second level of emotional appraisal involving complex perceptions and concepts received from the cortex following a more immediate 'intuitive' appraisal by the emotional brain from the initial input (LeDoux, 1993). As LeDoux (1993) emphasized, the initial 'pre-cognitive' emotional processing is highly adaptive because it allows people to respond quickly to important events before complex and time-consuming processing has taken place. Thus it is adaptive to jump back quickly from a sinuous-looking form in the forest, even if, on closer analysis, one discovers that it is a circular branch rather than a snake. Preconscious apprehension of a pattern therefore generates emotion. Therapy needs to work with this precognitive apprehending process if it wishes to access people's constructions of their lived world.

Research in the bioevolutionary domain suggests that there are a number of innate, primary, biologically adaptive emotions, each with a characteristic action tendency and facial expression (Ekman & Friesen, 1975; Izard, 1977). Different action tendencies correspond to different emotions. For example, fear is associated with the mobilization for flight, while anger involves the urge to attack, repel or break free. Examples of primary emotions include sadness, fear, joy, disgust and anger. With their attendant action tendencies, primary emotions are thus 'hard-wired' expressive-motor responses that mobilize the individual for adaptive action, and convey pertinent information to others. Primary emotions focus attention, interrupt other behavioral and cognitive activities, and prepare the organism for the execution of adaptive action. Other, more complex emotions, like pride and jealousy, are less obviously associated with concrete or particular action tendencies, or with facial expressions. Instead, these emotions are defined more by a given context or script but are still based on appraisals of the relevance of a situation to a need/goal/concern, are motivational in nature and inform us of the significance of events to us.

Emotion is thus a primary meaning system. Emotions are like barometers of meaning providing affective feedback on states of body and mind. Primary emotions can be viewed as biologically based adaptive relational action tendencies resulting from the appraisal of a situation in terms of a concern or need (Frijda, 1986; Greenberg & Korman, 1993; Greenberg & Safran, 1987; 1989; Oatley & Jenkins, 1992; Safran & Greenberg, 1991). Emotions give us information about what concerns us, and evaluate the significance of events to our well-being. The generation of much emotional experience is driven initially by automatic processes that produce primary responses following simple perceptual appraisals (Greenberg & Korman, 1993; Scherer, 1984). Automatic processes are followed immediately by more complex activity in which sensory, memorial and ideational information is integrated, yielding a felt sense of our self and of the world. This higher-level synthesis of a variety of levels of processing has been referred to as an 'emotion scheme', and has been identified as a principal target of intervention and therapeutic change (Greenberg, Rice & Elliott, 1993; Greenberg & Paivio, in press).

Emotions are important in therapy because they tell people something about their automatic appraisals of themselves and their worlds, inform them that an important need, value or goal may be advanced or harmed in a situation (Frijda, 1986), and are involved in setting goal priorities (Oatley & Jenkins, 1992). Promoting clients' access to their emotions in therapy serves a number of important functions. First, it provides the therapist and the client with information about the meaning to them of events, and also about the client's needs, desires, beliefs and values. Second, access to emotions guides decision-making and action as it helps set priorities about what requires immediate attention and what actions should be performed. Third, access to emotion tells clients when there is something wrong, and this awareness of existential/experiential problems motivates problem-solving. Finally, expression of unexpressed or stifled emotional responses helps access dysfunctional beliefs and can mobilize unexpressed needs and goals that address the future (Greenberg & Korman, 1993; Greenberg & Paivio, in press). Therapy therefore needs to access and work with emotions in different ways depending on the type of emotion and its function (Greenberg & Safran, 1987; Greenberg & Paivio, in press).

A DIALECTICAL CONSTRUCTIVIST VIEW

In a dialectical-constructive view (Greenberg & Pascual-Leone, 1995; Greenberg, Rice & Elliott, 1993; Pascual-Leone, 1980; 1983; 1984; 1987; 1990a; 1990b; 1991; Watson & Greenberg, 1996) emotions are seen as the primary generator of personal meaning. Personal meaning involves the self-organization and explication of one's own emotional experience. It involves an integration of the head and the heart. Personal meaning is generated ultimately by a conscious cognitive explaining function acting on emotional experience to construct different 'selves' at different times (Hermans, Kempen & Van Loon, 1992); and it does so by drawing on a variety of sources and levels of information. People constantly represent themselves to themselves and to others in images, actions and narratives; they continuously construct views of themselves in consciousness.

In our view consciousness is a significant arbiter of meaning by way of selecting the source of information attended to, and the interpretation to be favoured. This partly conscious process involves components of *will* and *choice*; with them, people bring their effortful mental attention under the control of internal executive-like processes. Will operates essentially by allocating attention to schemes *not* activated in a situation so that they can override schemes activated in the situation. By being able to regulate their attentional allocation people are therefore able to be agents in the construction of their experience. Consciousness, however, is influenced by a number of other factors: by immediate emotional experience, by deliberate, controlled, processing, and by such factors as the salience of certain external stimuli, the views and attitudes of others toward self, the past responses of the self in similar situations, and many other factors. Consciousness is the arena for a final dialectical synthesis of different sources of sensory, kinaesthetic, emotional, cognitive, and conceptual information about the self and the world, and provides for an element of self-determination. This occurs as the person encounters and resolves felt contradictions between aspects of self, and between self and world, and organizes these into a particular view of reality.

People are not simply passive information-processing systems determined by inputs. Driven by affect, they are active constructors of meaning. By attending to certain elements of information and disattending from some, or interrupting the emergence of others they can create truly novel performances and configurations of experience. Therapists in turn engage with clients in this process, influencing what clients attend to and the meaning they make of this, thereby becoming co-constructors in the meaning-making process.

In summary, self-organizing, tacit (unconscious) processes therefore produce a performance, or an experienced sense of self, a sense that is experienced by us as simply 'happening' to us. Consciousness then often selects aspects to amplify or symbolize. This interaction produces our final view of ourselves. At any moment, there are always more processes occurring in the internal field than can be simultaneously symbolized into complete consciousness. Generally it is only aspects that are consistent with a preferred view of self that are so amplified and symbolized. The individual is thus continually constructing a particular view of self by constantly selecting some elements of experience (internal or external) and ignoring other aspects. Meaning, emerging from these selected processes, is therefore neither simply imposed by language and consciousness, nor is it wholly contained in automatic 'raw' experience. Rather, it results from repeated dialectical synthesis of the many different levels of information processing. Conscious construction of meaning is continually guided by an implicit emotionally based 'felt sense' of meaning, and culminates perhaps in the capturing of this 'felt sense', often in language.

THE INTERNAL DIALECTICS OF MEANING MAKING

The Three Vital Moments

Construction of conscious personal meaning involves three vital moments of importance in therapy (Watson & Greenberg, 1996): first, the synthesis of a feeling, or 'felt sense'; second, a moment of attending to this bodily felt sense and consciously symbolizing it to form a subjective reality; third, a moment of generating explanations of the symbolized experience to produce a coherent narrative and/or conceptualized self-identity. It is the combination of these three processes of attending to and synthesizing feeling, symbolizing and explaining, that leads in therapy and life to the stable construction of new views of self and reality. Each of these moments offer different opportunities for therapeutic intervention.

Synthesis of bodily feelings

Not all emotions arise as discrete emotions, such as anger and sadness. Rather, with development, emotion schemes generate complex feelings based on the person's emotional learning history. These high-level feelings, one's sense of things or 'gut feelings', become available as a bodily felt referent to which one can attend to create meaning. A bodily felt sense or a feeling arises by means of the dynamic synthesis of an internal set of emotionally based schemes with other cognitive schemes activated in a particular situation. Imagine, for example, telling the story to a friend of an occurrence the previous evening—one of standing in line for a movie—and then turning around and suddenly seeing someone whom you either wished desperately to avoid or whom you were amorously longing to meet. Depending on which occurred you might be able to speak at length from two entirely different senses of internal complexity generated in the moment. You could talk about how you felt in, and about, this moment, drawing on all kinds of different images and explicating complex felt meanings and their implications. All these tacit meanings occurred in the field of internal complexity but were not necessarily processed consciously in the moment before opening your mouth and greeting the other person. What is said could be either coolly dismissing or charmingly disarming, if you have your wits about you, or it could be clumsily awkward, if you are overwhelmed by your own internal complexity. Thus, beyond the specific performance generated, there lies, at the periphery of awareness, a host of bodily felt meanings that, with attentional allocation, can be brought to focal awareness and articulated (James, 1895; Perls, Hefferline & Goodman, 1951).

The bodily felt referent (Gendlin, 1962), to which one can attend, and from which one speaks in order to unpack the host of situated meanings, is filled with the implications of the components of which it has been constituted. Thus in the case of seeing the desired person the situation is filled with one's feelings, wishes, hopes, dreams and evaluations of self-worth, including evaluations of one's looks, body, intelligence and social abilities, as well as many other idiosyncratic feelings and meanings. In the case of seeing the dreaded person, one's fears and resentments, evaluations of one's self-worth, competence, rights, abilities to deal with this aversive situation. The first step in therapy is focally to attend to one's bodily felt sense of experience. It is from this that meaning emerges and towards this that progressive attempts at symbolization reach.

Symbolizing and explaining

Within a dialectical perspective we view people not only as living their lives—the first stream of consciousness—but also as being compelled to evaluate and make meaning of their lives—the second stream. In order better to understand themselves, people continually symbolize and explain themselves to themselves—forming an ongoing narrative of who they are as they become. In this manner their stable identity emerges.

Symbolizing

Tacit or implicit meaning and the accompanying bodily felt sense, when attended to and symbolized in awareness, are referred to by therapists as 'experiencing' (Bohart, 1993; Gendlin, 1962; 1964; Greenberg, Rice & Elliott,

1993). This experiencing results from the automatic activation of schemes in the individual's repertoire. This experiential (holistic) processing of patterns of emotional relevance is different from a reflective (often sequential and propositional) level of conceptual processing (Epstein, 1993; Greenberg, Rice & Elliott, 1993). In experiential processing the bodily felt sense acts as a constraint on the possible conscious conceptual constructions that can satisfy it, eliminating many other possible meanings. A crucial part of this meaning-making process is the production of linguistic distinctions to express this implicit bodily felt sense of meaning. For instance, one might symbolize a given internal sense as 'feeling tired' or as 'feeling overwhelmed'. Both synthesized meanings reflect the experiential constraints in a way that saying that one is feeling 'happy' or 'afraid' would not. The symbols 'tired' or 'overwhelmed' are each adequate, but capture different aspects of the total experience. Conscious experience is thus not simply 'in' us, fully formed, rather it develops further as we put words to our feelings. How we articulate our feelings, most often in language, is thus crucial in the creation of new conscious experiential meaning.

Human nature does, however, have its own order, based on inborn emotional/motivational tendencies; it does not always follow the order imposed upon it by language and culture. Not any socially derived symbol can 'accurately' reflect a given experience. An 'inaccurate', externally imposed, symbol cannot create new lived experience, and it might ultimately cause greater disturbance and confusion if mistakenly accepted. People must be guided by their own emotionally based 'internal complexity' arising from interaction with the particularities of the situation. This internal complexity induces a 'bodily felt sense' of meaning (Gendlin, 1962; 1964; 1968), which must be attended to in therapy and symbolized to help conscious experience to unfold.

Explaining

Self-explanations of experience can be more or less veridical. A dramatic illustration of this is offered by Gazzaniga (1985) who showed in split-brain patients that the left hemisphere makes up rational, but false, reasons to explain actions verbally, driven, unknowingly, by the right hemisphere.

Once clients have expressed and clearly articulated their feelings, they are in a position to reflect on and evaluate their experiences and actions, in the light of current goals, needs and values. These activities produce cognitive reorganization. Pennebaker (1990) has shown that talking and writing about emotionally traumatic experience immediately cause a drop in skin conductance and blood pressure, and affect long-term health and immune function. Particularly striking are the results of subjects writing for 15 minutes a day, for four days, about the most traumatic experience of their lives. They consistently evidenced significant drops in the number of visits to physicians, and showed enhanced immune functioning. Analysing these subjects' essays, Pennebaker (Pennebaker & Traue, 1993) observed that the writing appears to force people to stand back and reorganize their thoughts and feelings. Subjects commented that the process of writing made them think things out and look at themselves from outside; it helped them sort out their thoughts. This report suggests that reflective elaboration and meaning creation are important therapeutic consequences of emotional expression. But to achieve them, psychotherapeutic interventions need to go beyond techniques that simply encourage emotional expression or self-disclosure; they also need to focus clients on the creation of new meaning of aroused emotional material.

In healthy meaning-making, people's self-reflections are based predominantly on their bodily felt sense, generated bottom-up by emotional and sensorimotor processing. Explaining, however, can also be based on more socially acquired cognitive schemes that were obtained from others or inferred from past experience. Although often useful, these may be sources of psychological difficulty. Those explanations that favour image maintenance over experience, and interfere with here and now perception, have been viewed as guided by 'learned conditions of worth' (Rogers, 1951) or 'introjects' (Perls, Hefferline & Goodman, 1951), or 'faulty assumptions' (Beck, 1976). Whenever identity is overly controlled by these determinants people are not grounded in their own primary experience, and dysfunction may result.

The synthesis

Infants' emotional systems are involved in rapid evaluation of what is good or bad for them. Thus infants, right from birth, experience feelings and, as soon as they can construct schemes of sufficient complexity, they use these feelings to construct a conscious personal sense of self. A major determinant of this self construction is their intersubjective experience, with their caretakers, associated with their own automatic emotional reactions. An individual's sense of self is primordially organized around emotional schemes formed in primary-attachment relationships. Affect regulation develops with maturation but also with the way caretakers react to the child's emotions; these experiences determine the affectively based sense of self. The views of others about one's emotional experience are synthesized with one's own internal experience to form emotion schematic records of self and circumstance. These emotional schemes become the core structures of the person and guide further growth. How one symbolizes one's internal states evolves in an intersubjective manner, and the 'I' comes to see itself as a particular 'me', mediated through others' views of, and responses to, the self (Guidano, 1987; 1995; Stern, 1985).

Language and bodily experience, derived respectively from culture and biology, therefore both play a critical role in constituting people's identities. Immediate experience influences, but is also influenced by, how identity is formulated. This circumstance sets language and experience in a circular causal relationship. Identity results from dynamic syntheses of direct experience with learned views of self. But people do not only synthesize self-representations. They also consciously examine them and select syntonic views of self and alternatives for action. Therapy thus involves, as a final step in the change process, the generation of new explanations, new narrative constructions that reorganize experience into a new view of self, past and future. This helps consolidate experienced change, and acts as a guide for future action.

Thus when a person experiences an event in life, such as not getting a hoped-for promotion or not receiving a grant, this may generate a complex bodily felt response. This response represents the synthesis of a host of emotion schemes. Attending to this the person may say 'I feel disappointed' or 'I expected this' but may continue to be plagued by a felt sense, not yet fully articulated. As the day proceeds the person may feel alternately numb or drained. Continued focusing on the felt sense can lead to further symbolization such as 'I have failed, I am never going to get where I was aiming'. Although this appears to be a feeling of defeat it may bring a real sense of relief. The person may feel lighter and clearer and acknowledge 'That's it, that's what I feel, I'm never going to get there'. Now a process of re-evaluation begins. The person begins to ask 'What do I really what? What is most important to me?' and begins to create a new view of self, of the past and of the future. This is a meaning-making step that involves emotional arousal, symbolizing and reflecting.

Psychotherapy and Emotional Meaning

A pivotal task of therapy is the symbolizing of subjective emotional experience, so as to understand it and unfold its implicit action tendencies (Greenberg, Rice & Elliott, 1993). The primary objectives of an emotionally focused approach to therapy are to evoke emotional experience in order to increase awareness of emotion and to integrate reason and emotion. These are the key processes in meaning construction (Greenberg, Rice & Elliott, 1993). In therapy clients are encouraged, in a safe environment, to focus their attention on their always evolving internal emotional experience, to symbolize it in words, with the aim of using this as an aid in solving specific cognitive-affective problems that are causing distress (Greenberg, Rice & Elliot, 1993).

Change in psychotherapy in our view results from the symbolization in awareness of truly novel experiential syntheses that occur tacitly. By attending to and reprocessing experience, new felt experience is synthesized and people just feel differently. Therapy involves attending to previously unacknowledged emotions for their adaptive information, such as when a client accesses and attends to the primary anger they felt at being abused or violated, an anger that was unable to be experienced at the time of maltreatment. This anger then acts to provide a new response to, and a new view of, the situation, a view that helps overcome a previous sense of helplessness. In addition, therapy often involves a process of activating and restructuring emotion schemes (Greenberg & Paivio, in press). Here, for example, maladaptive shame-based structures, such as feeling unworthy and ashamed, or anxiety-based structures, such as feeling insecure and afraid, are evoked in therapy in order to make them more amenable to change. Once evoked both the emotional response patterning and the dysfunctional beliefs embedded in these structures are restructured by exposing them to new information. Thus a client who was humiliated by her father may re-experience this shame in therapy, in an imaginary dialogue with the father, but may also come to access her disgust, anger and sadness associated with the experience. In our approach to treatment the challenge to old structures comes from access to alternative internal resources based on biologically adaptive feelings and needs in the personality. For example, the shamed client may access her needs for comfort through experiencing her sadness at the loss of parental protection and her needs for inviolacy through anger at her father's violation of her. Accessing these primary adaptive emotions and needs helps to restructure the person's weak or bad sense of self (Greenberg & Paivio, in press).

Emergence of new meaning is greatly facilitated by vivid evocation in therapy of emotionally laden experience; this helps bring emotions into contact with reflective processes. The integration of emotion and reflection is, in our view, the key to therapeutic change. Neither catharsis nor reasoning alone is sufficient. It is the ability to be aware of feelings that helps us regulate them. Our view, however, is not one of needing to improve control of emotions, rather it is that awareness of emotions allows people to integrate emotions with reason, providing a more balanced response than that dictated by emotion or reason alone.

Processes generating emotional experience occur independently of, and often prior to, conscious, cognitive operations. Therefore, working only at the cognitive level to effect affective/emotional change is likely to prove ineffectual. Instead, interventions need to target the emotion schematic processes that automatically generate emotional reactions and the felt sense of oneself in the world. Change in these schemes is produced by accessing them so they are 'up and running', and by making new information and experience available to them so that they accommodate (learn) to construct new adapted schemes (Greenberg & Safran, 1987; 1989; Greenberg, Rice & Elliott, 1993; Greenberg & Paivio, in press). Thus therapy has to facilitate clients' access to their emotions and inner experiencing during the session; a variety of techniques can be used, including requesting them to evoke events vividly and concretely, to focus on a bodily felt sense or to imagine a significant other to evoke an emotional response (Greenberg, Rice & Elliott, 1993).

Emotions, then, are evoked in experiential therapy so that they can be represented symbolically. Clients' attention to their emotions in therapy and their ability to represent and reflect on them, lead to accessing previously unavailable internal resources that produce novel responses and can lead to enduring change. Clients use re-evoked emotional experiences to differentiate meanings implicit in their reactions, and to discern the impact on them of events, internal processes and significant others. Negative emotions, in particular, often alert people to problematic aspects of experience that require attention. Affects and emotions often signal that one's needs/goals have not been attained; sadness signals that something important is lost, anger that one's goals are being thwarted—and this sets a problem for reason to solve. We thus see that much cognition is in the service of affective goals, and that emotion needs to inform reasoned action (Greenberg & Paivio, in press; Pascual-Leone, 1991). Emotions might, for example, tell one that something is wrong in the domain of interpersonal relations, for instance that an interpersonal bond has been ruptured or endangered. Thinking then needs to be applied to create a solution. For example, a client in therapy attended to and felt a sense of fear in response to imagining a demand made on him by his wife, a demand to give her more support in having their child learn her native language. His fear helped him to identify that a problem existed. It informed him that he felt very concerned that not learning his wife's native language would make him feel isolated, as if he did not belong in his own family. This was a feeling he had had in his family of origin. He then needed to evaluate how disappointed and angry his wife would be if he decided not to learn a second language. He also needed to decide what he felt his obligations were, to his wife, to learn the language. This then all needed to be integrated with the degree to which he, himself, desired to learn the language and the concrete possibilities of taking on this venture. This is a complex affective/cognitive problem-solving process.

To summarize, meaning creation in therapy relies on three critical moments: *The activation and synthesis of emotion schemes* to produce emotional arousal, the *symbolization in awareness of bodily felt experience* to create conscious awareness and *the evaluation of and reflection on symbolized material* to provide explanation and identity. This involves the ongoing tacit synthesis of tacit or preconscious schemes to form a sense of internal complexity, and a more conscious synthesis process in which generated experience and symbolization and explanation are integrated. This final synthesis provides integrated emotionally motivated, reasoned action. It is this synthesis that also gives birth to a narrated view of self.

Therapy Session Example

A brief segment of the beginning of a transcript from an actual session of psychotherapy is provided below. In this transcript we see the moment-by-moment process of the symbolization of emerging experience, and reflection on it, to produce new meaning, which in turn evokes new experience for further symbolization in an ongoing process of the creation of meaning.

TRANSCRIPT

T: What's happening now?

C: Just like I mentioned, um, uneasiness or I guess maybe anxiety comes up because, um—there's a bit of, it's frightening or, um. *(Symbolizes emerging experience.)*

T: Can you kind of go to that place right now? (C: Um—no.) Is it hard to go there? *(Attend to bodily felt sense.)*

C: Yeah, it's like, well it's not hard, it's, it's the loneliness is there and I feel like what I'm looking for *is comfort* . . . (T: Uh, huh.) . . . *um, being told that I matter* . . . (T: Yeah, that's what you'd like) . . . *reassurance, I guess. (Emotion scheme activated and symbolized in consciousness.)*

T: Yeah, somebody to say 'Yeah, it's okay, Cindy'. *(Evocative intensification.)*

C: Yeah (crying) I'm just, I guess, to just hear it from somebody else and . . . (T: Uh huh.) . . . and, um I mean, just repeating to myself. *(Reflexive elaboration-explaining.)*

T: Uh huh, it's like hard to keep doing it all on your own . *(Exploration.)*

C: Yeah yeah, it is, that's right, it's like . . . always there. *(Attend to bodily felt experience.)*

T: Sort of a constant feeling of wanting something? *(Explore goals/needs.)*

C: Yeah, yeah, that's always there . . . (T: Uh huh.)—I guess I just need to reassure myself that, you know, it's going to be okay. (T: Mm mm hm hm) You

know, that—*you do have friends that care and, um, family and, yeah, I guess I just need reassurance. (Reflexive examination and explaining.)*
T: But just something, there's something you want out there . . . some kind of reassurance. *(Explore and encourage symbolization.)*
C: Mm hm, yeah, I guess I'm the type of person that needs to hear that or, again, because I've always been, always been giving and, um, not, I guess I didn't get it back to me, um, that make makes me feel maybe like, um, you know *I've been ripped off* or . . . (T: Mm hm). *(Reflexive examination activates new emotion scheme which is symbolized.)*
T: So there's a feeling of being cheated too? (C: Cheated, yeah!) What's that like? 'I've given and given and given and what have I got for this?' kind of thing? *(Attend to and explore emotion scheme.)*
C: Right, yeah, 'Why isn't it coming back to me?' or . . . (T: Mm hm.) . . . it's prolonging, like *it's been a very long time. (Reflexive examination.)*
T: So you're getting a bit fed up with it, like, 'It's been a long time since I've been giving and putting out'? *(Intensify attentional allocation.)*
C: Yeah, 'when is it going to be my turn to?', not that I want to receive, as in gifts and stuff, but just . . . (T: Yeah) . . . to *mean that I count, that I'm there for a reason* . . . (T: Yeah.) . . . to be told that . . . (sniff). *(Reflexive examination.)*
T: Yeah, like you've sort of become more aware now of what you need, right?
C: Yeah, um, and maybe this is why, um, *I give, give because I guess the emptiness—it makes me feel good like when I do that, but then inside, um, well it seems like a hole. (reflexive examination then attends to bodily sense of emotion scheme.)*
T: Yeah, so you're saying you sort of would try to fill it before by giving and now that you're not doing it you're kind of left with this big open gap? *(Understanding and evocation.)*

The transcript continues a few minutes later after discussing a specific incident of overextending herself.

C: That feeling creeps up on me, and you know, I will think, when you know, um, I've given and given—*'When is it my turn to receive?' (Reflexive examination.)*
T: Yeah, so it sounds like a little bit of almost anger or like . . . (C: Uh.) It's like 'What about me?' *(Empathic conjecture about emotion not yet symbolized.)*
C: Yeah.
T: So you sort of . . . (C: Cut myself up) . . . . and tell yourself like—'No, that wasn't nice . . . (C: Yeah.) . . . you're mean, C'. *(Co-construction of meaning.)*

C: (crying) So it's actually—*I guess, being myself,* you know, why can't I just (crying) do that, why do I have to feel this, you know, it's just common sense, it's something that is minor. *(Emotion scheme activated.)*

T: So, it's like just being yourself and saying what you want to say is difficult? *(Understanding and exploration.).*

C: Yeah (crying) (sniff) (T: Try to take a breath.) (crying) (T: Yeah, just breathe.) I guess you just, you *just hit the spot,* like when you said (crying) um, *be myself.* (T: Uh, huh.) (sigh) *(Emotion scheme fully accessed.)*

T: There's something about being yourself that's difficult. *(Understanding.).*

C: Yeah, it's like, um, I feel restrained . . . (T: Uh huh.) . . . um . . . *(Explore elements of scheme.)*

T: Is there some feeling of, uh, you're clamping down? *(Empathic conjecture.)*

C   No, (crying) you know, it's *bad to say what I think* that, or . . . (T: Uh huh.) . . . (sniff) but then it worries me because then I say to myself, you know, *'Don't you have any respect for yourself?'* *(Access maladaptive belief and alternate internal resource.)*

T: Uh huh, that's the other side of it, but there's something about it, like it's bad to be yourself or . . . *(Exploration.)*

C: Yeah, yeah, that's it, it's bad to speak your mind . . . (T: uh huh) . . . um, again, because (sniff) it's, um, *getting it from my parents,* saying, you know, 'Don't', and then getting it from A. (T: Mm hm.). I just have a hard time (sigh)— you know, even though it's in my mind I want to express it but it's, *I hold back.* (T: Mm hm.)

(Identification of source of belief and of a self-interruptive conflict).

In this excerpt we see the client continually creating new meaning as she proceeds in the session. As this co-constructive process unfolds she attends to aroused, bodily felt sensations, symbolizes them in words, and then reflects on them. She moves from a place of feeling uneasy and lonely to activating her dependent, unsure sense of self that needs reassurance. She moves from feeling the unmet need for support to evaluating that it is unfair that she gives but does not get back. This evokes anger and a sense of entitlement as well as a realization that giving is an attempt to fill her emptiness. Her anger informs her that she feels taken advantage of and that she has a need to receive as well as give. This leads to her examining why she cannot be herself and begins to access her negative self-view that prevents her from feeling worthy. This complex process all unfolds in a brief few minutes and represents a microcosm of the larger, complex, dynamic process of meaning transformation that occurs in therapeutic dialogue.

Elsewhere we have detailed the more molar change processes that occur in therapeutic episodes and more complete therapies (Greenberg,

Rice & Elliott, 1993; Greenberg & Paivio, in press). A number of different episodes have been investigated in which the meaning transformation process discussed here is involved in helping people resolve more molar problems. Thus meaning transformation processes might be involved first in the identification of a particular type of cognitive/affective problem, such as unfinished business with a significant other. Continual moments of arousal, symbolization and reflection could then promote resolution by facilitating steps of accessing previously disowned feelings and disclaimed action tendencies, such as accessing anger at the significant other and the associated tendency to separate or attack. This would be followed by accessing a new emotion/need/belief complex such as sadness, the associated unmet needs for nurturance and the belief that one is undeserving. The mobilization of the unmet need then acts to motivate and empower people to challenge dysfunctional beliefs from the newly found internal sense of entitlement and worth. This leads to change in the view of self and other, and to a new narrative construction of one's past, present and future (Greenberg, Rice & Elliott, 1993; Paivio & Greenberg, 1995). Change over the course of whole treatments has been shown to follow similar paths (Greenberg & Paivio, in press). Here presenting problems are generally secondary 'bad' feelings, such as feeling depressed and anxious. These are evoked in therapy and explored to access underlying, more primary adaptive feelings and needs. The more primary feelings act as internal resources, which help combat negative cognitions. This leads to a final reconstruction of a person's self-view.

CONCLUSION

Affects and emotion serve as organizing forces in human functioning and play a key role in the development of personal meaning. Emotion in conjunction with the allocation of mental attentional energy guides conscious cognition and makes individuals active determiners of their conduct rather than passive reactors to stimuli. One of the primary goals of an emotionally focused, experiential therapy is the evocation of various emotional states in a variety of different in-therapy contexts. This is done to help clients become aware of the adaptive tendencies emanating from their own emotional states. This helps to restructure their emotional experience, to challenge negative self-views and to create new meaning by understanding the impact of events on them, and the significance to them of events and of people. Informed by their emotional responses, people can analyse and reflect on their experience to solve the vital problems of living.

REFERENCES

Beck, A.T. (1976). *Cognitive Therapy and the Emotional Disorders*. New York: International Universities Press.
Bohart, A. (1993). Experiencing: A common factor. *Journal of Psychotherapy Integration*, 3, 51–68.
Ekman, P. & Friesen, W.V. (1975). *Unmasking the Face*. Englewood Cliffs, NJ: Prentice-Hall.
Epstein, S. (1993). Integration of the cognitive and the psychodynamic unconscious. *American Psychologist*, 49(8), 709–724.
Frijda, N.H. (1986). *The Emotions*. Cambridge: Cambridge University Press.
Gazzaniga, M.S. (1985). *The Social Brain: Discovering the Networks of the Mind*. New York: Basic Books.
Gendlin, E.T. (1962). *Experiencing and the Creation of Meaning: A Philosophical and Psychological Approach to the Subjective*. New York: Free Press of Glencoe.
Gendlin, E.T. (1964). A theory of personality change. In P. Worchel & D. Byrne (eds), *Personality Change*. New York: John Wiley.
Gendlin, E.T. (1968). The experiential response. In E. Hammer (ed.), *Use of Interpretation in Therapy* (pp. 208–227). New York: Grune & Stratton.
Greenberg, L. & Korman, L. (1993). Integrating emotion in psychotherapy integration. *Journal of Psychotherapy Integration*, 3, 249–267.
Greenberg, L. & Paivio, S. (in press). *Working with the Emotions*. New York: Guilford Press.
Greenberg, L. & Pascual-Leone, J. (1995). A dialectical constructivist approach to experiential change. In R. Neimeyer & M. Mahoney (eds), *Constructivism in Psychotherapy*. Washington, DC: American Psychological Association.
Greenberg, L.S. & Safran, J.D. (1984). Integrating affect and cognition: A perspective on the process of therapeutic change. *Cognitive Therapy and Research*, 8, 559–578.
Greenberg, L.S. & Safran, J.D. (1987). *Emotion in Psychotherapy; Affect, Cognition, and the Process of Change*. New York: Guilford Press.
Greenberg, L.S. & Safran, J.D. (1989). Emotion in psychotherapy. *American Psychologist*, 44, 19–29.
Greenberg, L.S., Rice, L.N. & Elliott, R. (1993). *Facilitating Emotional Change: The Moment by Moment Process*. New York: Guilford Press.
Guidano, V.F. (1987). *The Complexity of the Self*. New York: Guilford Press.
Guidano, V. (1991). *The Self in Process*. New York: Guilford Press.
Guidano, V. (1995). The constructivist psychotherapy: A theoretical framework. In R. Neimeyer & M. Mahoney (eds), *Constructivism in Psychotherapy*. Washington, DC: American Psychological Association.
Hermans, H.J.M., Kempen, H.J.G. & Van Loon, R.J.P. (1992). The dialogical self: Beyond individualism and rationalism. *American Psychologist*, 47, 23–33.
Izard, C. (1977). *Human Emotions*. New York: Plenum.
James, W. (1895). *The Principles of Psychology*. New York: Holt. (Reprinted, New York: Dorer, 1950).
LeDoux, J.E. (1993). Emotional networks in the brain. In M. Lewis & J.M. Haviland (eds), *Handbook of Emotions*, (pp. 109–118). New York & London: Guilford Press.
Mahoney, M. (1991). *Human Change Processes: Notes on the Facilitation of Personal Development*. New York: Guilford Press.
Oatley, K. & Jenkins, J.M. (1992). Human emotions: Function and dysfunction. *Annual Review of Psychology*, 43, 55–85.
Paivio, S. & Greenberg, L. (1995). Resolving unfinished business. Experiential therapy using empty chair dialogue. *Journal of Consulting & Clinical Psychology*, 63(3), 419–425.

Pascual-Leone, J. (1980). Constructive problems for constructive theories: The current relevance of Piaget's work and a critique of information-processing simulation psychology. In R. Kluwe & H. Spada (eds), *Developmental Models of Thinking* (pp. 263–296). New York: Academic Press.

Pascual-Leone, J. (1984). Attentional, dialectic and mental effort: Towards an organismic theory of life stages. In M.L. Commons, F.A. Richards & G. Armon (eds), *Beyond Formal Operations: Late Adolescence and Adult Cognitive Development* (pp. 182–215). New York: Praeger.

Pascual-Leone, J. (1987). Organismic processes for neo-Piagetian theories: A dialectical causal account of cognitive development. *International Journal of Psychology, 22,* 531–570. Also in A. Demetriou (ed.), *The Neo-Piagetian Theories of Cognitive Development: Towards an Integration* (pp. 531–569). Amsterdam: North-Holland.

Pascual-Leone, J. (1990a). An essay on wisdom: Toward organismic processes that make it possible. In R. J. Sternberg (ed.), *Wisdom: Its Nature, Origins, and Development* (pp. 244–278). New York: Cambridge University Press.

Pascual-Leone, J. (1990b). Reflections on life-span intelligence, consciousness and ego development. In C. Alexander & E. Langer (eds), *Higher Stages of Human Development: Perspectives on Adult Growth* (pp. 258–285). New York: Oxford University Press.

Pascual-Leone, J. (1991). Emotions, development and psychotherapy: A dialectical constructivist perspective. In J. Safran & L. Greenberg (eds), *Emotion, Psychotherapy and Change* (pp. 302–335). New York: Guilford.

Pascual-Leone, J. & Irwin, R. (1994). Noncognitive factors in high-road/low-road learning: I. Modes of abstraction in adulthood. *Journal of Adult Development, 1(2),* 73–89.

Pascual-Leone, J. & Johnson, J. (1991). The psychological unit and its role in task analysis. A reinterpretation of object permanence. In M. Chandler & M. Chapman (eds), *Criteria for Competence: Controversies in the Assessment of Children's Abilities* (pp. 153–187). Hillsdale, NJ: Erlbaum.

Pennebaker, J. (1990). *Opening Up: The Healing Power of Confiding in Others.* New York: Morrow.

Pennebaker, J.W. & Traue, H.C. (1993). Inhibition and psychosomatic processes. In J.W. Pennebaker & H.C. Traue (eds), *Emotion, Inhibition and Health* (pp. 146–163). Gottingen, Germany: Hogrefe & Huber.

Perls, F., Hefferline, R. & Goodman, P. (1951). *Gestalt Therapy.* New York: Dell.

Rogers, C.R. (1951). *Client-centered Therapy.* Boston: Houghton-Mifflin.

Safran, J. & Greenberg, L. (1991). *Emotion, Psychotherapy and Change.* New York: Guilford Press.

Scherer, K.R. (1984). On the nature and function of emotion: A component process approach. In K.R. Scherer & P. Ekman (eds), *Approaches to Emotion* (pp. 293–317). Hillsdale, NJ: Erlbaum.

Stern, D. (1985). *The Interpersonal World of the Infant: A View from Psychoanalysis and Developmental Psychology.* New York: Basic Books.

Watson, J. & Greenberg, L. (1996). Emotion and cognition in experiential therapy: A dialectical-constructivist position. In H. Rosen & K. Kuelwein (eds), *Constructing Realities: Meaning Making Perspectives for Psychotherapists* (pp. 253–274). San Francisco: Jossey Bass.

Chapter 11

THE TRANSFORMATION OF MEANING: A PSYCHOANALYTIC PERSPECTIVE

*Phil Mollon**

WHAT GOES ON IN PSYCHOANALYTIC THERAPY?

For the benefit of readers who may not be familiar with psychoanalysis from their own experience, it is necessary to describe something of what actually goes on. One problem is that, after a hundred years of psychoanalysis, there is much variation in both theory and technique. The following general account probably applies reasonably well to most versions of psychoanalysis.

The psychoanalyst offers a regular and consistent *frame*, involving the timing, setting and behaviour of the analyst. Psychoanalysis takes place five times per week; *psychoanalytic therapy* may be much less frequent and may be time-limited. The patient may sit or lie on a couch. He or she is invited to speak of whatever comes to mind, the process of *free-association*. The analyst does not structure the session or provide any kind of agenda. The patient may speak much or very little, but on the whole will speak more than the analyst.

The analyst is attentive to boundary issues in relation to the setting and the restrictions on the analyst's behaviour (which is limited primarily to listening, interpreting and maintaining the setting). Boundary keeping and boundary violations have been found to be loaded with meaning (Epstein, 1994; Langs, 1985). A patient may push for a boundary violation but might actually feel quite unsafe if this were successful; for example, a patient repeatedly berated the analyst angrily and scornfully for his

*Department of Clinical Psychology, Lister Hospital, Stevenage, UK

The Transformation of Meaning in Psychological Therapies.
Edited by Mick Power and Chris R. Brewin. © 1997 John Wiley & Sons Ltd.

failure to touch her and for being 'rigid', but she eventually acknowledged that it was only because the analyst stuck to his framework that she felt safe enough to express her rage, which had its roots in childhood deprivations.

The analyst's main skill is the mode of *listening*. Analytic listening involves an 'evenly suspended attention' (Freud, 1912b)—listening to the flow of the patient's thoughts, to the emotions expressed, to the expected emotions which are not expressed, to the themes which recur and coalesce, to the words used, especially the images and metaphors. The analyst listens with an attitude of not presuming to know or understand, but waiting, 'without memory or desire' (Bion, 1967), to see what emerges. The analyst also monitors his or her own feelings, thoughts, fantasies and state of mind in response to the patient (the *countertransference*) and also the experience of pressures towards particular roles and behaviours (*role responsiveness*; Sandler, 1976)—and uses these to inform an understanding of what is being communicated.

In understanding the *material* (words, affects, behaviours) of the session, the analyst proceeds from the surface (the manifest content) to the depth (the unconscious or latent content). It is assumed that whereas conscious communication follows a linear sequential thread, unconscious representation is elliptical, metaphorical, both allusive and elusive, involving dense networks of strands of meaning. Moreover, it is assumed that the unconscious contains not just psychodynamics, emotional forces which are not conscious, but also has its own mode of representation, particularly through displacement (from one representation to another) and condensation (one representation containing many meanings)—a mode which Freud (1900) called 'primary process thinking'. The patient's references to other people may sometimes be taken as representations of parts of the patient's own personality.

As the analyst listens, his or her attention will eventually discern a structure of emotional dynamic conflict—usually consisting of an impulse/need, an anxiety associated with the impulse, and a defence against the anxiety, this defence being the manifest symptom or behaviour. The analyst may then, when the material is clear enough, *interpret* this conflict, showing how it is represented in the material. Through this interpretation, which aims to enlarge the patient's consciousness (the provision of *insight*), it is hoped that the patient may be able to test the anxiety against reality and arrive at a better resolution of the conflict. (A view of the function of consciousness which is highly relevant to the role of insight is provided by the cognitive psychologist Bernard Baars (1988).)

The dynamic conflict may be apparent in relation to various people described by the patient, but privileged status is given to the way the conflict is manifest in relation to the analyst (the *transference*). In general it is considered that interpretations in the transference are more effective, more *mutative* (Strachey, 1934) than other interpretations because the *cognitive* insight is combined with interactional *experience*.

The analyst's understanding of conflict is embedded in knowledge and theories of child development from birth onwards. Analysts in training often study babies with their mothers for the first year or two of life, again with a kind of free-floating observational stance. However, different groups of analysts will emphasise different aspects of development and employ different theories. The analyst may offer reconstructions— speculative pictures of conflictual relationships and developmental difficulties in the past. The analyst may also speak of the child or infant parts of the patient in the present.

Most analysts employ some kind of theory of the patient's internal representations of relationships—inner models of needs, fears, expectations and defensive adaptations in relation to others. These are perhaps similar to the deep schemas which cognitive therapists have more recently begun to address in relation to personality disorders. (There are in fact a number of cognitive reformulations which deal with aspects of psychoanalytic theories (e.g. Horowitz, 1988). There are also simplified psychodynamic models, such as Luborsky's work with the Core Conflictual Relationship Theme, which permit easier research study whilst jettisoning much of the theoretical complexity of psychoanalysis (e.g. Luborsky & Crits-Christoph, 1990).)

SIGNAL AND NOISE AND THE BABEL OF PSYCHOANALYSIS

When I set myself the task of bringing to light what human beings keep hidden within them, not by the compelling power of hypnosis, but by observing what they say and what they show, I thought the task was a harder one than it really is. He that has eyes to see and ears to hear may convince himself that no mortal can keep a secret. If his lips are silent, he chatters with his finger-tips; betrayal oozes out of him at every pore. And thus the task of making conscious the most hidden recesses of the mind is one which it is quite possible to accomplish. (Freud, 1905, pp. 77–78)

Thus wrote Freud, in the case of 'Dora', demonstrating that he saw the analytic task as one of revealing and decoding that which a patient has hidden from him/herself. At this point apparently he believed that the unconscious will reveal its secrets easily to those who can observe and decode. When one means of communicating anxiety-laden mental content is blocked, the unconscious will speak through some other mode. A little earlier, Freud had written his great book on *The Interpretation of*

Dreams (1900), in which he described how, by following certain principles of pursuing free associations to all the element of a dream, it was possible for the analyst to arrive at the unconscious meaning of a dream. Few analysts would appear so confident today, finding that whilst unconscious meaning is sometimes revealed clearly, often it is obscure, dreams and narratives being open to a wide range of differing interpretations. Even the matter of what constitutes the material for interpretation of meaning is open to much variation among analysts. A recent entire issue of the *International Journal of Psycho-Analysis* (1994, **75** (5/6)) was devoted to the question of 'What is a clinical fact?' The Sandlers (1994), amongst others, point out that selection and selective perception of clinical material are inevitable; analysts, guided by their own theories, both official theories and unconscious private theories, will make their own choices over what they regard as signal and noise in the analysand's material.

After a century of clinical work, psychoanalysis is no longer *a* theory, but a myriad of interwoven strands of theory. Different groups of analysts are located at different areas of the tapestry, some individuals having a broader view of the whole than others. It is still possible for analysts from different traditions to communicate and understand each other, but only just—and it takes much effort. To deconstruct the babel, it is still necessary at times to return to the root language of Freud.

FREUD ON DREAMS, MEANING AND ENERGY

In the origins of psychoanalysis there is a pervasive tension between the *hermeneutic* (to do with the uncovering of meaning) and *economic* (to do with the quantity and distribution of instinctual energy) dimensions of the theory. Whilst the title of Freud's book on dreams suggests that the analytic material was like a 'text' that needed to be interpreted, this analogy was only partially apt. Freud did write of dreams as having a language-like structure, and described the rules of that language of the unconscious in terms of displacement, condensation and so on. However, these quasi-linguistic processes were also concerned with the transformations of psychic 'energy', the *libido*. In his thinking about dreams, Freud introduced not only a linguistic dimension, but also an economic one, concerned with 'quantities' of energy. Indeed he regarded dreams as having primarily an economic purpose—to act as a discharge for psychic energy, through disguised expression of wishes, so that sleep would not be disturbed. It is rather startling to realise that Freud did not consider that dreams are *intending* to communicate, but rather are a means of discharge of instinctual tension through the use of a kind of scrambled visual representation which provides hallucinatory satisfaction. In that respect dreams are not like a language. To interpret the *meaning* of a dream would then seem to be a most unnatural and intrusive activity—like surgery, necessary perhaps, but nevertheless an inherently violating activity. This view of dreams is in contrast with that of most analysts today, and also that of Freud's own contemporary, Jung. There are still some who articulately hold to this view. For example, not long ago I heard an eminent Freudian analyst remark that he did not believe that patients in analysis *intend* to communicate anything; he believed that what the analyst hears are the *leakages from the defences*.

In certain ways, dreams can be taken as a model of neurosis. According to Freud's model, the meaning of the dream is that an infantile wish hooks into a suitable element of present reality and attempts to mould it into a fulfilment of that wish; in order to accomplish this hallucinatory fulfilment, distortion and disguise of the wish must take place in order to avoid 'censorship'. This is the notion of *defence mechanism*. The work of analysis is to unravel and decode the distortions and reveal the true meaning of the wish. Why? So that the person can deal with their infantile wishes and fears more consciously and realistically and be less driven by internal forces beyond their awareness.

To the end of his life, Freud's method was to use the provision of *meaning* (through interpretation) to alter the *dynamic* and *economic* dimensions of the mind. The following quote from his final paper illustrates this:

> To start with, we get the patient's thus weakened ego to take part in the purely intellectual work of interpretation . . . We . . . transform what has become unconscious and repressed into preconscious material and thus return it once more to the possession of his ego. . . .
> We shall not be disappointed, but, on the contrary, will find it entirely intelligible, if we reach the conclusion that the final outcome of the struggle we have engaged in depends on quantitative relations—on the quota of energy we are able to mobilize in the patient to our advantage as compared with the sum of energy of the powers working against us. (1940, pp. 181–182).

He added, in answer to his question as to why neurotic people experience more difficulty, anxiety and pain:

> Quantitative *disharmonies* are what must be held responsible for the inadequacy and sufferings of neurosis. (1940, p. 183)

Perhaps anticipating contemporary psychopharmacology, he suggested:

> The future may teach us to exercise a direct influence, by means of particular chemical substances, on the amounts of energy and their distribution in the mental apparatus. (1940, p. 182)

DISPLACEMENT OF MEANING

The Freudian theory of dreams suggests that what the forbidden wish presses to express undergoes disguise through displacement (amongst other mechanisms of defence). Robert Langs (e.g. 1978) has adapted this model slightly in order to argue that the structure of neurosis (whether in the form of dreams, neurotic symptoms, parapraxes such as slips of the tongue, or the free-associative narratives in the consulting room) consists of a wish, a thought or a perception, which is felt to be dangerous to express directly (to the self or the other) and which is therefore expressed in disguised, displaced, form. This is perhaps analogous to the conscious process of *hinting*, which we do when we want to communicate something but feel that to say it directly would be embarrassing. Neurosis is perhaps a kind of unconscious hinting. For example, following a summer break in her therapy, a patient commented that her boyfriend had been a 'complete bastard' through his abandonment of her in various ways during the previous four weeks. After she had talked for some time about this, the therapist commented that perhaps she had also felt that the therapist was a 'complete bastard' because he had not been available to her. She replied that she thought this was correct. She then went on to say that she thought there was a similar pattern in relation to her boyfriend, her therapist and her mother; she suspected that when she felt angry with any one of them she would displace her anger onto one of the others whom she was not at that moment with.

Langs has also emphasised that the object of unconscious defence is not only forbidden wishes and fantasies, but often forbidden and unconscious *perceptions*. During therapy the patient is continually observing and monitoring the therapist's functioning, partly consciously and partly unconsciously. The patient unconsciously perceives and processes much more of the therapist's unconscious communications than is registered consciously. According to Langs' conclusions from extensive examination of clinical material, the patient is often exquisitely sensitive unconsciously to the therapist's deviations from an appropriate and consistent frame for the therapy. Boundary deviations may be welcomed consciously but condemned unconsciously. Langs (1985) gives an example of a therapist who, in response to the patient's distress over the ending of a relationship, disclosed some of her own experience of divorce; consciously the patient felt supported by this self-disclosure, but that night had a terrifying nightmare of hands reaching up from the ground to capture him and drag him down, suggesting that unconsciously he had perceived the therapist's interventions as invasive and threatening. Langs' work leads the therapist to a stance of continually monitoring the patient's communications for unconscious commentary upon the process, rather as if the patient can be an unconscious supervisor. Other analysts also listen in this way (see especially Casement, 1985) but it is Langs who has most explicitly and relentlessly pursued the implications of this.

Attention to the patient's unconscious commentary can be extremely illuminating, revealing complex interweaving of the childhood past with contemporary reality, as well as helpful prompts regarding therapist errors.

Illustration of the Patient's Unconscious Supervision of the Therapist

The patient was a medical practitioner with a male therapist. Part of the context for the following material was that the patient had recently requested an additional session each week. The therapist had not really had the extra time available, but for various reasons wished to try to accommodate the patient's need. Therefore, an additional early (7 a.m.) time had been offered and this session was the first of these.

The patient arrived about a minute late. He remarked that he had not yet mastered the art of arriving exactly on time. The therapist commented that he seemed to be judging himself against a very high standard of precision! In reply the patient said that it was hard for him to adapt to being a patient; as a doctor he must not be late for his patients. He then talked of how, as a GP, he cannot easily take time off; he is often exhausted; GPs are notoriously bad at seeking help and looking after themselves. Next he spoke of a patient of his who used to be seen by a psychologist privately; the psychologist used to say to her 'Phone me any time', but when she attempted to do so he was never available. He talked of the reassurance this woman felt when he, in contrast with the psychologist, offered her a definite time with limits; he thought that she felt safer with that, even though she might pressure him for more time. Then he added 'I feel safe here'.

The therapist pointed out that the context for what had been said was that this was the first of the additional sessions—that the patient had talked of a psychologist who was unrealistic about his own availability—and about GPs who cannot look after themselves. He then interpreted that perhaps the patient felt that he had pressurised the therapist into agreeing to the extra sessions, which were at a very early time—and that perhaps he was wondering whether the therapist can say 'No' to demands, and whether he can look after himself; in this way perhaps the patient did *not* feel 'safe'.

The patient agreed with this, saying that he had indeed felt he had pressurised the therapist. He then talked about his childhood feeling that he had to look after his mother, and also spoke of occasions when his father had not stood up to him sufficiently.

The process of meaning transformation was as follows. By taking the change in the session schedule as the context around which the patient's unconscious communications might organise, and by abstracting the schematic and thematic meanings from the patient's remarks, it became possible to see clearly that he was presenting his worry that the therapist could not say 'No' to a burdensome request; the patient's assertion that he felt 'safe here' was understood as a simple denial or negation of his true feeling. Thus the context provided the key to obtaining the *latent* meaning from the *manifest* meaning. After this had been interpreted, the patient provided further associations to similar worries in relation to the original figures in his childhood.

TRANSFERENCE—SHIFTING VIEWS, FROM LIBIDO TO RELATIONSHIP

One of the most central of psychoanalytic concepts is that of transference. The patient begins by talking about his/her relationship to symptoms, but through transference, and the analyst's attention to it, the talk shifts to the relationship to the analyst. This surely is a most remarkable transformation of meaning, which is at the very heart of the psychoanalytic endeavour.

It is in the transference that the neurosis is unravelled, for it is in this domain that the patient's patterns of unconscious conflict become available for scrutiny and influence. But what exactly is this 'transference'?

Freud (1912a) introduces the notion of the 'stereotype plate' or template, determining the pattern of the individual's love relationships. He goes on to describe how the analyst is assimilated to this stereotype plate and becomes the new love object. At this point he considered that a person becomes neurotic when, in the face of frustration or disappointment in love relations, an increased amount of libido is withdrawn from reality and invested in the neurotic symptoms. He explains the therapeutic strategy: 'The analytic treatment now proceeds to follow it; it seeks to track down the libido, to make it accessible to consciousness and, in the end, serviceable for reality' (1912a, p. 102). Freud's view of the function of transference in the treatment appeared to be that it became a *vehicle for the liberation of the libido* through enticing the libido into a new and more accessible battleground.

> In place of his patient's true illness there appears the artificially constructed transference illness, in place of the various unreal objects of the libido there

appears a single, and more imaginary object in the person of the doctor. (Freud, 1917, p. 454)

Through the analytic work of interpretation, repression is lifted and conflicts become conscious.

> When the libido is released once more from its temporary object in the person of the doctor, it cannot return to its earlier objects, but is at the disposal of the ego. (1917, pp. 454–455)

A point to be emphasised again here is that Freud saw the work of interpretation (hermeneutics) as a means to liberate energy, libido (the economic dimension). He did not see neurosis as essentially a problem of conflictual relationships that have been internalised (an 'object relational' conflict), but as a problem of libido being withdrawn from reality and unavailable to the ego. Later, with the development of his structural model (of id, ego and superego) (Freud, 1923), he saw the neurotic ego as torn between contradictory demands from the id (the source of instinctual energy, the libido), the superego (the conscience) and the outside world, and enfeebled by expenditure of energy in vain attempts to fend off the demands of the id. This was still an *economic* model. The therapeutic task was one of strengthening the ego, through the undoing of repression, so that the ego could establish a better distribution and expression of libidinal energy.

However, in Freud's 1923 presentation of the structural model, there can also be discerned the beginnings of an object-relational (i.e. internal representations of relationships) model of mental life, the superego being the first notion of an internal object (representation of a parental figure). He was now able to describe how this internal object (derived from a weave of fantasy and identification with a parent) can be re-externalised onto the perception of the analyst.

He goes on to explain the therapeutic implications:

> If the patient puts the analyst in the place of his father (or mother), he is also giving him the power which his superego exercises over his ego. The new superego now has the opportunity for a sort of *after education* of the neurotic; it can correct mistakes for which his parents were responsible in educating him.' (p. 175) [Freud cautions the analyst:] In all his attempts at improving and educating the patient the analyst should respect his individuality. (p. 175)

So there is the therapeutic process according to Freud's final description; the analyst takes the place of the internalised parent and carries out a re-education of the patient, albeit from a position of analytic neutrality; this re-education allows the patient's ego to become friendlier to the libido.

Most contemporary analysts use concepts of transference that in certain ways are fundamentally different from Freud's conception (without this change of meaning always being fully explicit). The original libido theory has evolved into various forms of object relational theory—the idea that neurotic problems are to do with conflictual relationships in childhood, which become internalised to form the basis of persisting structures of unconscious fantasy which distort relationships in current reality. Although this might appear to be implicit in Freud's theory and to amount to little more than a slight adjustment of emphasis, there is a fundamental shift of assumptions. The analysis of a relational conflict is no longer viewed as a means to the liberation and redistribution of libido under the direction of the ego, as it was for Freud, but as a means of releasing the patient's capacity for more mature and more free relationships; in particular, especially in Britain, the emphasis is upon enabling the patient to establish healthy dependence on others, including the analyst—the implicit paradigm used here being that of the baby's dependence upon, and communicative interaction with, the mother. In this framework the economic as a *purely intrapsychic dimension* has all but gone. It is replaced largely by a concern with structures of emotional meaning—the *wish/need* for certain kinds of responses from others (including the wish to be understood), the *fear* of encountering emotional pain (e.g. of loss, of guilt, of rejection, of failed empathy, of derailed communication), and the *defences* against the feared pain, this constellation being represented unconsciously in the patient's words and actions in the consulting room. The economic dimension is still present implicitly, but now interpersonally, in the concern with the *functions* of the caregiver (or the analyst) in regulating tension states; these functions are implied in the use of concepts such as 'containment', 'mirroring' and the emphasis in some quarters on the role of empathy in development (cf. Mollon, 1993).

One crucial implication of this is in relation to *timing* of interpretation of the transference. The analyst who is truly following Freud's position will wait for the transference to develop into the *transference neurosis*, when the patient's wishes, fears and fantasies about the analyst will be near to consciousness. The term 'transference meurosis', which is rarely used now, only makes sense in terms of the libido theory: '. . . all the libido is forced from the symptoms into the transference and concentrated there . . .' (1917, p. 455). However, for the analyst who draws upon an object relations theory (a theory based around the primacy of relationships rather than drives), the patient is seen as bringing his/her characteristic relationship conflicts into the relationship to the analyst *from the beginning*; in particular the infantile dependent parts of the personality relate conflictually to the analyst, who is unconsciously perceived as a parental figure. The patient is seen as having a problem because his/her relationships are distorted by infantile fantasy and projective (i.e. attributive) processes. This is a common contemporary view of transference: the unconscious persistence of infantile patterns of relationship, existing as structures of inner fantasy, which colour the perception of other people. It is seen as present from the beginning of analysis and in many other areas of life as well as the consulting room. From this point of view, transference interpretations—i.e. interpretations about conflicts and anxieties in relation to the analyst—will seem perfectly appropriate from the first session.

What the contemporary analyst does retain from Freud's view is that something from the childhood past is transferred into the relationship to the analyst. Much more than was the case with Freud, however, the relationship with the analyst is itself seen as an important context for understanding the patient's unconscious allusions to that relationship; in the present view, the transference does not evolve purely intrapsychically and is not static, but is part of an ongoing interaction with the analyst that is often pervaded with tension and discomfort for both. Because the immediate relationship with the analyst is fraught with conflict and anxiety, the patient will often refer to the transference unconsciously by speaking of other relationships. Part of the analyst's task is to undo this displacement, and to connect and differentiate past and present. Sometimes the patient will speak more directly of feelings about the analyst, but a reconstruction of the conflictual relationships of the past may be necessary for a full understanding of the transference in the present; the elucidation of past and present are each used to illuminate the other. This probably corresponds to what Cooper (1987) refers to as the 'modernist' model of transference: '. . . a new experience rather than an enactment of an old one. The purpose of transference interpretation is to bring to consciousness all aspects of this new experience including its colourings from the past' (p. 81). Another model which is implicit in much contemporary analytic thinking is of the analysis as a kind of *theatre* (McDougall, 1986), in which complex interpersonal situations from childhood are played out (Klein, 1952; Joseph, 1985).

Clinical Illustration—The Meaning of the Present as a Reworking of the Past

The context for the following clinical material, from two sessions, is the imminent planned end of the therapy. The patient is a refugee woman in mid-life. Part of the historical childhood context which informs the patient's and therapist's understanding is that as a very young child she appeared to have had a close and sexualised relationship with her father which had abruptly ended when her brother was born; she believed that at this point her father had devastatingly turned away from her.

The patient talked first of her feeling that the therapist must be disappointed with her for not having achieved more in the therapy. She also spoke resignedly of a feeling that men will always leave her. She talked of a sense that the therapist was letting her go because he had no interest in her, even though the ending had been at her initiative and its meaning had been much explored already. She remarked that there had been much change through the therapy, but she had not produced 'a glittering object'—elaborating on this odd phrase by saying that she had not produced a baby, she had not produced any revelatory new memories of childhood, and that she felt 'barren'. She further associated to the idea of a child performing on the potty as a 'gift' for the parents.

The therapist commented: 'You feel that nothing has come from our therapeutic intercourse.' The patient replied: 'That's right—and part of me feels that you must be fed up with me.' The therapist then said: 'I think the way you are feeling may be modelled on how you felt when your father turned away from you [she agreed]. In your child's thinking at the time, it probably seemed to you that your father turned away from you to your mother because you didn't produce a baby and your mother did.' The patient replied that this would be perfectly logical reasoning for the baby.

The patient then went on to speak of how devastated she had felt when the therapist had recently changed one of her session times to 15 minutes later. She had felt that he had turned away from her to a baby sibling, a rival patient. She also then went on to reflect upon a long period when the analytic work had seemed very stuck, when nothing seemed to be happening, and when she had been struggling with little success to remember more of her childhood. On looking back she realised how desolate she had felt because she had not been able to produce a memory (faeces/baby) for the therapist.

The next day the patient talked of feeling dead, and also that she had made the therapist dead and that she had sent him to sleep. She talked of feeling poisoned inside and of a sense that she had been somehow withholding from the therapist. The therapist enquired whether the patient had been constipated as a child. She replied that she had had serious problems with constipation and that she thought this had dated from when her father abandoned her—'I just wouldn't let it out'. She went on to speak of further thoughts of feeling abandoned by the therapist. The therapist commented: 'You held on to your faeces, partly out of resentment, but perhaps also because you felt so lost and disoriented that you clung to the only thing you felt you had, your faeces inside. But then you may have felt even more that people would want to abandon you because you were full of shit.' The patient replied: 'I used to fear that I smelt—I couldn't produce a nice shiny baby—I could only produce something nasty.' She went on to reflect further upon her lifelong resentment of men and her feeling that men would always want to abandon her and that she could never have a good and creative intercourse with a man.

This concludes the clinical material. So what have the patient and therapist done together with the meaning of the material of the session? The material has consisted of the patient's mood, free-associative feelings, thoughts and images, partly brought to the session and partly emerging in response to the therapist's comments. The patient's first remarks are consciously related to the therapist, her feelings that she is a disappointment to him; she goes on to associate to babies and faeces and implies a metaphor of the therapy as an intercourse which has failed to be fruitful. An interpretive shift then occurs as the therapist places the patient's current feelings and fantasies in the historical context of having been emotionally abandoned by her father when her brother was born. The patient goes with this new line of thought and reflects upon other ways in which she has felt abandoned by the therapist whom she has experienced, in the transference, as her father. She sees that she has felt useless and 'barren' because of a childhood comparison with her mother's capacity to produce a baby; here the fantasies and thought processes of the child are reconstructed. She realises how she has wished to produce baby-equivalents for the therapist. In the following session she talks of feeling dead and poisoned and of withholding. The therapist sees this as possibly reflecting a fantasy of constipation. The patient acknowledges that this was a serious problem as a child. Patient and therapist then begin to reconstruct the childhood clinging to faeces, the sense of being able only to produce dirty and smelly objects, and the painful comparison with her mother's capacity to produce a baby. Thus the patient's low mood and self-esteem is revealed to be the product of a complex of *historical* childhood perceptions, thoughts, feelings and fantasies which are alive in the *present* transference to the therapist. The understanding of this material appears to be crucially dependent upon a grasp of the relevant context, the ending of the therapy.

REPRESENTATIONS OF PARTS OF THE SELF AND STATES OF THE SELF IN DREAMS AND FREE ASSOCIATIONS

The shift from a libido to an object-relational theory of mental life has also enabled dreams to be viewed differently. Fairbairn (1952) was perhaps the first analyst to suggest that the various characters in a dream can represent different parts of the self, and that the dream may portray an internal relationship conflict between parts of the self and internal objects. A dream may also be seen as representing, sometimes very clearly, a situation between patient and therapist, as illustrated in the following.

In supervision, a therapist talked of how she felt very stuck with her patient who seemed unable to make any change in his rather restricted life. She described how she had attempted a number of lines of approach, none of which had been fruitful. In particular she had tried to find ways of engaging the child parts of the patient. The supervisor commented that perhaps the patient wished to remain in a kind of cocoon and did not want to be helped out of this—that perhaps his endeavours were entirely at odds with hers, being devoted to maintaining the status quo rather than achieving change. In response, the therapist recalled a dream the patient had reported some weeks previously: the patient is in a self-contained flat which contains absolutely everything he needs; there is a small window and looking out he sees children trying to get in; he shoots at them. A clearer representation of the situation in the patient's mind and in relation to the therapist could hardly be imagined. He is attempting to live in a fantasy of a narcissistic cocoon, self-contained, with no need of another person, but in so doing he has to project outside the needy and lively child parts of himself; these are located in the therapist and in her attempts to engage him; he is shooting at the child parts of himself that are attempting to return. Thus patient and therapist are pursuing completely opposing agendas—hence the therapist's sense of frustration.

An example of how parts of the self may be represented in the patient's free-associative talk is as follows. A man, with some perverse aspects to his character, talked at length to his therapist about a friend who was trying to persuade him to accompany him on a trip to the Far East where they could spend time with the local prostitutes and engage in a variety of sexual activities, including group sex. He described this friend as a bisexual cross-dresser. It was not difficult to see that as well as talking about this actual friend, the patient was also unconsciously representing his struggle with a perverse part of his own mind which continually pulled him towards perverse sexual activity.

INTERPRETATION OF *BEHAVIOUR* IN THE TRANSFERENCE

Some psychoanalysts, particularly those within the British Kleinian school, have developed an emphasis upon the importance of attending not only to the words a patient presents, but also to the *way* in which something is said. Betty Joseph is perhaps the most notable proponent of this technical style, in which the analyst pays exquisitely close attention to the way the patient responds to the analyst and the state of mind which he/she attempts to produce in the analyst. Joseph looks for the unconscious enactments in the transference of the patient's character structure.

One example she gives (Joseph, 1971) is that of a perverse man with a rubber fetish, whom she describes as highly narcissistic, attempting to retain an attitude of superiority, whilst projecting his infantile needs and desires into others, such as his girlfriend and the analyst. He would respond to interpretations with a polite 'How interesting" but appear quite unmoved by them. He would often appear to retreat into wordy theories which were unproductive of any change. Part of the detailed material Joseph describes is as follows; for reasons of space the extensive basis for her interpretations cannot be described.

The patient began one session with talk about his sexual difficulties with his girlfriend. He described how he had been lying next to her and stroking her and she had indicated a wish to make love, but then he had stopped. Joseph comments: 'I showed him that this apparent passivity was going on in the sessions. It seemed to be assumed that I wanted him to get on in the analysis, to use the session to get on with understanding and with his sexuality, as if he were verbally stroking me as he stroked Pat, thus trying to stimulate and frustrate me, to make me want something and to withhold it from me, and that this was all part of his sexual excitement and was going on on the couch.' (p. 60) After further material from the patient, both verbal and non-verbal, Joseph adds: 'I could then show him that we, in the quietest possible manner, were locked in a sado-masochistic relationship, in which I was to be excited and tormented, and that it was far more difficult for him to give up this gratification and have a real relationship with his analytic material and me as a woman and an analyst than to retreat into his heavy silence, his words, and his theories, which I believe are actually being used as the rubber fetish into which he can withdraw from contact.' (p. 60).

Thus Joseph is arguing that a sado-masochistic relationship of quiet excitement is being maintained in place of a real relationship—and that this takes place in relation to the analyst as well as the patient's girlfriend. Moreover, she suggests that the patient's use of words and theories has a function in the analysis something like that of the rubber fetish, into which he can withdraw from real contact. In arriving at these conclusions, she takes account not only of the patient's words, but also his manner, attitude, way of using words, the emotional reactions he creates in the analyst, the general atmosphere and mood of the session—and indeed almost every dimension of interpersonal experience that is available for scrutiny. Joseph attempts to find a way of describing the entire experience in the consulting room.

THE DEEPENING OF EMPATHY—THE SELF-PSYCHOLOGICAL SCHOOL

One further school of analytic work which needs mention is that of 'self-psychology', developed by Kohut (1971; 1977). To give an adequate account of this theoretical and technical position is beyond the scope of this chapter, but it can be said that the self-psychologist aims, not so much at interpreting defences, but at deepening the patient's empathy with his/her own experience. Like Joseph, the self-psychological analyst follows the patient responses very closely, carefully monitoring the relationship between the analytic partners, but there the similarity ends. Lichtenberg (1992) describes his approach thus:

> I attempt to follow closely the analysand's precise words, affect displays and shifts in theme that are consequent to both the interventions made and the communications of the patient not responded to. I am sensitive to trying as much as possible to comprehend meanings from within the patient's point of view rather than as external observer and arbiter of 'reality'. I believe that when I succeed in maintaining this way of listening, the interpretive sequence deepens the inquiry into a patient's mode of experiencing and simultaneously invites the patient to sharpen his or her own self-reflection.' (p. 250)

He goes on to explain:

> As a working analyst I do not think of myself as concerned with encouraging destabilization of the status quo . . ., finding chinks in the defensive armour . . ., or applying optimal frustration . . . Rather I am guided by an attempt to maintain an optimal responsiveness . . . to the patients' inner state of mind, especially her affects and her intentions as *she* would recognize them to be. (p. 270)

There is one immediate difference between this stance and that of most other psychoanalytic positions. Since Freud, the psychoanalytic interpretation has been along the lines of 'You think you are talking about A, but unconsciously you are talking about B'. By contrast, the self-psychologist aims to expand the patient's awareness of their subjective experience and its origins; the interpretation is not from A to B, but from A to a greater awareness of A. There are, I think, some implied meanings in this empathic stance. The analyst is implicitly conveying: 'What you are experiencing can be understood and accepted by another human being and is not therefore shameful; your expectation that I will respond to you without empathy and understanding is incorrect; therefore your inner model of relationships can be revised; moreover, if I can understand and accept your experience, then you can be more empathic with yourself as well.' The assumption in the self-psychological position is that the expectation of a lack of empathy is, in many instances, what makes defences and distortions of mental life necessary.

CONCLUSIONS

In its beginnings, Freud's psychoanalysis was both a theory of meaning and a theory of mental energy (the libido). He presented a view of dreams as employing a kind of 'text', through which the mind deceived itself and maintained sleep, by a disguised hallucinatory expression of wishes which would otherwise evoke anxiety. By and large the libido theory has been left behind, sometimes explicitly, but more often implicitly, being replaced by a variety of object-relational theories. As a result, the notion of the transference neurosis, the concentration of libido on the figure of the analyst, has given way to the view of transference as the unconscious repetition of complex patterns of experience of relationships in childhood; the analytic setting is seen as a kind of theatre in which conflictual and painful scenarios of the past are reworked. In understanding the unconscious repetition of the past in the present, contemporary analysts take account of many details of behaviour, mood and experience in the consulting room, and also link the patient's communications closely to events in the analysis itself. The patient can also be understood at times as offering a perceptive, yet unconscious, commentary upon the analyst's activity. In contrast with the prevailing emphasis upon interpreting *disguised* meaning in the patient's communications, the relatively new school of self-psychology emphasises an approach which aims at deepening the patient's awareness of his/her subjective experience.

REFERENCES

Baars, B. (1988). *A Cognitive Theory of Consciousness*. New York: Cambridge University Press.

Bion, W.R. (1967). Notes on memory and desire. *Psychoanalytic Forum*, **2**: 271–280.

Casement, P. (1985). *Learning from the Patient*. Routledge: London.

Cooper, A.M. (1987). Changes in psychoanalytic ideas: transference interpretation. *Journal of the American Psychoanalytic Association*, **35**: 77–98.

Epstein, R.S. (1994). *Keeping Boundaries. Maintaining Safety and Integrity in the Psychotherapeutic Process*. Washington: American Psychiatric Press.

Fairbairn, W.R.D. (1952). *Psychoanalytic Studies of the Personality*. London: Routledge.

Freud, S. (1900). *The Interpretation of Dreams. Standard Edition*, Vol. 4–5. London: Hogarth Press.

Freud, S. (1905). Fragment of an analysis of a case of hysteria. *Standard Edition* Vol. 7, pp. 7–122. London: Hogarth Press.

Freud, S. (1912a). The dynamics of transference. *Standard Edition*, Vol. 12, pp. 99–108. London: Hogarth Press.

Freud, S. (1912b). Recommendations to physicians practicing psycho-analysis *Standard Edition*, Vol. 12, pp. 111–120. London: Hogarth Press.

Freud, S. (1917). Analytic therapy. Introductory lectures on psychoanalysis. *Stand ard Edition*, Vol. 16, pp. 448–463. London: Hogarth Press.

Freud, S. (1923). The ego and the id. *Standard Edition*, Vol. 19. London: Hogarth Press.

Freud, S. (1940). An outline of psycho-analysis. *Standard Edition*, Vol. 23, pp. 144–207. London: Hogarth Press.

Horowitz, M. (ed.) (1988). *Psychodynammics and Cognition*. Chicago: University o Chicago Press.

Kohut, H. (1971). *The Analysis of the Self*. New York: International University Press

Kohut, H. (1977). *The Restoration of the Self*. New York: International University Press.

Joseph, B. (1971). A clinical contribution to the analysis of a perversion. In: E.B Spillius & M. Feldman (eds), *Psychic Equilibrium and Psychic Change. Selecte Papers of Betty Joseph*, pp. 51–66. London: Routledge, 1989.

Joseph, B. (1985). Transference: the total situation. *International Journal of Psycho Analysis*, **66**, 447–454.

Klein, M. (1952). The origin of transference. *International Journal of Psycho-Analysis* **33**: 433–438.

Langs, R. (1978). *The Listening Process*. New York: Jason Aronson.

Langs, R. (1985). *Madness and Cure*, Emerson, NJ: New Concept Press.

Lichtenberg, J.D. (1992). The interpretive sequence. *Psychoanalytic Inquiry*, **12(2)** 248–274.

Luborsky, L. & Crits-Christoph, P. (1990). *Understanding Transference: The CCR Method*. New York: Basic Books.

McDougall, J. (1986). *Theatres of the Mind. Illusion and Truth on the Psychoanalyti Stage*. London: Free Association Books.

Mollon, P. (1993). *The Fragile Self. The Structure of Narcissistic Disturbance*. London Whurr.

Sandler, A-M. & Sandler, J. (1994). Comments on the conceptualisation of clinica fcts in psychoanalysis. *International Journal of Psycho-Analysis*, **75**(5/6): 995–101C

Sandler, J. (1976). Countertransference and role-responsiveness. *International Re view of Psycho-Analysis*, **3**, 43–47.

Strachey, J. (1934). The nature of the therapeutic action of psychoanalysis. *Interna tional Journal of Psycho-Analysis*, **15**: 117–126.

Chapter 12

FOUNDATIONS FOR THE SYSTEMATIC STUDY OF MEANING AND THERAPEUTIC CHANGE

M.J. Power* and Chris R. Brewin†

In the introductory chapter we posed a number of core questions about the causal status of meaning, the types of meanings implicated in psychopathology and their origin, the cognitive processing of meaning, and the implications for psychotherapy. We will now attempt to summarise some of what we have learned from individual chapters. Although the causal status of meaning remains hotly debated by philosophers, in Chapter 2 Bolton and Hill have outlined a persuasive case for the study of meaning alongside biological determinants of behaviour. We share their view that meaning frequently does have a causal role in the production of symptoms and behaviour, and that it is central to many cognitive accounts of abnormal psychological processes.

SOURCES OF MEANING

Innate Sources

As Bolton and Hill emphasised in their chapter (see also Bolton & Hill, 1996), 'meanings' are derived from a range of different sources that include innate factors, maturation and learning. The brain is not a *tabula rasa* but instead provides a range and variety of innate starting points

---

*Royal Edinburgh Hospital and University of Edinburgh, and †Royal Holloway, University of London, UK

The Transformation of Meaning in Psychological Therapies.
Edited by Mick Power and Chris R. Brewin. © 1997 John Wiley & Sons Ltd.

which are then shaped by maturation and experience. These innate factors include the bases for low-level cognitive processes that cover perception, memory, motor coordination, and so on. There is also increasing evidence for the possibility of a number of innate basic emotions such as sadness, happiness, anger, fear and disgust (e.g. Power & Dalgleish, 1997). Again, recent research emphasises that these innate basic emotions provide organising principles around which cognitive-affective development is coordinated (M. D. Lewis, 1996). Although each of these five basic emotions appears in the first year of life (M. Lewis, 1993), a combination of personal, familial and cultural factors interact with each other across the lifespan to influence their experience, meaning and expression. Cognitive theories of emotion now focus on the role that emotions play in personal meaning (e.g. Oatley & Johnson-Laird, 1987); thus, an event may be experienced as positive if it aids the individual's goals and plans, but be experienced as negative if it blocks or threatens goals and plans. In Chapter 3, Paul Gilbert described in detail the biological basis for a number of universal biosocial goals that are central to the experience of a wide range of emotions. These biosocial goals include care-seeking, caregiving, cooperation, mating and social ranking behaviour.

Early Experience

Our early experience in each of these domains provides the basis for future development. As described by Andrews in Chapter 5, initial exposure to abusive, neglectful or excessively critical caretakers is associated with the development of cognitive and behavioural risk factors for subsequent psychopathology. There are a number of different ways in which this may happen. Later adversity may mirror early stressful experiences, which are either explicitly recalled in the form of persistent intrusive memories or shape the meaning assigned to adult adversity. Alternatively, early stressors may lead to the development of negative behavioural patterns (e.g. concerning the use of social support) and negative beliefs about the self and others. Hackmann's chapter also provides a number of excellent examples of how early experiences are linked to potent images and metaphors that trouble adult clients.

Recent evidence is strongly supportive of the idea that negative cognitions in adulthood are associated with specific negative childhood memories (Strauman, 1992), with childhood adversity (Andrews & Brewin, 1990; Kuyken & Brewin, 1995, 1996) and with recall of negative parental attitudes (Brewin, Andrews & Furnham, 1996a; Brewin et al., 1992). In addition, positive cognitions associated with good mental health are associated with positive parental attitudes (Brewin, Andrews & Furnham, 1996b).

However, as noted by Andrews, the effects of early adversity and attachment problems are not immutable. In a number of longitudinal studies of disadvantaged children, the importance of the capacity for planning in different domains, especially that of close relationships, has been found to be protective despite early vulnerability (Champion, Goodall & Rutter, 1995; Rutter et al., 1995). These longitudinal studies provide some optimism in that they demonstrate both that early adversity does not inevitably lead to subsequent psychopathology, and that protective factors such as the capacity for planning and engagement in optimal close relationships can be highlighted in psychotherapies which attempt to address these developmental, emotional and interpersonal problems.

A TAXONOMY OF THEMES

The confluence of innate appraisal mechanisms that give priority to events that have important implications for survival, and of specific types of early adversity that are regularly associated with psychopathology, yields a small number of themes that will be familiar to the experienced psychotherapist. Although we do not claim that our taxonomy is original or all-embracing, and indeed all the individual themes have been extensively discussed by many authors, it may be helpful to bring together some of the most important meanings associated with psychopathology under seven headings. Four of these are primarily concerned with the self, and three with other people.

We assume that the meanings that clients assign to their experiences are phenomenological events that will differ markedly between individuals. Nevertheless, they are likely to share commonalities that can be expressed as themes, and the themes can be then used to guide research and clinical work. Specific meanings may be associated with one or more themes. They may be associated with a variety of sometimes contradictory emotions and behavioural strategies—meanings cannot be reduced to emotions, although accessing emotions may result in the discovery of new meanings.

The Self as Powerless

The theme of the self as powerless to achieve life goals, as unable to prevent the occurrence of aversive events, or as lacking in control over the physical and social environment, is a ubiquitous one. Some of the most influential theories in clinical psychology, such as learned helplessness theory and social learning theory, have been centrally concerned with expectations of being unable to influence important outcomes.

The Self as Inferior

This theme has been addressed by an enormous amount of research on negative evaluation of self and on discrepancies between the actual self and the 'ideal' or 'ought' self (e.g. Strauman, 1992). Inferiority or lack of status may be reflected in many ways, among the most common of which are perceived physical or mental weakness, incompetence, unattractiveness, stupidity, unloveability and moral degeneracy.

The Self as Non-existent

Loss of identity has been described by family and marital therapists as a feared consequence of being overwhelmed by a more powerful personality. Similarly, individuals brought up in two cultures or in two households may complain that they do not know who they are, and they cannot identify with a core group or family to whom they feel they belong. Loss of core goals or core attachments may also provoke a response that the person is no longer sure of his or her identity, and loss of identity is commonly feared as a result of 'going mad' or 'losing control'.

The Self as Futureless

Negative life events often lead individuals to feel that they have no future, either because their major life goals are now unattainable or because the world has ceased to be an orderly, meaningful place. This profound sense of existential disorientation has been well described by writers such as Frankl, and by Janoff-Bulman in this volume. Hopelessness about the future is often associated with suicidal impulses. Faced with events or human actions that were previously unimaginable, individuals struggle to create, or undergo conversions to, new ways of looking at the world that restore some meaning and purpose to living.

The Other as Abandoning

The theme of loss, rejection and abandonment is one of the cornerstones of psychotherapeutic practice, being particularly associated with attachment theory. Fear of abandonment may be expressed in a number of ways, including excessive jealousy, anger and dependency.

The Other as Betraying

The theme of being 'let down' by a core attachment figure has been shown empirically to be strongly associated with depression (Brown et al., 1986). Similarly, several researchers writing about the impact of child abuse have emphasised that it is the sense of betrayal by a previously trusted figure that makes the abuse difficult to come to terms with (Finkelhor & Browne, 1986; Freyd, 1996).

The Other as Hostile

Misperception of events as involving hostile intent by others is a defining feature of persecutory delusions, and has been found to mediate the influence of physical abuse on conduct disorders in childhood (Dodge et al., 1995).

It will be evident that these themes can occur together in many different combinations. Feelings of inferiority often appear to be attempts to explain rejection or abandonment by close others, for example. It is noteworthy that the most noxious negative experiences, such as those consisting of humiliation and entrapment, are likely to involve multiple themes with the self being perceived as powerless and inferior, and the other as hostile and betraying.

COGNITIVE PROCESSING OF THEMES: SINGLE-VERSUS MULTI-LEVEL APPROACHES TO MEANING

Cognitive approaches to therapy have generally focused on a single level of meaning, such as the schema, and the role that it plays in the origin, occurrence and maintenance of psychopathology (e.g. Beck et al., 1979). One of the key aims for the therapist therefore in cognitive therapy is to identify and then work with the patient to challenge dysfunctional schemas that are considered to have arisen in childhood. Although the patient is unlikely to be aware of these schemas at the beginning of therapy, through a variety of techniques this awareness should be eventually achievable. More recent cognitive therapists have further subdivided schemas into different types such as in Young's (e.g. 1994) distinction between 'unconditional' (I Am Unloveable) and 'conditional' (If I Am Criticised, That Means I Am Unloveable) schema. Such distinctions are clinically useful in that, for example, unconditional schema may be more difficult to work with than conditional ones, though this approach to meaning continues to be a single-level one.

An explicit schema-based model of therapeutic change that can be applied across all therapies has been developed by Stiles & Shapiro and their colleagues (Shapiro et al., 1992; Stiles et al., 1990). In the so-called 'Assimilation Model' problematic experiences are considered to be gradually integrated into schemas which may exist already or which may develop during the course of therapy. A sequence of stages occurs which begins with the experience being warded off, entering awareness as unwanted thoughts, being clarified as a problem, understanding and insight, working through, problem solution, and, finally, mastery. Clients may enter therapy with one or more problems at different stages along this continuum; nevertheless, the therapeutic aim is to help the client move further along the continuum with these problems. The Assimilation Model, although it provides a useful integrative approach to therapeutic change, shares the same problem noted above for the cognitive therapies in that the approach to meaning utilises a single level.

There have now been several critiques of single-level approaches to meaning representation in models of therapy and therapeutic change (e.g. Brewin, 1989; Power & Champion, 1986; Teasdale & Barnard, 1993). In Chapter 9, Teasdale has summarised a number of arguments against single-level models. He has argued persuasively that at least two levels of meaning representation need to be considered (in addition to lower-level modality-specific forms of representation) in any adequate model. Within his Interacting Cognitive Subsystems framework, these two levels are the propositional and the schematic model. Whereas propositional level representations can be represented in a linguistic form which has true–false truth value (e.g. I Am Worthless), schematic models are syntheses of a variety of inputs from internal and external sources that are experienced holistically. The advantage of this approach to meaning is that it offers the possibility of a more sophisticated account of conflicts, for example, those experienced between 'intellectual' and 'emotional' beliefs and the problems these may lead to in therapeutic change. However, we have argued both here (see Power, Chapter 4) and elsewhere (Power & Dalgleish, 1997) that not only should meaning be represented in this dual form, but also the generation of emotion should be modelled similarly, as we will consider next. Greenberg and Pascual-Leone (Chapter 10) have similarly argued the case for two different systems based on automatic versus conscious processes involved in the generation of emotion.

One of the clear messages that arise from the biological and developmental literatures is that an innate starting point for meaning generation lies in a rapid and automatic information-processing system. As summarised by Power in Chapter 4, this unconscious system continues to develop through maturation and learning; the continued automatisation of cognitive and cognitive-affective sequences throughout life considerably adds to and alters the content and form of this system. The purpose of this system remains that of implementing procedures likely to ensure survival, even though automatic sequences developed in one context (e.g. surviving one's parents) may prove to be maladaptive in other contexts. The individual's experience of the existence of this system often arises because of uncontrollable reactions that seem irrational, for example, knowing that butterflies are harmless or that flying is the safest form of transport while experiencing complete panic.

The fact that we are able to experience such automatic reactions as irrational is part of the evidence for the existence of a second, qualitatively different processing system which is based on the capacity for consciousness and involves a slower, controlled processing of information. One of the functions of this evolutionarily later system may indeed be to monitor automatic reactions, so that they can be re-evaluated, prioritised or ignored. The automatic reaction can therefore become part of a schematic model which, in the case of anxiety for example, could amplify the reaction into a catastrophic one, or minimise it as benign and non-threatening.

In summary, therefore, we and others have argued that dual-level or multi-level approaches to meaning and the generation of emotion must be considered in place of a number of current single-level approaches. Teasdale (see Chapter 9) has argued that meaning should be represented at two levels, that is, the propositional and the schematic model levels, though in the ICS model emotion only arises from the schematic model level. Brewin's (1989, 1996) dual representation theory proposed that meaning is represented both in a verbally accessible form and in a situationally accessible form, i.e. a representation that can be triggered by external cues but is not available to conscious inspection. Power & Dalgleish's (1997) SPAARS model proposes that there are multiple levels of representation of meaning, two of which (the schematic model and the associative levels) can provide routes to the generation of emotion. One of the major consequences of these and other dual-level or multi-level approaches is that the process of therapeutic change may become more complex and potentially conflict-ridden than the single-level approaches propose.

CONFLICT, MEANING AND THE SELF

The existence of at least two qualitatively different types of meaning and two routes to the generation of emotion has a number of interesting consequences for models of psychopathology and for mechanisms of change in therapy. One obvious consequence mentioned above is that the two levels or routes may be discrepant with each other. For example, the individual may experience two discrepant emotions towards an event, situation or person such as both sadness and happiness in reaction to another person's adversity. The capacity to experience and acknowledge mixed emotions towards others is in fact a late-developing capacity (e.g. Harris, 1989). Indeed, Harter (1977) reported that the inability of children to experience such mixed emotions was frequently associated with subsequent psychopathology. Another variant of this problem is that some individuals may experience particular emotions such as anger or anxiety as ego-alien; that is, the key problem when the individual becomes angry or anxious is that there is a loss of the sense-of-self, which some individuals may experience as going mad or becoming someone else. It seems likely that such emotions have been rejected from early in development onwards, perhaps under familial and cultural pressure. These disavowed emotions remain unintegrated therefore with the self and fail to develop as part of the self (Power & Dalgleish, 1997). In such cases, the patient typically attends therapy with the expectation that the therapist will remove the unwanted emotion so that the individual can 'live happily ever after'. The work of therapy is to help the individual move towards an acceptance of these unwanted emotions as part of the self. As Greenberg & Pascual-Leone state (see Chapter 10), emotions help to promote problem-solving and occur for constructive reasons if the individual can make use of them in this way. These authors argue that the vivid evocation in therapy of emotion and emotion-containing experience is a key part of therapeutic change, because it allows the therapist to work with the patient to develop new 'experiential syntheses' of these emotions and associated events.

Another important aspect of more sophisticated approaches to meaning arises from the possibility that only one meaning may be available for the individual's introspection, while other possible meanings are not consciously available. As Brewin has summarised in Chapter 7, the traditional psychoanalytic approach has been to identify a number of defence mechanisms such as denial, repression, sublimation, projection and regression. Each of these defences potentially distorts meaning in characteristic ways such that the individual appears to gain in some way from the distortion. More recently psychologists have become interested in additional ways that individuals may distort the world and their role in it in order to maximise their perceived contributions to positive outcomes and to minimise their contribution to negative outcomes (e.g. Taylor & Brown, 1988). Measures such as the Self Deception Questionnaire (Sackeim & Gur, 1979) have been developed to assess the degree to which individuals deceive both themselves and others. Experimental demonstrations have also shown that manic and paranoid patients may defend themselves against low self-esteem (Bentall, Kinderman & Kaney, 1994; Winters & Neale, 1985) and similar predictions may be applicable to individuals with narcissistic-type personality problems (e.g. Mollon, 1993). The convergence of the psychoanalytic and social psychological approaches has led to an increasing number of attempts to operationalise and measure the use of defence mechanisms and the extent of the typical distortions. For example, although Freud used the term 'repression' loosely to cover almost any defence mechanism, recent attempts to operationalise repression suggest that it is possible to identify a group of individuals who are unaware of their own negative emotional states (see Brewin, Chapter 7). This strategy is successful in protecting the individual from remembering negative experiences, but the price paid is that repressors may run higher risks of developing a number of physical illnesses (e.g. Weinberger, 1990; Vaillant, 1990).

Dual- and multi-level models of meaning and emotion have substantial implications for normal models of the self, not just for models of psychopathology. As Bargh (e.g. 1989) has shown, aspects of the self may become so automatised that one may only be aware of subsequent emotions rather than what aspect of the self led to the generation of a particular emotion. One of the functions of close relationships may well be to monitor and help the individual become more aware of such automated reactions; in the absence of such close relationships the individual may be more likely to enter therapy in order to increase awareness of these automated aspects of the self. Stein & Markus (1994) have also made the important observation that while many psychoanalytic and cognitive models of the psychopathology of the self have focused on the *content* of the self-concept, it is also important to consider the *structure* of the self and the possibility that some types of self-structure may, for example, be more resilient in the face of adversity than others.

Rather than the self being seen as a stable monolithic structure that is consistent across the lifespan, recent social cognitive views emphasise the multifaceted and complex nature of a collection of 'possible selves' that may vary across domains and contexts. Indeed, Stein & Markus (1994) summarise a range of studies that demonstrate that low self-complexity may be less protective in the face of adversity than high self-complexity. In a related proposal, Champion & Power (1995) have argued that definition of the self in relation to one particular overinvested role or goal is a risk factor for the development of depression, whereas a healthier pattern is to invest in a range of roles and goals; thus, if one particular role or goal falters or stops, other alternatives are already available for the individual. In summary, therefore, the issue of levels of meaning, conflicting emotions, and the self or possible selves involves a complex set of interacting factors that are poorly understood both in normal and abnormal states.

One area that clearly deserves more research is the experience commonly reported by patients of emotion-laden states which are not experienced as part of the self; although self-complexity may be protective, complexity that involves the rejection of particular states of the self leaves the individual both frightened and vulnerable. We should add, however, in defence of more recent psychoanalytic approaches that the idea of self-complexity and of different possible selves is also apparent in the work of analysts such as Fairbairn (1952) and Kernberg (1975). As Mollon summarises in Chapter 11, Fairbairn was the first to point to the possibility that different characters in dreams may represent different parts of the self, and that different aspects of early relationships are re-enacted in the transference relationship (cf. Beach & Power, 1996). Perhaps again this convergence from different approaches can be taken as a sign that more unitary or integrated approaches to therapeutic change can be taken.

CHANGE PROCESSES

The multi-level approaches to meaning contained within Brewin's (1989, 1996) dual representation theory or Power & Dalgleish's (1997) SPAARS model suggest that clients' problems must first be analysed in terms of their underlying representations. In particular, to what extent are the beliefs and memories that give rise to symptoms verbally accessible or unavailable to conscious introspection?

In many cases clients will have consciously held models of the reasons for and consequences of their problems. In some cases these will amount to misconceptions that fully account for the symptoms and that can be readily altered by verbal persuasion or the presentation of new evidence. In the majority of cases, however, these conscious models of what the symptoms mean will not account for the observed pattern of symptoms, suggesting that the clients' behaviour is at least partly under the control of unconscious representations or unconscious associative links.

Much therapeutic work is devoted to uncovering evidence for the existence and likely nature of these unconscious links. As discussed by Greenberg & Pascual-Leone, important information about the meaning of symptoms can be derived from facilitating emotional expression, particularly where this appears to have become blocked. Hackmann notes that recurrent images and metaphors may be associatively linked in unexpected ways to significant, emotion-laden childhood experiences. In psychoanalysis, as described by Mollon, the analyst elicits and observes the material provided by the client in the form of free associations and transference reactions and by the analyst in the form of counter-transference reactions.

In all these examples activation of the relevant unconscious representations leads to observable products in the form of emotions, thoughts,
images, expectations, and impulses or behaviours. These products, which
occur spontaneously and sometimes without any awareness on the part
of the client, may be considered as the expression of implicit emotional
memories, goals or plans. Analysis of these products, whether reported
by clients, their friends, and families, or observed by therapists themselves, permits the formation of clinical hypotheses about the nature of
the underlying representations. These hypotheses essentially attempt to
explicate the tacit meaning of the symptom, often in terms of the core
themes described above.

Tacit meanings, unlike verbally accessible meanings, cannot be negoti-
ated, reinterpreted, or reconstructed. Tacit meanings either are or are not
automatically accessed by relevant external stimuli such as the behaviour
of significant others or media messages or by internal stimuli such as
thoughts. One possible therapeutic strategy may therefore be to block
access to the relevant unconscious representations. Traditionally, behaviour therapists have treated the memories underlying specific phobias
by creating new memories through imaginal or *in vivo* exposure. The new
experiences were designed to be as similar as possible to the original fear-
producing situation in all respects other than in outcome. Thus new memories in which fearful stimuli were associated with mastery and relaxation
blocked access to the old memories in which the same stimuli were associated with anxiety and helplessness. This process is discussed in greater
detail by Brewin (1989).

Alternatively, access may be blocked by training clients to reinterpret
aspects of the current environment that tend to trigger unconscious representations, using standard cognitive therapy techniques. Additionally,
detailed examination of the similarity between past situations eliciting
powerful negative emotions and the client's current situation may help the
client to discriminate the two instead of overgeneralising from the past.
This process will often need to be repeated many times in order for the new
concepts and categories agreed in therapy to become automatised, over-
write old appraisal patterns, and thus interfere with the retrieval of unwanted representations. If this is to be done successfully, psychological
defences that may be impeding examination of the past or present will
have to be weakened. As illustrated by Hackmann, the changing of an
image, a metaphor, or a narrative may also be effective at blocking the
retrieval of emotional memories. Recent evidence confirms that cognitive
therapy, unlike pharmacotherapy, appears to change clients' automatic
responses to negative self-related cues (Strauman & Kolden, 1996).

Dual-level models of meaning suggest, however, that even when tacit,
unconscious memories exert an influence, there may be consciously

accessible beliefs and representations that will also have to be addressed in therapy. Brewin, Dalgleish & Joseph (1996) have presented a detailed model of the treatment of post-traumatic stress disorder. They distinguish interventions such as exposure aimed at blocking access to unconscious memories from cognitive interventions aimed at altering consciously accessible maladaptive beliefs. Whereas exposure is likely to be effective in reducing meanings such as powerlessness and emotions such as fear experience during the trauma itself, cognitive interventions may be necessary to reduce secondary meanings and secondary emotions that arise from subsequent conscious appraisal of events. These would include the maladaptive metacognitive beliefs discussed by Hackmann in Chapter 8.

Constructivist therapies emphasise the importance of creating new and more positive meanings for symptoms and experiences, and recent evidence from the treatment of rape victims suggests that the creation of more organised, less fragmented trauma narratives is associated with a reduction in symptoms (Foa, Molnar & Cashman, 1995). From the multilevel perspective on meaning, however, it is important to recognise that the construction of a successful narrative may have a positive impact in a number of quite different ways, both altering conscious appraisals and blocking the reactivation of unconscious representations.

CONCLUSIONS

There is now considerable agreement among different schools of psychotherapy on the importance of constructing adaptive meanings rather than eliminating logical errors, on the need sometimes to address existential issues, on the frequent problems created by some kinds of defensive processes, on the value of the therapeutic relationship as a source of information about the client's past experience and current expectations, and on the existence of tacit meanings that may have a causal impact on client's behaviour without their awareness. Despite the continued divergence of opinion on such matters as therapeutic technique and the origin of maladaptive emotions, this represents a considerable step forward.

The study of meaning, we believe, holds much promise for integrating different approaches to psychotherapy. It need not involve the abandonment of a scientific project to determine what therapy does and why. Rather, as our contributors have so concisely and eloquently described, it is possible to identify a core set of themes and processes that are not only highly clinically relevant but are consistent with knowledge in biological, cognitive and social psychology. We hope that this volume will stimulate further attempts to use the concept of meaning to study and integrate different therapeutic processes.

REFERENCES

Andrews, B. & Brewin, C.R. (1990). Attributions of blame for marital violence: A study of antecedents and consequences. *Journal of Marriage and the Family*, **52**, 757–767.

Bargh, J.A. (1989). Conditional automaticity: Varieties of automatic influence in social perception and cognition. In J.S. Uleman & J.A. Bargh (eds), *Unintended Thought*. New York: Guilford.

Beach, K. & Power, M. (1996). Transference: An empirical investigation across a range of cognitive-behavioural and psychoanalytic therapies. *Clinical Psychology and Psychotherapy*, **3**, 1–14.

Beck, A.T., Rush, A.J., Shaw, B.F. & Emery, G. (1979). *Cognitive Therapy of Depression*, Chichester: Wiley.

Bentall, R.P., Kinderman, P. & Kaney, S. (1994). The self, attributional processes, and abnormal beliefs: Towards a model of persecutory delusions. *Behaviour Research and Therapy*, **32**, 331–341.

Bolton, D. & Hill, J. (1996). *Mind, Meaning, and Mental Disorder*. Oxford: Oxford University Press.

Brewin, C.R. (1989). Cognitive change processes in psychotherapy. *Psychological Review*, **96**, 379–394.

Brewin, C.R. (1996). Theoretical foundations of cognitive-behavior therapy for anxiety and depression. *Annual Review of Psychology*, **47**, 33–57.

Brewin, C.R., Andrews, B. & Furnham, A. (1996a). Self-critical attitudes and parental criticism in young women. *British Journal of Medical Psychology*, **69**, 69–78.

Brewin, C.R., Andrews, B. & Furnham, A. (1996b). Intergenerational links and positive self-cognitions: Parental correlates of optimism, learned resourcefulness, and self-evaluation. *Cognitive Therapy and Research*, **20**, 247–263.

Brewin, C.R., Firth-Cozens, J., Furnham, A. & McManus, I.C. (1992). Self-criticism in adulthood and recalled childhood experience. *Journal of Abnormal Psychology*, **101**, 561–566.

Brewin, C.R., Dalgleish, T. & Joseph, S. (1996). A dual representation theory of post-traumatic stress disorder. *Psychological Review*, **103**, 670–686.

Brown, G.W., Andrews, B., Harris, T., Adler, Z. & Bridge, L. (1986). Social support, self-esteem, and depression. *Psychological Medicine*, **16**, 813–831.

Champion, L.A., Goodall, G. & Rutter, M. (1995). Behaviour problems in childhood and stressors in early adult life. 1. A 20 year follow-up of London school children. *Psychological Medicine*, **25**, 231–246.

Champion, L.A. & Power, M.J. (1995). Social and cognitive approaches to depression: Towards a new synthesis. *British Journal of Clinical Psychology*, **34**, 485–503.

Dodge, K.A., Bates, J.E., Pettit, G.S. & Valente, E. (1995). Social information-processing patterns partially mediate the effect of early physical abuse on later conduct problems. *Journal of Abnormal Psychology*, **104**, 632–643.

Fairbairn, W.R.D. (1952). *Psychoanalytic Studies of the Personality*, London: Tavistock.

Finkelhor, D. & Browne, A. (1986). Initial and long-term effects: A conceptual framework. In D. Finkelhor (ed.), *Sourcebook on Child Sexual Abuse* (pp. 180–198). Newbury Park, CA: Sage.

Foa, E.B., Molnar, C. & Cashman, L. (1995). Change in rape narratives during exposure therapy for posttraumatic stress disorder. *Journal of Traumatic Stress*, **8**, 675–690.

Freyd, J. J. (1996). *Betrayal Trauma: The Logic of Forgetting Childhood Abuse*. Cambridge, MA: Harvard University Press.

Harris, P.L. (1989). *Children and Emotion: The Development of Psychological Under-standing.* Oxford: Blackwell.

Harter, S. (1977). A cognitive-developmental approach to children's expression of conflicting feelings and a technique to facilitate such expression in play therapy. *Journal of Consulting and Clinical Psychology,* 45, 417–432.

Kernberg, O. (1975). *Borderline Conditions and Pathological Narcissism.* New York: Jason Aronson.

Kuyken, W. & Brewin, C.R. (1995). Autobiographical memory functioning in depression and reports of early abuse. *Journal of Abnormal Psychology,* 104, 585–591.

Kuyken, W. & Brewin, C.R. (1996). Self-esteem, coping and attributional style in currently depressed women with and without a history of early abuse. Manuscript submitted for publication.

Lewis, M. (1993). The emergence of human emotions. In M. Lewis & J. M. Haviland (eds), *Handbook of Emotions.* New York: Guilford.

Lewis, M.D. (1996). Self-organising cognitive appraisals. *Cognition and Emotion,* 10, 1–25.

Mollon, P. (1993). *The Fragile Self: The Structure of Narcissistic Disturbance.* London: Whurr.

Oatley, K. & Johnson-Laird, P.N. (1987). Towards a cognitive theory of emotions. *Cognition and Emotion,* 1, 29–50.

Power, M.J. & Champion, L.A. (1986). Cognitive approaches to depression: A theoretical critique. *British Journal of Clinical Psychology,* 25, 201–212.

Power, M.J. & Dalgleish, T. (1997). *Cognition and Emotion: From Order to Disorder.* Hove: Psychology Press (Erlbaum, UK).

Rutter, M., Champion, L.A., Quinton, D., Maughan, B. & Pickles, A. (1995). Origins of individual differences in environmental risk exposure. In P. Moen, G. Elder & K. Luscher (eds), *Perspectives on the Ecology of Human Development.* Ithaca: Cornell University Press.

Sackeim, H.A. & Gur, R.C. (1979). Self-deception, other-deception, and self-reported psychopathology. *Journal of Consulting and Clinical Psychology,* 47, 213–215.

Shapiro, D.A., Barkham, M., Reynolds, S., Hardy, G. & Stiles, W.B. (1992). Prescriptive exploratory psychotherapies: Toward an integration based on the assimilation model. *Journal of Psychotherapy Integration,* 2, 253–272.

Stein, K.F. & Markus, H.R. (1994). The organization of the self: An alternative focus for psychopathology and behavior change. *Journal of Psychotherapy Integration,* 4, 317–353.

Stiles, W.B., Elliott, R., Llewelyn, S.P., Firth-Cozens, J.A., Margison, F.R., Shapiro, D.A. & Hardy, G. (1990). Assimilation of problematic experiences by clients in psychotherapy. *Psychotherapy,* 27, 411–420.

Strauman, T.J. (1992). Self-guides, autobiographical memory, and anxiety and dysphoria: Toward a cognitive model of vulnerability to emotional distress. *Journal of Abnormal Psychology,* 101, 87–95.

Strauman, T.J. & Kolden, G.G. (1996). Preliminary evidence for differential effects of psychotherapy versus medication on cognitive structures associated with vulnerability to depression. Manuscript submitted for publication.

Taylor, S.E. & Brown, J.D. (1988). Illusion and well-being: A social psychological perspective on mental health. *Psychological Bulletin,* 103, 193–210.

Teasdale, J. & Barnard, P. (1993). *Affect, Cognition and Change.* Hove: Erlbaum.

Vaillant, G.E. (1990). Repression in college men followed for half a century. In J.L. Singer (ed.), *Repression and Dissociation.* Chicago: University of Chicago Press.

Weinberger, D.A. (1990). The construct validity of the repressive coping style. In J.L. Singer (ed.), *Repression and Dissociation.* Chicago: University of Chicago Press.

Winters, K.C. & Neale, J.M. (1985). Mania and low self-esteem. *Journal of Abnormal Psychology*, **94**, 282–290.

Young, J.E. (1994). *Cognitive Therapy for Personality Disorder: A Schema-focused Approach* (revised edn). Sarasota, FL: Professional Resource Press.

AUTHOR INDEX

SUBJECT INDEX

Related titles of interest from Wiley...

Trends in Cognitive & Behavioural Therapies

Edited by Paul M. Salkovskis

"... a welcome addition to the library of professionals involved in the application of psychological strategies to understanding and treating psychological disorders."

Aaron T. Beck, University of Pennsylvania Medical Center

0-471-96172-8 174pp 1996 Hardback
0-471-95788-7 174pp 1996 Paperback

Cognitive Therapy for Delusions, Voices and Paranoia

Paul Chadwick, Max Birchwood and Peter Trower

Guides professionals towards better practice by treating the individual symptoms of delusions, voices and paranoia, rather than by the categorisation of schizophrenia.

Wiley Series in Clinical Psychology
0-471-93888-2 230pp 1996 Hardback
0-471-96173-6 230pp 1996 Paperback

The Hidden Mind

Psychology, Psychotherapy and Unconscious Processes

Israel Orbach

Provides a concise and scholarly critique of the psychoanalytic, cognitive, humanistic and dissociation models of human thought and behaviour, focusing on the unconscious.

0-471-95578-7 228pp 1995 Hardback
0-471-95864-6 228pp 1995 Paperback

The Therapeutic Relationship in Behavioural Psychotherapy

Cas Schaap, Ian Bennun, Ludwig Schindler and Kees Hoogduin
0-471-92458-X 202pp 1993 Hardback

Visit the Wiley Home Page at http://www.wiley.co.uk